Changing London

Edited by

Hugh Clout

University College London

University Tutorial Press

Published by
UNIVERSITY TUTORIAL PRESS LIMITED,
842 Yeovil Road,
Slough SL1 4JQ.

Gerald Manners, John Salt, John Adams, Peter Wood, Jacquie Burgess, Richard Dennis, Richard Munton, Carolyn Harrison, Ted Hollis, John Thornes, Eric Brown in their respective chapters

ISBN 0 7231 0762 9
Published 1978

Printed in Great Britain by
Cox & Wyman Ltd, London, Fakenham and Reading.

Cover photograph courtesy of National Westminster Bank

Contents

“To our Colleges”

Preface

Residents and visitors across the centuries have written of London as a city of contrast. At the heart of the most affluent region of the UK it contains the wide range of government offices, wealthy residential districts, entertainment facilities and other features that one associates with the national capital of a world power. But, with a population greater than that of many individual nation states, London also has a large share of social, economic and environmental ills, associated with unemployment, housing, public transport and many other matters. Indeed, two recent books have drawn attention to the capital's ailments by viewing London as a 'heartless city' in a 'problem region'. Such descriptions reflect both the advantages and the disadvantages that have accrued to Britain since World War II and have, of course, affected London. The nation has long recovered from wartime devastation and the British have become more emphatically a post-industrial society. Living standards have improved substantially and greater affluence has been accompanied by a rise in car ownership, more leisure time and ever greater demands on space. Post-imperial Britain has received new elements of social diversity associated not only with successive waves of immigrants but also with the tourists who arrive each year. Planning, in one form or another, has assumed major importance in managing or creating the environments in which the British live their everyday lives.

Those of us who live in and around London and work in its central area are aware that London contains much that makes it a unique city but, to echo Emerson's words, it is also 'the epitome of our times'. It may be seen as a kind of massive 'laboratory' in which the general features of our changing and increasingly urbanized society may be observed and analysed. This book has been written with such a point of view in mind. Its authors teach in the Department of Geography at University College London and are concerned with introducing students to the processes at work in changing the environment of our urban region. As might be expected, there is a large body of rather dispersed literature that is of interest to geographers as they undertake this task, but there is little by way of up-to-date, moderately priced and easily accessible synthesis. The chapters that follow have been written in the hope of filling part of that gap. They cover a *selection* of systematic and spatial themes that are of importance in trying to understand the changing and increasingly planned environment of the capital. No claim is made for them to represent a 'complete' geography. It is hoped that the book may serve three purposes: to provide information on their home region for sixth-formers, students and teachers in South East England; to offer a framework within which fieldwork may be set; and to characterize urban changes that are to be found, to one degree or another, in each of Britain's major cities and thus be relevant to an audience outside the South East region.

The first four chapters present systematic information on planning, population and employment, transport and the decline of manufacturing. Then follow seven chapters that examine recent changes in selected parts of the London region (the central area, dockland, suburbia old and new, the green belt and the urban fringe). The latter chapter, with its emphasis on recreation and ecology, forms a transition to the final section of the book which discusses aspects of change in the man-modified physical environment and concludes by examining the resources of that environment and the ways in which they have been put to use as London has grown. A number of accessible items for further reading, such as may be found in many public libraries, are listed at the end of each chapter. As a matter of policy, detailed reference to research documents and articles in learned journals has been excluded.

As editor, I owe thanks to my colleagues for writing their chapters, to the secretaries in the Department of Geography for typing the manuscript, to Tina Hill and Lisa Greenwood for drawing the illustrations under the supervision of Ken Wass in the Cartographic Unit at UCL, to Martin Ferguson and Gerald Manners for advising on several chapters, and to my mother for critically reading and checking each section of the book.

HUGH CLOUT

List of Abbreviations

CDA	Comprehensive Development Area
DSPSE	Development of the Strategic Plan for the South East
GLC	Greater London Council
GLDP	Greater London Development Plan
HPA	Housing Problem Area
ILEA	Inner London Education Authority
LB	London Borough
LCC	London County Council
MELA	Metropolitan Economic Labour Area
NNI	Noise and Number Index
PLA	Port of London Authority
pphm	parts per hundred million
ppm	parts per million
ROSE	Rest of South East England
SEG	socio-economic group
SMLA	Standard Metropolitan Labour Area
SSSI	Site of Special Scientific Interest
tcmd	thousands of cubic metres per day
WHO	World Health Organization

1 London: World Capital and Regional City

Gerald Manners

Introduction

London, one of the world's most important centres of banking, insurance, finance and commerce, plays many other roles as well. An outstanding node of international and national transport and communications, it is the location of the headquarters of many major manufacturing companies, of important professional and consultancy services, and of advanced industrial and commercial research. It is the home of a surprisingly wide range of manufacturing activity, and a centre of medical and educational excellence. It affords the resident and the visitor alike an extraordinary concentration of theatres, concerts, exhibitions, fine arts and museums, plus a cultural heritage that draws increasing numbers of tourists each year from all over the globe. London is also the centre of what was, until only a generation ago, one of the world's most extensive colonial empires, with all the connections and residual functions that such a role was bound to bestow. And it is the home of British government—with the Houses of Parliament, the principal courts of both civil and criminal law, and the greater part of the country's civil service. The functions of London, in other words, are of outstanding international and national importance; and their range is demonstrably diverse. The geographical extent of London, on the other hand, eludes ready definition.

The city region of London provides the most relevant intellectual context for an understanding of its economic and social characteristics and their dynamics. This is, of course, a very different area from the historic square mile of the City of London, or the 'central' area that is usually defined as the streets and buildings lying within a zone bordered by the major railway termini. The city region is also much more extensive than the inner London boroughs that until 1964 made up much of the territory of the London County Council (LCC), or the even larger area of Greater London that is currently administered by a metropolitan authority, the Greater London Council (GLC). This is the area that, in fact, provides the focus for much of the rest of this book (see Fig. 1·1). The London city region is a huge non-administrative area within South East England that looks to a considerable degree towards Greater London in general—and its central area in particular—for its white collar employment opportunities, for its commercial and industrial linkages, for its higher-order shopping facilities and for many of its recreational and cultural activities. Clearly, no understanding of London can ignore the fact that a significant and increasing proportion of its workforce live outside the formal boundaries of the GLC. Each day some 750 000 people commute into the central area alone. And millions more, living in such Home Counties as Surrey and Hertfordshire, Essex and Buckinghamshire, contribute regularly to the economy and the society of the capital and depend upon its proximity for their jobs and for its services. The extent of this city region in some places is 100 km or more from Charing Cross;

irregular in its geographical extent, and penetrating farthest into the Home Counties along the major lines of rail and motorway communication, it embraces such important urban centres as Southend and Reading, Canterbury and Oxford, Brighton and Luton. As communications have improved and standards of living risen, so has the population and the influence of London spread outwards, extending the city region wider and wider until it now embraces the greater part of South East England. Figure 1·2 illustrates the variety of spatial subdivisions within the South East.

The Expanding Metropolis: Decentralization and Renewal

The relentless expansion of the London city region does not reflect a new spatial process. Rather, it expresses a tendency that has been going on for centuries, albeit one that has quickened in recent decades. The process can be summarized in two words: decentralization and renewal. Stimulated by both economic and social forces, the process involves substantial changes in the geographical patterns of residence, of job opportunities, of journeys to and from work and of social provision. It can also create substantial social and economic problems in particular localities where obstacles to a satisfactory adjustment of land uses and human activities persist.

For centuries London has expanded outwards. As its population has increased, and as its wealthier inhabitants have demanded and acquired more residential space, so have a variety of activities seen advantage in operating from locations farther away from the centre of the capital. Shops, schools, surgeries and solicitors, amongst other activities, have moved out to serve the growing settlements on the

1·1 The London Boroughs.

periphery of London. They have subsequently been joined by other economic and social functions —repair shops, manufacturing establishments, local government services, hospitals, training colleges, research establishments and commercial offices. Some of these activities have been given birth in the suburban and ex-urban periphery. Others have moved their activities physically from sites nearer to the centre, and so left more room there for the remaining activities to expand or new ones to arrive, for old buildings to be converted or new ones to be built in their place. And with each innovation of transport technology—the train and the tram, the Underground and the bus, the trolley and the car—the pace of the process has quickened. Whilst the process might occasionally justify nostalgia, its logic cannot be denied.

For centuries the central area of London has adapted its functions and land uses to the opportunities of the day. The earlier coffee houses and trading functions of Fleet Street gave way to the newspaper industry, just as the residential role of Harley Street has been usurped by a much more profitable medical role. In the outer boroughs of south London especially, few can now regret the transfer of the country's principal airport just after World War II from the grass and cramped field near Croydon to the more distant but open spaces of Heathrow; and the logic of the downstream movement of London's seaport, first from the Pool of London and then from the up-river docks to the more convenient and more modern facilities at Tilbury, Felixstowe, Dover and Southampton, is all too apparent. Many manufacturing firms in the 1930s found the best mix of locational attributes on the Park Royal Estate adjacent to the main road leading west from London, or along the (then recently opened) North Circular Road. Today, in contrast, growing manufacturing concerns find their advantage best served and their productivity highest when they choose a location within the Home Counties with convenient access to the national motorway network, or in a new or expanded town with its ready provision of infrastructure and housing.

Population Changes

With decentralization in recent decades, many Londoners and an increasing proportion of their jobs, have not only been relocated within the Greater London area, but also beyond it into the Outer Metropolitan Area (OMA) and the Outer South East (OSE) (Fig. 1·3). It is there that many families, manufacturing firms, retail enterprises, transport activities and office functions are finding substantial

1·2 The South-East Region: Population Change, 1901–75.

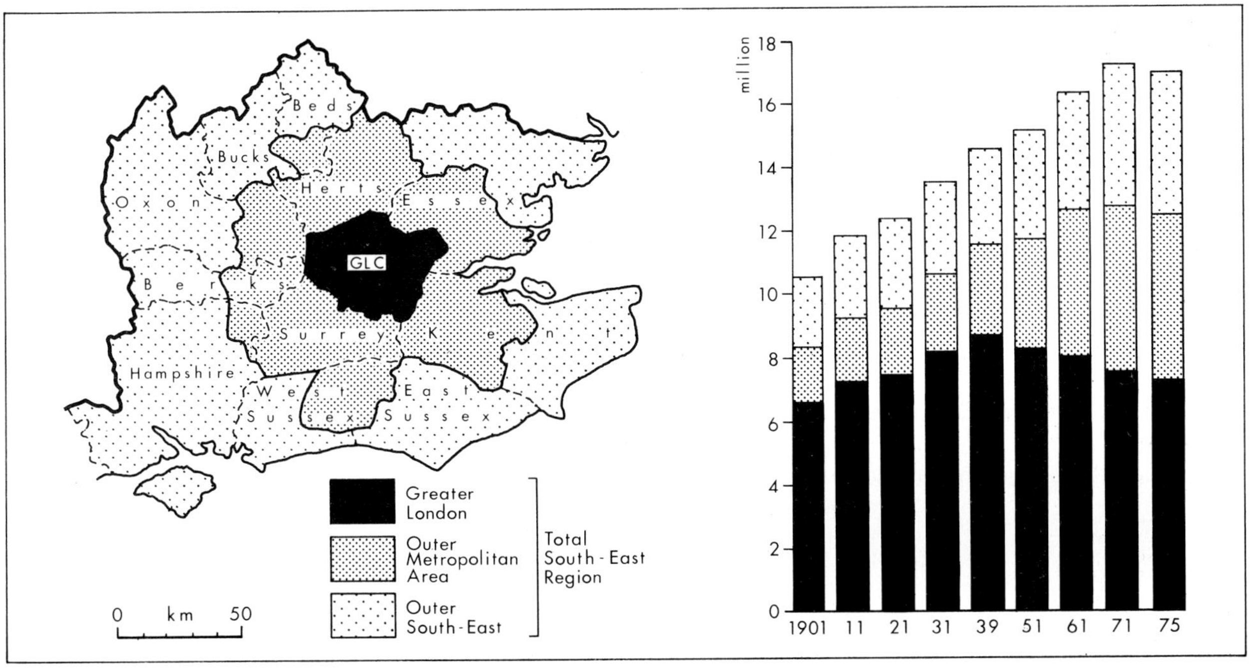

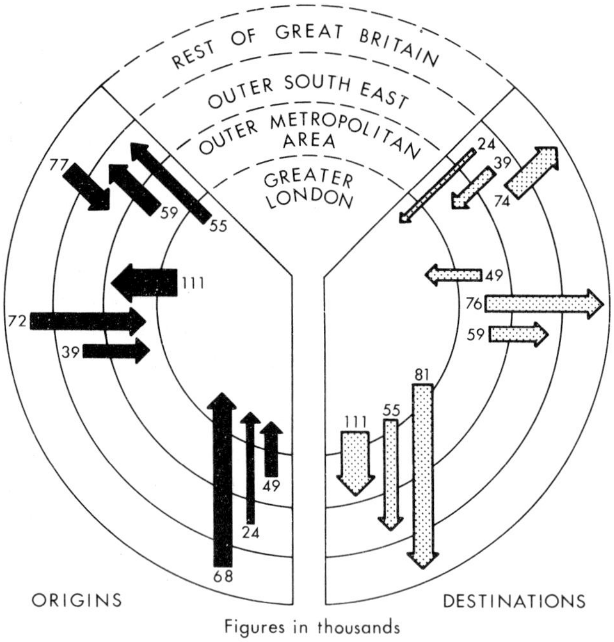

1·3 Migration to, from and within the South East, 1970–1.

advantages of position, of land availability, of costs and of environment, advantages that are not so readily available within the more densely settled Greater London. In consequence, the population of Greater London is falling markedly. It was 8 200 000 in 1951; it had declined to just under 8 000 000 in 1961; it had fallen further to 7 400 000 in 1971; and by 1976 it was down to barely 7 000 000. It could have shrunk to about 6 300 000 by 1981 according to some forecasts. But the characteristic of population decline at the heart of an urban area is not new. In the early years of the twentieth century, the decentralization of some central area functions and the redevelopment of the cities of London and Westminster especially at lower residential densities meant that the population of the inner areas reached its maximum in 1901; for nearly eighty years now, they have been in decline. The Greater London area was at its most concentrated in terms of population in 1939, when 8 600 000 lived there. For nearly forty years it has experienced decline.

It should be noted that these tendencies for decentralization to cause a fall in London's population were well established in a period when the British population as a whole was experiencing sustained, and, at times, vigorous growth. The experience of a declining birth rate in Britain during the last decade has tended to accelerate the process. Such a contraction in the population of Greater London should not be a cause for concern, however, provided that the process of land use and employment adjustments takes place reasonably smoothly, provided that those areas adjusting to lower residential densities are finding a new and successful role in the metropolis, and provided that the counterpart process of renewal is occurring at a comparable speed and with equivalent efficiency.

Planning Policies and Problems

Indeed, it should not be forgotten that during the first thirty years after World War II, it was the policy of both the central government and of the local authorities in South East England to assist and to encourage the process of decentralization. The formal physical planning objectives of the city region first set out by Abercrombie in 1944 in his *Greater London Plan*, and then later developed in a series of strategic planning documents for the whole of the South East, called for the creation of new towns and major growth centres in the OMA and the OSE to receive overspill population and industry from Greater London. The Abercrombie proposals led to the designation of the first generation of new towns in the OMA, places such as Stevenage, Harlow and Basildon, and were complemented by the development of other and smaller overspill arrangements under the Town Development Act; the mostly smaller expansion schemes at Aylesbury, Basingstoke, Kings Lynn and Luton, for example, fell into this category. Then in its 1964 *South East Study* the Ministry of Housing and Local Government proposed that this policy should be accelerated through the creation of additional and larger overspill settlements farther away from London and designed to serve as major counter-magnets to the conurbation, thereby to attract economic activity and population over a longer distance than market forces might advise. The 1967 *Strategy for the South East*, prepared by the region's Economic Planning Council, modified these proposals in detail by urging the channelling of London's overspill into those sectors that were best served by radial lines of road and rail communication; but the need to accept and even encourage decentralization remained its essential theme. The 1971 *Strategic Plan for the South East*, this time prepared by a joint team representing central and local government plus the regional economic planning council, advocated the concentration of overspill in major and medium growth areas within the region, as well as accepting population and employment movement out of the region into such planned reception centres as Peterborough (East Anglia), Northampton (East Midlands) and Swindon (South West). Most recently, the *Strategy for the South East: 1976 Review*—yet another team exercise—has confirmed the inevitability and the desirability of further London overspill. It stressed once again the advantages of the major and medium growth areas such as Milton Keynes, Southampton/Portsmouth, the Reading/Basingstoke area and Crawley/Burgess Hill that were designated in the earlier strategy, but in addition it proposed rather more spatial flexibility in overspill provision by suggesting that local authorities in the region might well find it advantageous to expand some of their existing towns in the light of local employment and environmental opportunities.

Thus, since 1945, the development of Bracknell and Basildon, of Hemel Hempstead and Welwyn Garden City, along with the other new and expanded towns, has given the changing pattern of settlement in the South East a distinctive spatial component that has been assisted by public policies—with funds to finance the construction of infrastructure and housing, and with policies that have encouraged the transfer of people and economic activities away from Greater London. These policies have come largely within the orbit of the Department of the Environment. In addition other government departments and public agencies have endorsed the decentralization strategy. The Department of Industry, for example, which can withhold permission for the construction of large factory premises through its administration of industrial development certificates, has restrained the growth of manufacturing jobs within London much more than in the rest of the South East (ROSE). And since 1963 a government commission, the Location of Offices Bureau (LOB), has been assisting the decentralization of office activities from central London by means of the provision of free information and advice to the business community on the advantages of alternative locations, and by drawing attention through advertising to some of the disadvantages of office location in the heart of the metropolis. These policies have met with considerable success. Since 1963 over 150 000 jobs in the office sector have moved or are in the process of being moved with the assistance of LOB; one-third of these went to the rest of the Greater London area, over 40 000 went to the OMA, and another 20 000 went to other parts of the South East. But the forces of the market have been just as powerful as public policy, if not actually stronger than it in recent years. The LOB has estimated that it handles only half of all the office jobs decentralizing from central London. The new towns of South East England have received only about 13 % of the population decentralizing from Greater London.

There is, therefore, an historical continuity in the process of decentralization and its implications for the population of London, and there has been a good deal of public encouragement of the process in the past. But there is a difference between present circumstances and historical experience in these matters. The difference lies in the scale and the speed of decentralization on the one hand, and the apparent failure of the mechanisms of renewal in some parts of London on the other. Particularly in some of the inner areas of London, developed mainly in Victorian times and formerly supported by an economic base of manufacturing industry and a range of activities in the transport and distribution sectors, there would appear to be a failure to adapt to changing economic and geographical circumstances, and an inability to find a viable role in the immediate future. An extreme case is provided by the Docklands of East London, considered in Chapter 6, where 2200 ha of land that were once substantially devoted to a transport function are to a large extent today without an alternative economic base to support their resident population of some 55 000. Perhaps modern societies, contemporary London included, are subject to many more rigidities than their predecessors, and the search for a new flexibility in land ownership and use, of labour and of capital, has become a major economic and social priority. Alternatively, new factors could have entered into the situation to demand a new analysis and new policies. Certainly, fears have been expressed that without deliberate political action, large areas of inner London could be subject to decline and decay for the want of viable land uses and the necessary incentives to renew the built environment.

In response, public policies came to be adjusted from 1976 onwards. An increasing number of measures have been introduced in the first instance to reduce the deliberate encouragement of decentralization by public actions and public agencies. The scale and the speed of the new towns programme, for example, has been reduced. The government has begun to steer additional financial resources into the inner London boroughs through adjustments to the annual rate support grant. Provision has been made for the actual encouragement of manufacturing industry in inner city locations, and the LOB has been given the task of trying to encourage offices to move from central London into inner London locations (as well as farther afield, especially the Assisted Areas). And central government has begun to develop 'partnership' agreements with inner city local authorities to prepare and finance jointly major renewal programmes—Lambeth and Docklands, for example, were singled out for early consideration and action. By these and other means, the government hope that the natural opportunities for inner urban adjustment and renewal might be grasped and accelerated, and that the not inconsiderable social problems associated with this process might be substantially ameliorated.

In sum, therefore, an understanding of London must begin with a recognition of its role within a broader city region embracing nearly the whole of South East England. Within this region, powerful economic and social forces are encouraging the decentralization of both people and of economic and social activity, with the result that the population of London is experiencing an accelerating decline. Of itself, this need not be a cause for concern. But since there is, in addition, evidence that the process of readjusting and renewing some of the inner areas of the capital city is not occurring at a speed and in a manner that is broadly acceptable, deliberate attempts are now being made to supplement market forces with public policies.

Against this background, therefore, this introduction to *Changing London* turns next to some of the more striking features of the economic geography of South East England. It then summarizes some of the more notable economic and social attributes of Greater London as a whole. Finally it examines the three major zones that exist within Greater London—the outer suburbs with their mixed attributes but not inconsiderable prosperity and economic success; the inner areas with their difficulties of economic and social adjustment; and then the central area with its buoyant economy and generally successful adaptation to changing national and international economic opportunities.

South East England

With a population of just under 17 000 000 in 1976, the South East of England is by far the most successful geographical component within the British economy. Its gross domestic product per head is 16 % above the national average; it has a highly diversified economy, with a concentration of higher-order, that is more specialized, job opportunities; unemployment has always been relatively low; and educational achievements have tended to rank outstandingly high. Greater London and the surrounding towns comprise the country's most important manufacturing complex. Here there are located a whole host of industries—including electrical and mechanical engineering, vehicles and aircraft, furniture, paper and printing, clothing, chemicals, food, drink and tobacco, iron and steel and oil refining —industries that produce goods for both the home and the export markets. The value of manufacturing output in the South East is worth twice that of manufacturing enterprise in any other region of the country. The importance of these industries in employment terms, however, is surpassed by the South East's service trades, some of which meet the needs of the resident population and industry, but more of which satisfy national and international demands. Apart from a cluster of research activities closely related to the needs of manufacturing activity—and it has been estimated that half of the country's research establishments, owned by both government and private enterprise, are to be found in the South East—the region provides transport and communication services that have enormous employment implications. The importance of passenger movements through Heathrow, Gatwick, Luton and the Channel ports are well known; by value, Heathrow is also the country's largest port for international trade (see page 11). In terms of traffic volume, of course, the seaport of London still has pride of place, whilst the ports of Southampton, Dover and Medway also have a considerable national significance. Most striking of all, perhaps, is the range of office employments in the region. Apart from national government administration, these include workers in the financial, banking and insurance sectors of the economy, major head office activities of the manufacturing and transport sectors, accountants, lawyers, advertising executives, business consultants and various other professional services. The South East provides about half of all the office jobs in the whole of England and Wales.

Within the South East, Greater London houses about 40% of the population and rather more of the region's jobs. It is considered later. The ROSE has been the scene of a remarkable surge of population and employment growth in the last two decades. With such new investments, and a growth-orientated industrial structure, it is one of Western Europe's greatest economic assets in an increasingly competitive world. Separated from Greater London by the Green Belt (see Chapter 10), the geographical development of ROSE has been a function of an earlier geography of settlement which has been allowed to expand as a consequence of its in-built momentum, plus the results of a set of public decisions which have sought to achieve two ends.

Planning policies in ROSE have sought, first, to protect large areas of rural territory from urban encroachment. As a result, the interests of the agricultural economy and community have been defended, and considerable areas of attractive and in some places outstanding natural beauty have been preserved for recreational purposes; in this latter category, for example, are the Chilterns, the North and South Downs and the New Forest. The same planning policies have also attempted to so concentrate urban growth that scale economies could be exploited in the provision of public services. At the same time it was hoped that relatively self-sufficient labour markets would evolve in these urban concentrations and thereby provide both a wide range of jobs for the employee and a wide range of skills for the employer; in the process longer-distance commuting would be minimized. In social terms such a form of urban growth is also seen to be advantageous, for a wider range of health, welfare, educational and cultural facilities could be provided than would be possible under a more dispersed urban form. And from the point of view of transport, the pattern was seen to facilitate the provision of public services both within and between urban centres. The five major growth areas of Reading/Basingstoke, Milton Keynes, South Essex, Crawley/Burgess Hill and South Hampshire are shown upon the map (Fig. 1·4), as are the six medium growth areas designated under the 1971 *Strategic Plan for the South East*. Between them can be seen the environmental and agricultural areas within which severe restraints are being imposed upon the urbanization and suburbanization processes.

ROSE, then, encircling Greater London, is a region of continuing growth. It is expected that, in the next twenty years or so, its population through natural increase and migration will increase from just under 10 000 000 today to approaching 11 500 000. Through the expansion of its existing economic base primarily, but also through the reception of overspill population and employment from Greater London, this outer zone of the London city region will progressively become the dominant element in the South East as a whole, in the sense of housing perhaps two-thirds or more of its population by 1991. With good motorway connections to the rest of the country and towards Continental Europe, with easy access to the nation's major international air and sea ports, with a pattern of land uses that is substantially adjusted already to the fuller use of the motor car, and with cost and environmental advantages for the conduct of many business and social pursuits, ROSE is the dynamic and successful context within which the tendencies, the problems and the challenges of Greater London have to be understood and assessed.

1·4 Main Aspects of the Strategic Plan for the South East as approved in 1971.

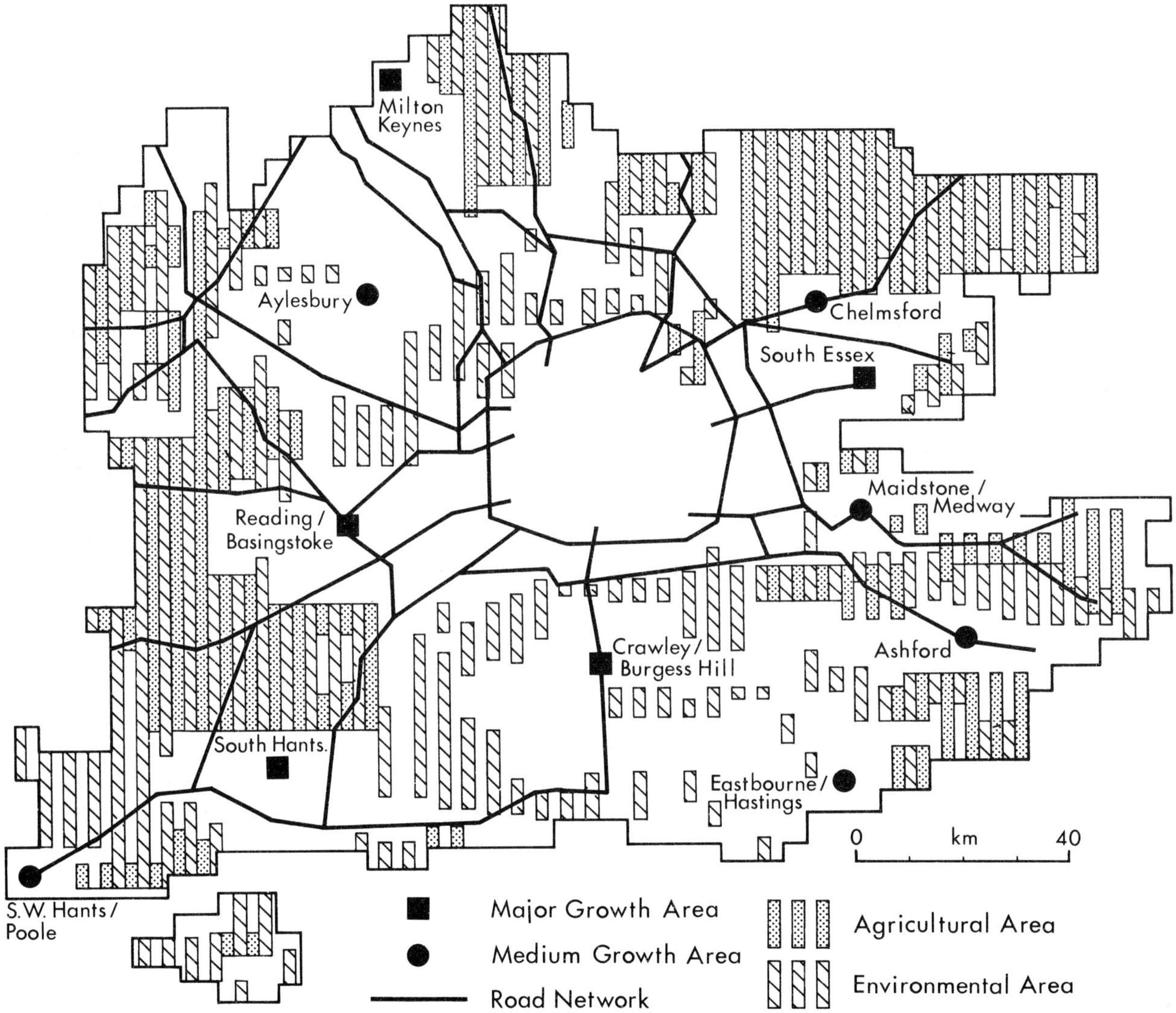

Greater London

One central feature of the changing geography of Greater London is its population. Its accelerating decline in recent years has already been noted. This overall decline, however, hides a much more complex reality in which there exist very substantial movements of people both in and out of London to live and work. In the early 1970s, some 350 000 residents were leaving Greater London each year; but another 250 000 people were simultaneously moving into the capital, some of them from new commonwealth countries to add to London's social variety and its social problems. And whereas the older age groups dominate the outwards movement, having found better homes, better jobs or possibly a more congenial location for retirement outside of London, it is the younger age groups, more especially young professional people, that dominate the inward flow. The net result, of course, is a loss of about 100 000 people from London each year by migration, a figure that is only slightly offset by the natural increase of the residential population, now running at about 6000 each year.

Simultaneous with the population decline, there has been a somewhat smaller contraction of employment opportunities within Greater London. The difference is explained by the growing tendency for more people to commute each day by rail and road into Greater London, especially its outer suburbs. Most of the contraction in jobs has been in the manufacturing sector of the economy—a fall of 27 % between 1966 and 1974, compared with a national decline of only 7 % during the same period—and in the less-skilled manual and clerical occupations. The service trades in general have been growing as employers, however, and they now represent some 70 % of London's jobs; this contrasts with their 60 % contribution in ROSE and the 51 % of the workforce that they employ in the whole of Britain. Within the service industries it is the skilled professional, administrative and managerial jobs that have been growing fastest, an expansion that is paralleled by a growing number of sales staff.

Such changes in the size and the structure of both the population and the workforce of Greater London have demanded a response by the local authorities responsible for physical planning. Responsibility is shared in these matters between the Greater London Council (GLC) which is responsible for the preparation of the overall London structure plan, and the thirty-two London boroughs (plus the City of London, which has a somewhat unique status in English local government) that are charged with the preparation and administration of detailed local plans. The role given to the GLC involves the development of broad population and employment policies for Greater London, the overall supervision of housing and environmental matters within the metropolis, and the preparation and implementation of a transport policy for its area. These policies are summed up in the *Greater London Development Plan* (GLDP), first produced in 1969 but subsequently modified by a variety of review procedures such as the public enquiry under Lord Layfield, the Department of the Environment, and the GLC itself in the face of new evidence. The Plan does not lay down a complete basis for the control of development in Greater London, but it does set a context within which local policies can be discussed and elaborated. Difficult though it has been to produce a plan to everyone's satisfaction, it is difficult to imagine rational planning at the level of the boroughs on such matters as transport, employment location and housing without some reasonably articulate and agreed overview.

By far the most contentious element in the original GLDP were the proposals for London's roads. Following very elaborate and expensive traffic surveys in the 1960s, the GLC proposed the construction of a series of ring and radial urban motorways to serve both industrial and private needs in the metropolis. The cost was enormous in financial terms. The estimates of the late 1960s put a price of £2 000 000 000 on the ringways, with the innermost motorway 'box' costing some £15 000 000 per km. The road proposals were judged by many to be even more costly in social terms—with the loss of thousands of homes, the increased pollution from vehicle exhausts, and the like—and so were strongly opposed by a variety of pressure groups first of all, and then, following a change of administration in 1973, by the Greater London Council itself. All that remains of the London road proposals today are some of the partly finished radials, such as the M1 to Brent and the M4 to Brentford; a programme to upgrade the North Circular Road (Fig. 1·5); an accelerated programme to construct the M25 that will encircle Greater London but along a route that is largely outside GLC territory; and a government expression of a need to improve lateral movement in inner London. The clash between housing and environmental issues on the one hand and transport and industrial needs on the other cannot be evaded. Certainly there are many who believe that only with the provision of better road facilities within Greater London will it be possible to retain many of the remaining manufacturing firms and attract new sources of employment. This issue is further explored in Chapters 3 and 4.

Other matters in the GLDP that provoked a good deal of public discussion concerned the tendency for employment, and in particular employment in manufacturing industry, transport and distribution in the inner areas, to decline, and the continuing problem of homelessness in a metropolitan area that appeared to have a more than adequate stock of houses in relation to its shrinking population. In both cases, the GLDP highlighted certain obstacles built into national policies that complicated the solution of London's problems. In the case of employment, for example, decades of public policies that have sought to restrain the growth of job opportunities in South East England, and deny the expansion of manufacturing plants there in order to steer employment into the

1·5 London's Primary Roads and Strategic Trunk Routes outside the GLC area.

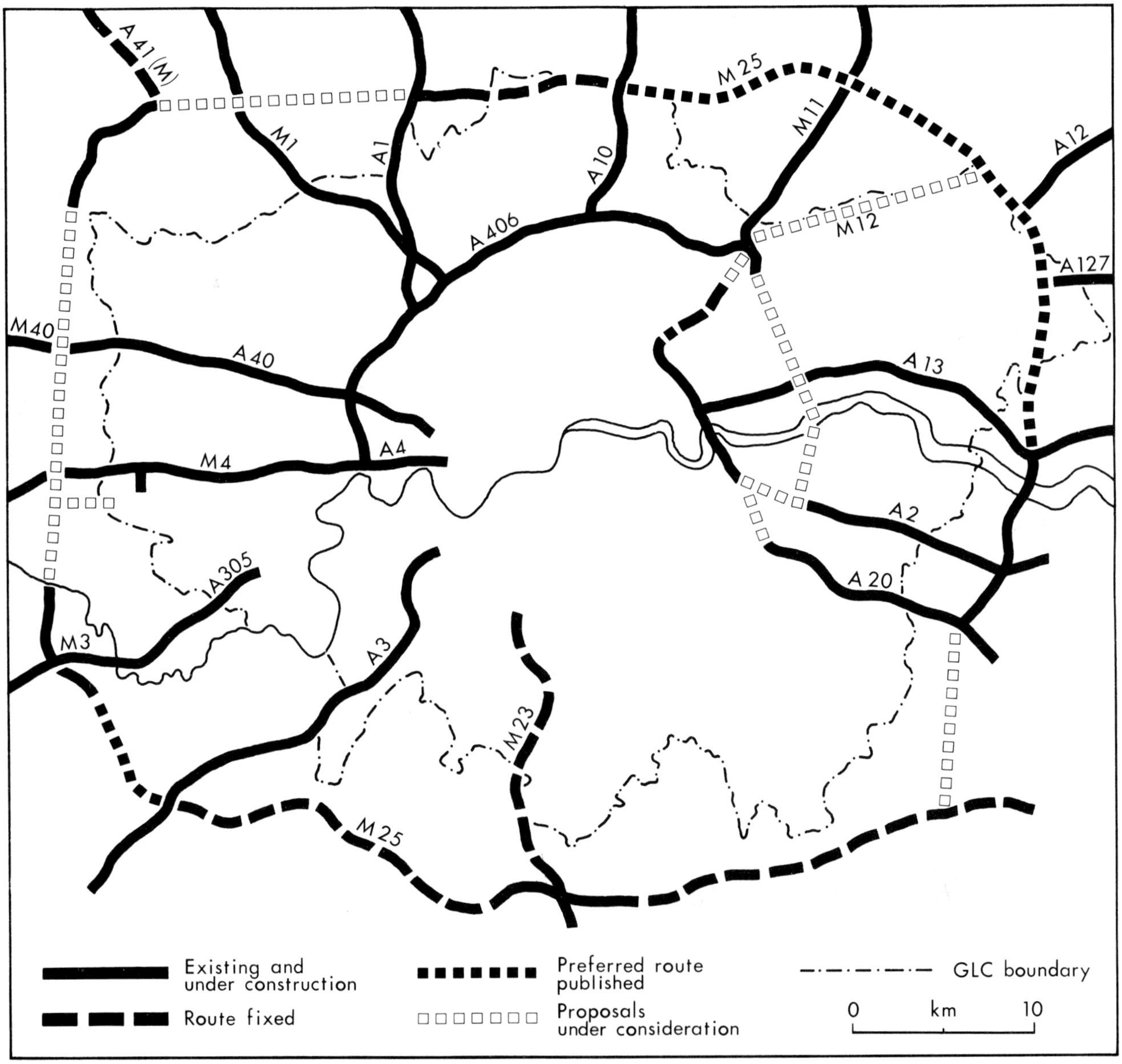

Assisted Areas, were seen to be starkly contrary to the interests of contemporary London; and the publication of the GLDP saw the beginning of articulate pressures to alter the policy of the Department of Industry in this regard. In the case of housing, the unique nature of the London market which has traditionally made available substantial amounts of rented accommodation for short stays in the metropolis and especially for younger members of the workforce was fully exposed, as were the difficulties of maintaining that supply in the light of national housing legislation that offered substantial security of tenure to tenants. On these and other issues, the solutions proposed in the GLDP have had to be modified in the light of fuller debate and the priorities of national policies. Their longer-term effects upon national policy, however, will not be denied—although such effects are more likely to be felt through shifts in the attitudes of government departments and the evolution of national policies, rather than in the precise wording of the GLDP as modified and approved by the Secretary of State for the Environment.

The extraordinary variety of Greater London, of course, in many matters precludes the formulation of policies that can have a relevance to the whole of the Council's area. For this reason, it is important to recognize at the very least three distinct zones within the built-up area. Each has a quite distinctive set of economic and social characteristics. Each has an equally contrasting range of planning problems. In the next section, the outer suburbs, the inner areas and the central area of London are discussed in turn.

The Three Zones of Greater London

The first component of Greater London is the outer suburbs. This is where the greater part of Londoners now live, either in owner-occupied premises or in GLC or borough public housing estates. This is also where most of London's manufacturing jobs are now to be found and where the contraction of job opportunities in them is being offset by the growth of office activities. Particularly in the strategic centres designated in the GLDP—centres such as Croydon, Ilford, Kingston and Wood Green—new office activities are being encouraged to expand in order to take advantage of the skills of the local workforce and in the hope that, by concentrating office work geographically, considerable use will continue to be made of public transport in the journey to work (see Chapter 3). As was noted earlier, some 39% of the firms and 33% of the jobs moving out of central London under the auspices of LOB have moved to locations within the GLC, and most of these locations have been in the outer suburbs. The need and the ability of these outer suburbs to adjust and renew their land uses is also to be seen in the retail sector. Rapid rationalization has been taking place, with a substantial renewal of facilities occurring in the strategic centres, and one entirely new shopping centre being built at Brent Cross; details of this latter development are discussed in Chapter 8.

There are, of course, contrasts between the various parts of the outer suburban ring of boroughs. The upgrading of the North Circular Road is giving the northern suburbs a lateral flexibility in job and social movement which is denied to the southern suburbs with their much inferior road system. To the west of London, the outer suburbs come under the unique influence of—and must weigh the costs and benefits of—the country's largest international airport at Heathrow. Whilst the quantification of its impact upon the surrounding boroughs is difficult, in terms of the direct employment on the airport, associated employment nearby, and attracted employment in the form of manufacturing and office firms that see some advantage in being located near to an airport, the influence of Heathrow is enormous. This is after all the largest international airport in the world. It currently handles 24 000 000 passengers each year, a figure that is expected to increase to 30 000 000 by 1980. It also handles over 400 000 tonnes of cargo each year, the value of which—some £7 000 000 000 in 1976—surpasses that of any other port in the country. As a result of these activities the airport directly employs a total of 52 000 people, half of them in the central terminal area. Employment off the airport, but related to it, could be of a comparable magnitude which means that through the multiplier effect—that is, the services demanded and the jobs created by this workforce—it is not unreasonable to think of Heathrow as having a dominant influence over the labour market in its immediate journey to work area where total employments number some 350 000. Heathrow represents one of the boldest contrasts between the London outer suburbs; but there are others, such as the Lee Valley Regional Park in the north-east and the new satellite community at Thamesmead, both of which are discussed in later chapters.

The second major zone within Greater London lies nearer the centre and is the inner area. It is here that, despite much continuing industrial vitality, the contraction of jobs in manufacturing industry, in transport and distribution has been at its most severe. Characterized by a relatively dense urban environment that has been bequeathed by Victorian and Edwardian history, manufacturing firms have been moving away or, in rather more cases, simply dying as a result of changing economic fortunes. As Chapter 4 explains, there are many factors that have been responsible for the recent demise of the manufacturing sector in this area. Relatively poor and inflexible factory premises (multi-storey buildings do not adapt well to modern, flow-line, production technology), a shortage of skilled labour, difficulties with road transport for the assembly of materials and components or for the delivery of finished products, planning difficulties with the local authorities, expansion constraints imposed by central government, and simply the superiority of other locations for the conduct of manufacturing enterprise in the second half of the twentieth century—all these and more are to blame. It is in this inner area that thousands of jobs in transport and distribution have also been lost, as the railways have shed labour and, more dramatically, as the port functions of London have moved downstream (see Chapter 6). But the problem is not so much these losses, which have an economic and a geographical logic, as we have seen. Rather the problem is the failure of alternative employments and activities to appear in their place. Some office jobs have moved to attractive locations in the inner areas—to Hammersmith, to Stratford centre or to Lewisham, for example—but many more firms in the office sector have transferred their operations to the outer suburbs where many of their workforce have tended to reside. And other activities in the growing service sector—tourism and entertainment, hotels and restaurants, for example—have generally found little to attract them to these inner areas.

The result has been the emergence of substantial problems. In the first place there is the relatively high level of unemployment, concentrated geographically in such areas of 'stress' as Stepney and Brixton, and concentrated socially amongst the relatively old, the unskilled and the coloured community (see Chapter 2). Unemployment levels of over 10% have been reported in some localities in recent years, and they have sponsored a government response in the form of encouragement to existing industries there, a more deliberate effort to help the workforce (and especially the unemployed) to acquire new skills, and encouragement to those without work to travel some distance within London to localities where jobs are available.

Associated with employment problems are a cluster of social problems. Family and group poverty, deteriorating housing conditions, vandalism and crime are locally severe in the inner areas. All of these difficulties resist ready solutions, but perhaps the most contentious set of uncertainties surround the issue of housing. Despite the accelerating decline of the inner areas' population, housing shortages remain as acute as ever. In theory, there appears to be a reasonable match of households and housing stock. But the institutional means of bringing them appropriately together has been lacking as the proportions of owner-occupied housing and local authority housing have increased at the expense of the more flexible private rented sector. As we saw earlier, to a considerable extent this is the result of national housing policies. And in this situation of mismatch there is evidence of a resultant deterioration of some of the housing stock.

The third and final zone within Greater London is its centre. Although it has seen a slight decline in its total employment opportunities over the last few decades, the central area of London has remained remarkably buoyant in economic terms. It remains the major source of jobs in the metropolis, and particularly the source of high income employment opportunities. A modest decline of small-scale manufacturing industry has been recorded there in recent years, as is only to be expected given the high land values, the lack of modern industrial premises and the difficulties of lorry transport upon a highly congested road system. Transport problems have also encouraged the decentralization of some wholesale trades, the most notable being the transfer of the country's premier fruit and vegetable market from Covent Garden across the Thames to Nine Elms (see Chapter 5).

Office activities, both private and governmental, have also moved out of central London as we have seen, but the dynamic expansion of this component in the metropolitan economy has meant that the total number of jobs has not fallen—for the remaining firms, or parts of firms, have continued to expand, and in addition many new firms have been born in the City or the West End or have moved into London from overseas. International banks and the international oil industry have been of outstanding importance in this latter category. The office jobs that have decentralized have included nearly every type of activity, but they have tended to be jobs associated with routine office operations; in contrast, the office jobs that have stayed and expanded have tended to involve more specialized activities and the application of higher skills. In addition, of course, central London's retail trade, entertainments, cultural activities and tourism have all grown in importance as creators of wealth and as sources of employment in the centre. In recent years they have added considerably to the diversity and economic strength of the centre of London. At the same time of course they have added to the diversity and economic strength of both Greater London and the South East.

To sustain this high level of activity in a very small area, whilst its workforce has been tending to decentralize, has involved the maintenance of a highly complex transport system focused upon the central area of the metropolis. This has posed a variety of problems, which are examined in Chapter 3. Whilst the use of public (road and rail) transport for journeys into central London has fallen slightly, the rail system both on the surface and underground still carries the greater part of the commuting burden. On the commuter network of London and the South East some 1 000 000 journeys are made each day which together make up about 43 % of the total passenger travel in the whole country. The convenience and often the lower marginal cost of car transport has meant that there has been a slight tendency for workers to switch from public to private transport—but this tendency has been resisted with quite rigorous measures to restrain the use of the motor car, especially by commuters into the greater part of the central area. A reduction in the number of parking spaces, both on and off street, the increase of parking fees, the designation of bus lanes and the pedestrianization of some streets have all been employed in an attempt to maintain a high level of public transport use and efficiency. But the management of central city traffic is in part an art as well as a science, and a totally satisfactory set of arrangements has yet to emerge.

Central London has other problems too. High land and property values have made it increasingly difficult to retain private homes in many localities and so preserve a desirable mixture of land uses. The divided views of planners, politicians and ordinary citizens on the aesthetics and ethics of redevelopment have left many prominent sites in a state of deterioration and ill-suited to contemporary needs—Piccadilly Circus is a classic example. The pollution of the air by the burning of coal may have been substantially reduced; but the equally serious air pollution from road vehicles has steadily worsened, as Chapter 13 explains. Despite these and other problems, however, the central area of London must be seen primarily for its strengths, its adaptability and its success as the focal point of a world, national and regional city.

Conclusion

A study of Greater London gives a somewhat arbitrary, even misleading, impression of London in its totality. Here is an ancient city which has adapted over the centuries to changing economic and social opportunities and challenges. It has grown through time to encompass an ever-larger number of people within its daily orbit, and lies today at the heart of the strongest, most modern, and most varied commercial and industrial component in the economic geography of Britain. Its city region now extends throughout the greater part of South East England. Seen in this wider context, Greater London is given its proper perspective. Interpreted through the dynamics of an expanding city region, the characteristics and the problems of the various parts of Greater London are afforded a fuller meaning.

Further Reading

Ash, M., *A Guide to the Structure of London*, (Adams and Dart, London, 1972)

Clayton, K. M. (ed.), *Guide to London Excursions: Twentieth International Geographical Congress* (LSE, London, 1964)

Clayton, R. (ed.), *A Geography of Greater London* (George Philip, London, 1964)

Coppock, J. T. and Prince, H. C. (eds.), *Greater London* (Faber, London, 1964)

Daniels, P., *Office Location* (Bell, London, 1975)

Goddard, J. B., *Office Linkages and Location* (Pergamon, Oxford, 1973)

Goddard, J. B., *Office Location in Urban and Regional Development* (OUP, Oxford, 1974)

Hall, J. M., *London: Metropolis and Region* (OUP, Problem Regions of Europe Series, Oxford, 1976)

Hall, P., *London 2000* (Faber, London, 2nd edition, 1969)

Hillman, J. (ed.), *Planning for London* (Penguin, Harmondsworth, 1971)

Hobhouse, H., *Lost London* (Macmillan, London, 1971)

Manners, G. (ed.), *Regional Development in Britain* (Wiley, London, 1972)

Pahl, R. E., *Whose City?* (Penguin, Harmondsworth, 1975)

Shepherd, J., Westaway, J. and Lee, T., *A Social Atlas of London* (OUP, Oxford, 1974)

Wilcox, D. and Richards, D., *London: the Heartless City* (Thames TV, London, 1977)

Young, G., *Tourism: Blessing or Blight?* (Penguin, Harmondsworth, 1973)

Young, P. and Willmott, P., *The Symmetrical Family* (Penguin, Harmondsworth, 1973)

2 Population and Employment in London

John Salt

Introduction

The life blood of any city is its people. It follows then that change in the numbers and characteristics of the inhabitants of a city will fundamentally influence not only its form and functions but its very *raison d'être*. During the period since World War II the major cities in the UK have undergone profound demographic change. At the same time, their economic bases have changed as many manufacturing industries have moved out and office employment has come to dominate most city centres.

The aim of this chapter is to review the main changes in population and employment in London. This is clearly a large topic as the vast amount of census data (to mention only one statistical source) testifies. Accordingly, attention will be focused on selected aspects of change which have given rise to expressions of concern in recent years. These are London's changing social composition, the growing significance of migrants from overseas in the capital's population, and the recognition of 'stress' areas, particularly in the inner city. These are highly complex and interrelated topics, which have become increasingly the subject of detailed analysis. The main concern here can be no more than to indicate dimensions and directions of change as pointers for the future social and economic development of the capital.

A review of aggregate change in the demographic and employment structure of British cities between 1951 and 1971 shows accelerating decentralization from the urban core. Table 1 summarizes population and employment change between 1961 and 1971 for 126 labour market areas, containing the vast majority of Britain's population. (Labour market areas are based on criteria developed by Political and Economic Planning in *The Containment of Urban England* (Peter Hall and others, 1973). Two principal types of urban area were recognized: (i) Standard Metropolitan Labour Areas—SMLA, consisting of a labour centre or core and a metropolitan ring of areas strongly related through journey to work to the core; and (ii) Metropolitan Economic Labour Areas—MELA, consisting of an SMLA and an outer metropolitan ring of areas less strongly related to the core.)

TABLE 1 Population and employment change in urban labour markets in Great Britain

	Population change (%)		*Employment change (%)*	
	1951—61	*1961—71*	*1951—61*	*1961—71*
Urban cores	1·9	−2·8	6·7	−3·1
Rings	13·3	17·2	6·6	15·0
SMLAs	5·7	4·4	6·7	1·4
Outer rings	3·1	9·8	−0·4	3·9
MELAs	5·3	5·2	5·6	1·8

Between 1951 and 1961 there was still some population increase in the urban cores but by the 1960s this had changed to decrease. By contrast, population increased considerably in the metropolitan rings. The same tendency was also in evidence for employment. In the 1950s employment increase was greatest in the urban cores but in the 1960s the trend was completely reversed. A very substantial increase in employment took place in the metropolitan rings and as far as the outer rings are concerned a small decline for 1951–61 became a marked increase in 1961–71. Hence the 1950s and 1960s mark a reversal in the long-established growth of population and jobs in British cities. There are many reasons for these changes and they include social attitudes to city living, developments in transport, housing aspirations and the housing supply, as well as greater social and occupational mobility. Technological development has changed the balance of locational advantage for employers, often to the detriment of older urban locations. Manufacturing has moved out, together with some tertiary sector employers, who are no longer willing or able to face the high costs of central locations. Such trends have major implications for any city, with respect to maintaining its economic base (and therefore its income) and planning its provision of schools, hospitals and other social or community facilities. Increasingly, city authorities are faced by the problem of planning for decline rather than growth, since the latter is now occurring in suburban and outer suburban areas which are often located in different administrative authorities.

The trends referred to so far have been especially obvious in the London region (Table 2, Fig. 2·1). During the 1950s loss of population in the core was more than compensated by increase beyond, resulting in a net increase in population for the London SMLA as a whole. By the 1960s things had changed: further massive losses in the core (GLC area) were not compensated in the metropolitan ring, where population increase was small. The capital and its immediate hinterland formed an area of population decline, suffering the largest loss of all the major urban labour markets in the country. After some hesitation came the out-movement of job opportunities to match the decentralization of London's population. During the 1950s the London labour market gained over

TABLE 2 Population and employment change for the London SMLA

	Population change		*Employment change*	
	1951—61	*1961—71*	*1951—61*	*1961—71*
Core	−293 000	−554 000	+129 000	−386 000
Ring	+349 000	+158 000	+134 000	+143 000
SMLA	+57 000	−396 000	+264 000	−243 000

250 000 jobs, more or less evenly split between core and ring. The next decade witnessed a dramatic turnround when overall loss almost equalled the gain of the previous decade. While the metropolitan ring managed to sustain its employment increase in the 1960s, the core suffered a massive loss of jobs. In aggregate then, the London labour market has undergone a traumatic change in its population and employment fortunes since the end of the last war. Gains in the 1950s were turned into losses in the subsequent decade, especially in London itself.

Change in London's Population and Employment

Between 1961 and 1971 London's population fell from 7 980 000 to 7 440 000, an average annual fall of 53 600 people. In the 1970s the decline gained momentum to 82 500 per annum, leading to a 1975 population level of 7 110 000. In contrast, the outer Metropolitan area and outer South East continued to increase in population although at a decreasing rate (Fig. 2·1). The scale of this change has consistently taken attempts to plan London and the South East by surprise and has led to a fundamental reappraisal of planning in the region. From the acceptance of Abercrombie's Greater London Plan (1944), until the end of the 1960s the planning philosophy for London was predominantly one of containment of growth. The methods used were Green Belt restrictions and the channelling of 'surplus' population to New and Expanded Towns. With this in mind, the South East Study and the South East Strategy proposed and endorsed a new generation of large expansion schemes such as Milton Keynes, Southampton/

Portsmouth and Ashford. These would not only cater for population increase generated in London, but also divert migration channels that might otherwise have ended up in the capital. However, as the expected population failed to materialize, so the reasons for the expansions became less pressing and several of the schemes were abandoned, *eg* Ashford, Southampton/Portsmouth. Those that remained, such as Milton Keynes, have found difficulty in meeting population targets.

What caused this decline in population in London? Figure 2·2 shows migration and natural change for London between 1961 and 1974. Both natural change and migration contributed to population decline, with the latter being of greater significance.

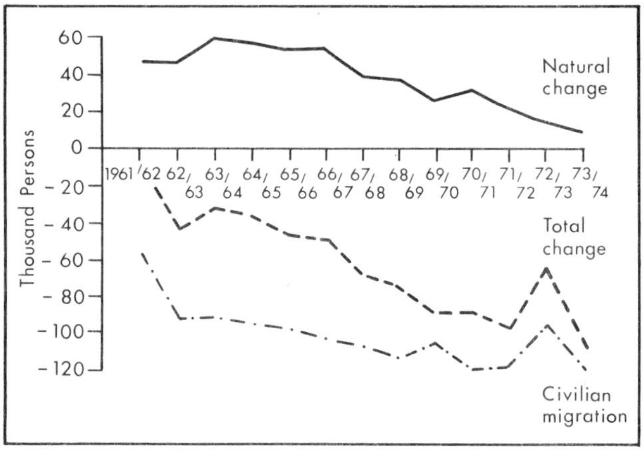

2·2 Civilian Migration (net) and Natural Change in London, 1961–74.

2·1 London: Core, Metropolitan Ring and Outer Metropolitan Ring.

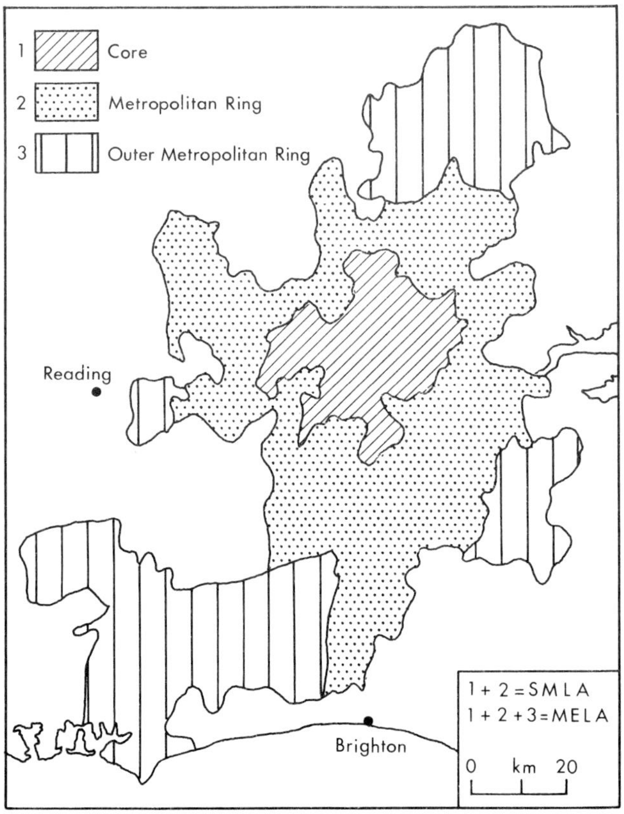

The summary picture for 1970–1, for example, shows net migration loss of 110 000, natural increase of only 31 000 and total annual loss of 79 000. Change in natural increase from a peak of 60 per thousand in 1964 to less than 20 per thousand in 1974 was because of falling numbers of births. Loss by migration was particularly rapid in the early 1960s and has continued to gain momentum in the 1970s. Comparison of 1965–6 and 1970–1 suggests the increased loss was because of emigration overseas, with comparatively little change in number of migrants from London going to other destinations in the UK being recorded in the censuses.

Trends in London's employment have been as profound as those in population. During the twentieth century the principal economic tendency has been for London to become a service centred city with an initial decline in the *proportion* of the workforce engaged in manufacturing becoming, since 1961, a decline in the *absolute* numbers employed in manufacturing. From 1966 to 1973 employment in the GLC fell by over 500 000 with 350 000 jobs being lost in manufacturing. This contraction in manufacturing has been examined for the period 1966–72, using redundancy records of the Department of Employment. It was estimated that about 50 000 redundancies per annum were taking place in London;

inner London was particularly affected, especially the industrial areas in the East End and inner ring where 200 000 jobs were lost during the period, the majority for male manual workers.

To some extent losses in manufacturing have been compensated by gains in the service sector, especially in finance, insurance and banking, professional and scientific services and, to a lesser extent, in public administration. Between 1961 and 1971 employment in these sectors grew by approximately 160–180 000 with the largest increase among professional and scientific workers. However, the expansion in office employment cannot compensate fully for the losses that have occurred in manufacturing because of mismatches in labour-force characteristics and skill requirements. Hence, some redundant workers have changed sector, others have joined the ranks of the unemployed, but many have migrated away from London, especially to outer suburban areas.

2·3 Wards of Housing Stress recognized in the GLDP.

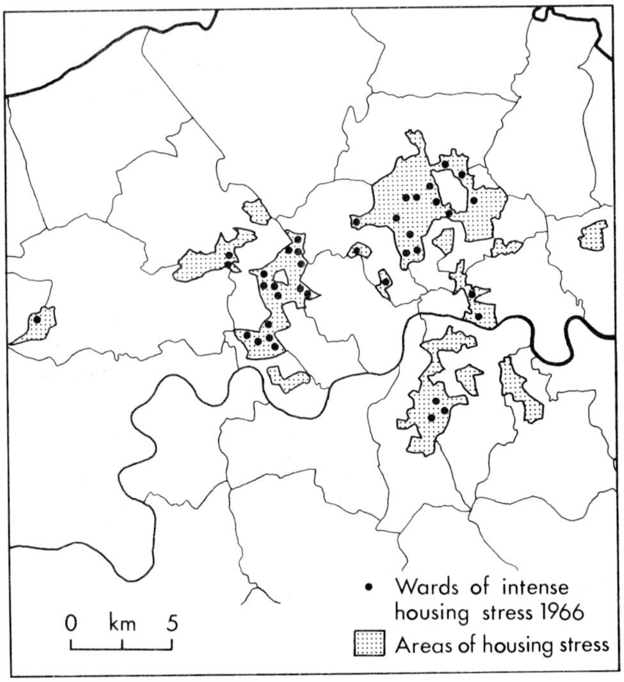

Problems in the Inner City

These aggregate figures hide variations within the city, particularly between inner and outer boroughs. Out-migration, for example, is especially from the city centre, a trend gaining in importance from 1965. At the same time the attraction of the city centre has also diminished for migrants from elsewhere, with increased numbers going directly to the suburbs. Only immigrants from overseas seem still to prefer inner areas. This seeming unpopularity of inner area living has contributed to a growing awareness that inner London, like the inner parts of other large cities, faces a formidable 'inner city' problem. One of the principal features of the inner city problem has been that of 'housing stress', a term usually synonymous with overcrowding, sharing of amenities and a high proportion of rented accommodation, but also applied in other ways, for example, to obsolescence. The GLDP (1969) described sixty-five wards as housing stress areas, mostly in thirteen boroughs in inner London (Fig. 2·3). More recently, researchers have been able to identify thirty-nine wards of intense housing stress based on sharing of accommodation and amenities and overcrowding, all in inner London (Fig. 2·3). These areas of intense housing stress conditions form a semi-circle running through the inner ring westwards from the Hackney–Tower Hamlets border and extending south of the river into Lambeth and Southwark. Only to the east is there any extensive break in the concentration of housing stress areas circling central London.

These stress wards are characterized by high proportions of poorer people and frequently have concentrations of coloured immigrants. In the mid-1960s up to one-third of coloured immigrants lived in stress wards, especially in the private rented furnished housing sector, compared with only 10% of British born population living in London. The inhabitants of stress wards are generally of low skill level and occupy poorly paid jobs. They are unable to compete for the most favoured sectors in the housing market and so are forced into decaying residential areas where either cheap owner-occupied property, frequently in multiple occupation, is available or, more commonly, the private rented sector provides overcrowded dwellings with few amenities. Local authority housing in such areas is usually in short supply and waiting lists are long. Over the years the housing problem in these areas has been exacerbated by the decline in the private rented sector due to rent controls, which has caused competition for the dwindling supply to intensify.

The other principal feature of the inner city problem has been employment stress, with high unemployment rates in some areas. In general London's relative unemployment position is not bad. In June 1975 it had nearly 10 % of national unemployment but 17 % of the national labour force. However, there are parts of the city where unemployment is high and *A Social Atlas of London* (1974) shows the high rates of unemployment for many wards in inner London in 1971. Figure 2·4 presents a more recent picture and is based on Department of Employment data for local office areas for June 1975. It shows the highest unemployment numbers and rates in a semi-circle of areas around the west side of central London, in Westminster, Hammersmith and St. Marylebone and also in Brixton, Holloway and Hackney. The highest rates occurred in Brixton, Poplar and Holloway, each having over 6 %. Four other areas (Camberwell, Lewisham, East Ham and Hornchurch) had over 5 %. Thus, within London there were areas in the mid-1970s which had much worse unemployment rates than those in many labour markets in officially designated 'development areas'.

The reasons for these high unemployment rates in parts of the capital are not entirely clear. The decline in employment, already referred to, is clearly important. However, despite the scale of redundancies in manufacturing there has been no great increase in numbers unemployed in the manufacturing sector; in fact, the sectoral distribution of the unemployed reflects almost exactly the broad employment structure of Greater London. Thus it seems that most of the manufacturing workers have moved out of the area or have moved into other sectors of the economy. This suggests that the unemployment figures reflect characteristics of supply rather than of demand. Researchers have used unemployment figures from the 1971 Census to try and explain variations in unemployment rates between boroughs and found that the personal characteristics of the unemployed, such as age and skill level, were more significant than factors of demand. They found that high proportions of immigrants from New Commonwealth countries were not usually associated with

2·4 Unemployment in the London Boroughs, June 1975.

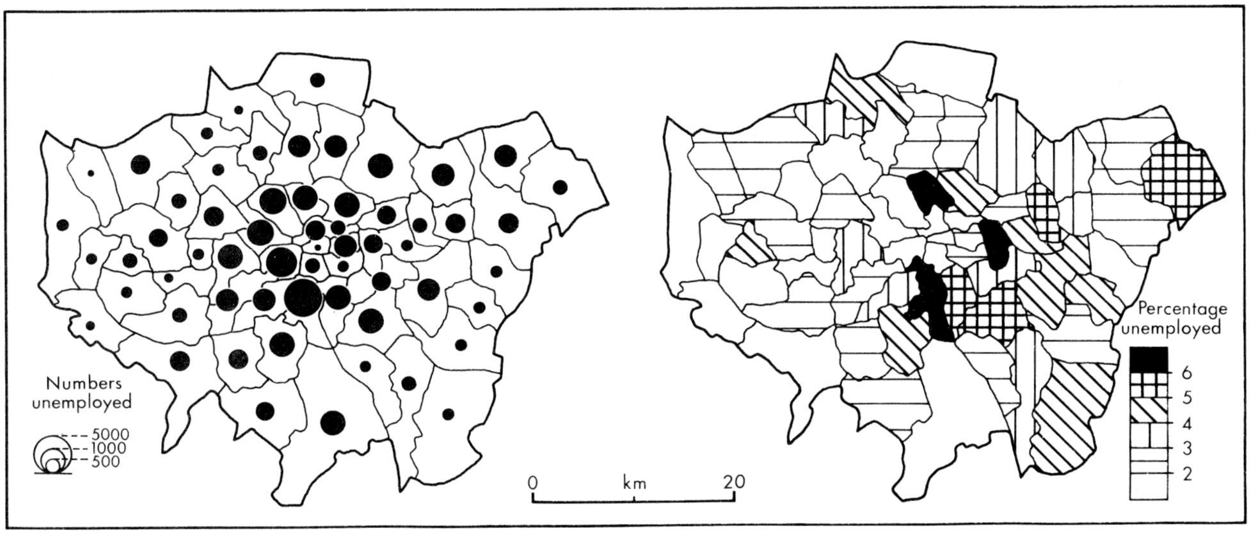

above average unemployment. Evidence from two recent studies of high unemployment areas suggests there is no uniform explanation. The Canning Town Community Development Project (1975) has suggested that out-migration there has not kept pace with the rundown in jobs, nor have the new jobs coming into the area matched the skills of the unemployed. A feature of male unemployment in Canning Town is the advanced age of the jobless (40 % were aged over 50) and their lack of skill (over 50 % were unskilled manual workers). In addition, the high proportion of people living in local authority housing in the area impedes mobility, while poor public transport restricts the size of the local labour market by making longer journeys to work more difficult. The Inner Area Study for the Stockwell area of Lambeth, sponsored by the Department of the Environment, presents a picture that has both similarities with and differences from Canning Town. In Lambeth the employment structure was more diversified but there was still a general problem affecting unskilled manual workers. However, the unemployed men were much younger, only a quarter being aged over 50, but 20–25 % of the unemployed in 1973 were West Indians, which is of particular importance.

Social Composition

The processes which have led to declines in population and employment and to the housing and employment problems described above have generated concern that the social composition of London as a whole may also be changing. Attention is normally directed to two questions. The first is whether the overall social balance in the capital has changed, with, for example, those who can afford to move to the suburbs and beyond, leaving behind a residue unable or not inclined to move. The second is whether change in the distribution of socio-economic groups in the city is leading to spatial polarization into 'rich' and 'poor' areas. Such changes may be due to many factors. These include the educational system and the jobs acquired by school-leavers. The Inner Area Study for Stockwell has suggested that one of the roots of the employment problem in parts of Lambeth is the low level of academic attainment, so that new entrants into the labour market tend to be predominantly unskilled. But at the same time, they are educated enough to reject what they see as the low status jobs (*eg* with London Transport) that were accepted by their parents. Other forces for change are the pattern of retirement from the labour force and general social mobility. Perhaps the most potent agent of social change, however, is the selective nature of migration. A fundamental distinction here is in the origins of migrants, particularly the proportions that come from overseas. The latter type of flow has received much publicity in recent years and there has been public debate about the build-up of ethnic and foreign minorities in British cities. It is also well established that migration is selective in a socio-economic sense, with certain groups, especially the better off, being more migratory than others. Hence, the social balance of the city and its constituent areas may be changed as a result of differential group propensities to migrate.

The evidence for spatial polarization of London's rich and poor does not present a clear picture. Willmott and Young (1973), looking at social class for pre-GLC boroughs in the period 1951–66, suggested that working-class people were becoming concentrated in a riverine 'cross', running roughly east–west along the Thames and north–south along the Lee and Wandle valleys, with higher social classes concentrating in the centre and suburbs. They attributed change to differential migration. Other workers, examining wards between 1961 and 1966, found no broad geometrical pattern and even a tendency for the social class distribution of small areas to approach the average Greater London distribution. They were also reluctant to ascribe the change observed to migration. This contradiction may be due to the differential geographical scales and time periods used in the two studies. More recently, data have been used from the 1961, 1966 and 1971 Censuses to try to verify social trends. The analysis is based mainly on the economically active male sector of the population, arguably the most important in determining the social character of an area. First of all the patterns of migration of the various socio-economic groups in the mid-1960s (using the 1965–6 migration information from the 1966 Census) are reviewed and attempts made to relate this to the observed social change in Greater London between 1961 and 1971.

The analysis began by collapsing seventeen socio-economic groups into the five categories used in an earlier study, namely, (a) professional and managerial (SEGs 1–4, 13), (b) skilled manual (SEGs 8–9, 12, 14), (c) non-manual (SEGs 5–6), (d) semi-skilled and service (SEGs 7, 10, 15), (e) unskilled manual, forces, inadequately described (SEGs 11, 16–17), while the thirty-three boroughs are aggregated into five sectors: north-west, north-east, inner-south, outer-north, outer-south. The general pattern that emerges is one of net decentralization for all groups, mainly of short distance moves. The north-west sector (City, Camden, Hammersmith, Kensington and Chelsea, Westminster) was an exception to the general rule, with net gains of white-collar workers moving from longer distances. The decentralization that occurred was distinctly and regularly selective, with the rank order of radial flows being professional and managerial (largest), non-manual, skilled manual, semi-skilled and service, and unskilled forces and others (smallest). The north-west sector had a regular outflow of skilled manual workers but gained professional, managerial and other non-manual workers from the rest of the UK. Some movement of professional and managerial workers into the north-east sector from the north-west may be associated with gentrification in parts of Islington.

When overall aggregate trends from the three censuses are considered a consistent story emerges. The general change through the decade was one of increase in the numbers of white-collar workers but decrease in the numbers of manual workers for London as a whole. Despite the overall fall in the economically active male population of 335 000 between 1961 and 1971, and despite the evidence of their net emigration in 1965–6, the proportions of managers of small establishments, professional employees, personal service and own account workers all increased consistently. In contrast, junior white collar and all manual workers decreased as a proportion of Greater London's economically active male population, while other groups showed no clear trend. This pattern was true for both inner and outer London, although between 1966 and 1971 the decrease in numbers of skilled manual workers in inner boroughs was large; from 30·6 % to 26·3 % of the total economically active male population.

When these changes are examined for individual boroughs for the period 1966 to 1971 (borough boundary changes prevent a 1961–71 comparison) it is seen that both the percentage increase in numbers of employers, managers and self-employed and the decrease in skilled manual workers are common to most boroughs. Increases in professional and non-manual workers were scattered throughout several boroughs including Islington, Lambeth and Wandsworth in inner London. Only in Ealing, Enfield, Haringey and Tower Hamlets did the proportion of semi-skilled increase and only in Newham and Redbridge did unskilled increase. In summary, it is suggested that the observed increase in white-collar workers in Greater London applied to both inner and outer boroughs. When individual boroughs are examined for 1966–71 there is no suggestion that any particular group of boroughs was subject to social change in contrast to patterns for the GLC as a whole.

This analysis suggests that there does not seem to be a tendency towards polarization of the city into social areas, at least at the borough level, but in order to test further whether or not this was so, uni-polarity scores have been calculated for the boroughs in 1966 and 1971. These relate the distribution of socio-economic categories for a borough to the distribution for the Greater London norm, producing a statistic that allows easy comparison between areas and between dates. Analysis for 1966–71 showed Camden, Richmond and Barnet becoming relatively more 'professional', while Tower Hamlets, Hillingdon and Hackney moved in the opposite direction. But the trends were not very great and on the whole do not suggest that boroughs were becoming more extreme, more polarized. However a note of warning must be injected into interpreting such analysis. It should be pointed out that although less-skilled male workers in outer London are an increasing proportion of all less-skilled workers in London, their presence in outer London is not increasing as fast as the rest of the working population in suburban areas. One may draw the tentative conclusion that the urban pattern of the 1950s and 1960s is being entrenched, with an increasingly hard line being discernible between the middle and outer ring of boroughs.

Migration from Overseas

The significance of the overseas migration stream in numerical population change in London has already been described, and it is recognized that the key element in social change in many parts of London over the last two decades has been immigration from overseas, especially from New Commonwealth countries. Most cities have historically had their immigrant 'quarters' and London has been no exception. However, popular concern in Britain has been voiced recently that out-migration of the indigenous population from some areas of London, combined with continued in-migration of people from overseas, might lead to the creation of ghettos in areas where immigrants have become established.

In analysing the geography of immigrants from overseas the first hurdle is that of data availability. The basic source is the Census of Population Birthplace Statistics, which must not be regarded as a direct surrogate for racial/ethnic status. There are difficulties in using these data comparatively; *eg* in the 1961 and 1971 Censuses people were asked in a similar manner to identify their place of birth, but there was a slightly different wording to the question in the 1966 Census. This may be a small problem when comparing large areas but it increases in magnitude when small areas are considered. Another major problem in studying the internal geography of London is that of boundary comparability between boroughs, which were changed by the London local government reorganization in the 1960s, and also between enumeration districts.

Analysis of census statistics shows that the decrease in Greater London's population is mainly the result of a net decrease in the capital's UK born citizens (Table 3). Between 1961 and 1971 there was a net reduction of these people by 850 000 (12 %). During the same period numbers born in other countries increased by 265 000 (31 %) with the increase being mainly those

TABLE 3 Greater London: Enumerated Population of Birthplace by 'A' and 'B' boroughs—1961 and 1971 (thousands of persons)

	Greater London			*'A' Boroughs*			*'B' Boroughs*		
Country of Birth	*1961*	*1971*	% *Change*	*1961*	*1971*	% *Change*	*1961*	*1971*	% *Change*
All Countries	7 997	7 452	−7	3 494	3 003	−13	4 503	4 420	−2
UK	7 119	6 270	−12	2 954	2 364	−20	4 165	3 906	−6
Outside UK	847	1 113	+31	522	622	+19	325	492	+51
Visitors	37	44	+19	26	35	+35	11	9	−18
Residents of England and Wales/UK*	810	1069	+32	496	587	+18	314	483	+54
Irish Republic	254	241	−5	150	126	−16	104	116	+12
Old Commonwealth	33	41	+24	17	22	+29	16	18	+13
New Commonwealth	242	476	+97	169	267	+58	73	210	+188
Other Countries and At Sea	281	311	+11	160	172	+8	121	139	+15
Not Stated	31	69	+123	18	47	+161	13	22	+69

* England and Wales applies to 1961 data; UK applies to 1971 data

born in New Commonwealth countries, 234 000 (97 %). These figures mean that while in 1961 the New Commonwealth born population was smaller than that born in other non-UK countries, by 1971 it was half as big again. By 1971, the proportion of London's population born there had fallen from 68 % in 1966 to 66 %.

Clearly during the 1960s there were important changes going on in the origins of the migration streams from overseas. These may be traced by looking at the proportions of migrants from various birthplaces who entered London after 1960. For Greater London as a whole 44 % of the migrants born abroad recorded in the 1971 Census had entered since 1960, but the proportions varied considerably among subgroups. Only 24 % from Eire entered after 1960, compared with 59 % of people born in New Commonwealth countries. The 'most recent' migrants were from Old Commonwealth countries (62 % entered post-1960), but the short lengths of stay of this group are probably explained by immigration of young people on working holidays. It does seem that more recent migrants have tended to settle in similar areas to their compatriots who preceded them, though with the inner boroughs outside the central area taking a slightly higher proportion.

Distribution of Immigrants

The various immigrant groups have not settled uniformly over Greater London. In 1971 21 % of the residents of the inner London ('A') boroughs were born outside the UK compared with 11 % in the outer ('B') boroughs (Fig. 1). There is marked variation, however, between the areas settled by specific immigrant groups. In general, European born and Old Commonwealth born live in the better housing areas, especially in the outer boroughs. New Commonwealth and Irish born concentrate in the inner ring. Both the 1966 and 1971 Censuses suggest that the Irish live in the worst housing areas.

The reasons for these concentrations vary but generally they are familiar: low standing in the labour market prevents immigrants effectively competing for the most favoured sectors in the housing market and channels them into the decaying inner residential areas. Once concentrations have become established they will tend to attract similar immigrants through the development of cultural and language ties, the provision of minority community services and the construction of social networks. The results are seen when individual wards are examined. For example, Golborne ward in Kensington and Chelsea had 22 % of its population in 1971 born in a New Commonwealth country; for Harrow Road ward in Westminster the figure was 28 %. Several wards in Haringey, Brent and Lambeth, and Spitalfields ward in Tower Hamlets had over 30 %. Extreme cases were Northcote and Glebe wards in Ealing with 63 % and 42 % respectively.

Study of individual migrant groups reveals clear concentrations, although these are not necessarily coincident (Fig. 2·5). West Indians congregated in three main areas: a west London concentration in southern Brent, northern Hammersmith and Kensington and Chelsea; a south London concentration in western Wandsworth, Lambeth, central Southwark and north Lewisham; and a north London concentration in Haringey, northern Islington and Hackney. Very few West Indians were found in the centre and in the outer suburbs. The Irish born population was spread throughout most of Greater London, though the main concentrations were in Brent (where in Kilburn ward 20 % of the population in 1971 had been born in the Irish Republic), Hammersmith and Ealing to the west, and in some wards of Camden, Islington, Kensington and Chelsea and Westminster. The lowest proportions of Irish were to be found in south-east London, in Havering, Bromley and Bexley, and in east London. Concentrations of Asian born were smaller than for the other two groups and their distribution was somewhat different. Asians tended to be less located in the inner boroughs than other immigrants, being especially found to the west, in central Hounslow and south Ealing. Other boroughs, such as Brent, had incipient concentrations in 1971, which subsequently increased with the settlement there after 1973 of Ugandan Asians.

Of importance for the social geography of the capital is whether or not the distributions described above represent a stage in the entrenchment of ghettos. If, in fact, it is true that concentrations of specific immigrant groups are becoming increasingly focused in the inner boroughs, it could be expected that those boroughs would have had a greater increase between 1961 and 1971 in the immigrant population than London as a whole. *A Social Atlas of London* includes a series of maps showing the relationship of immigrant population observed in 1971 to the immigrant population that might have been expected had increases in the immigrant population since 1961 been the same in the borough as in London as a whole. In 1961 the percentage of West Indian immigrants in all inner London boroughs (excluding Greenwich) was higher than the corresponding percentage for Greater London. West Indians were also concentrated in Brent and Haringey. Between 1961 and 1971 there was no uniform pattern of change. Only in Lewisham and Wandsworth (in inner London) and in Brent and Haringey did the concentrations of West Indians increase, while in Camden, Westminster, Kensington and Chelsea and Tower Hamlets there was an absolute decline, so that by 1971 their proportions of West Indian immigrants were less than for London as a whole. Other inner boroughs remained with higher than average proportions of West Indians, but their rates of increase

2·5 Residential Patterns of West Indians, Asians and Irish, 1971 (From *A Social Atlas of London*).

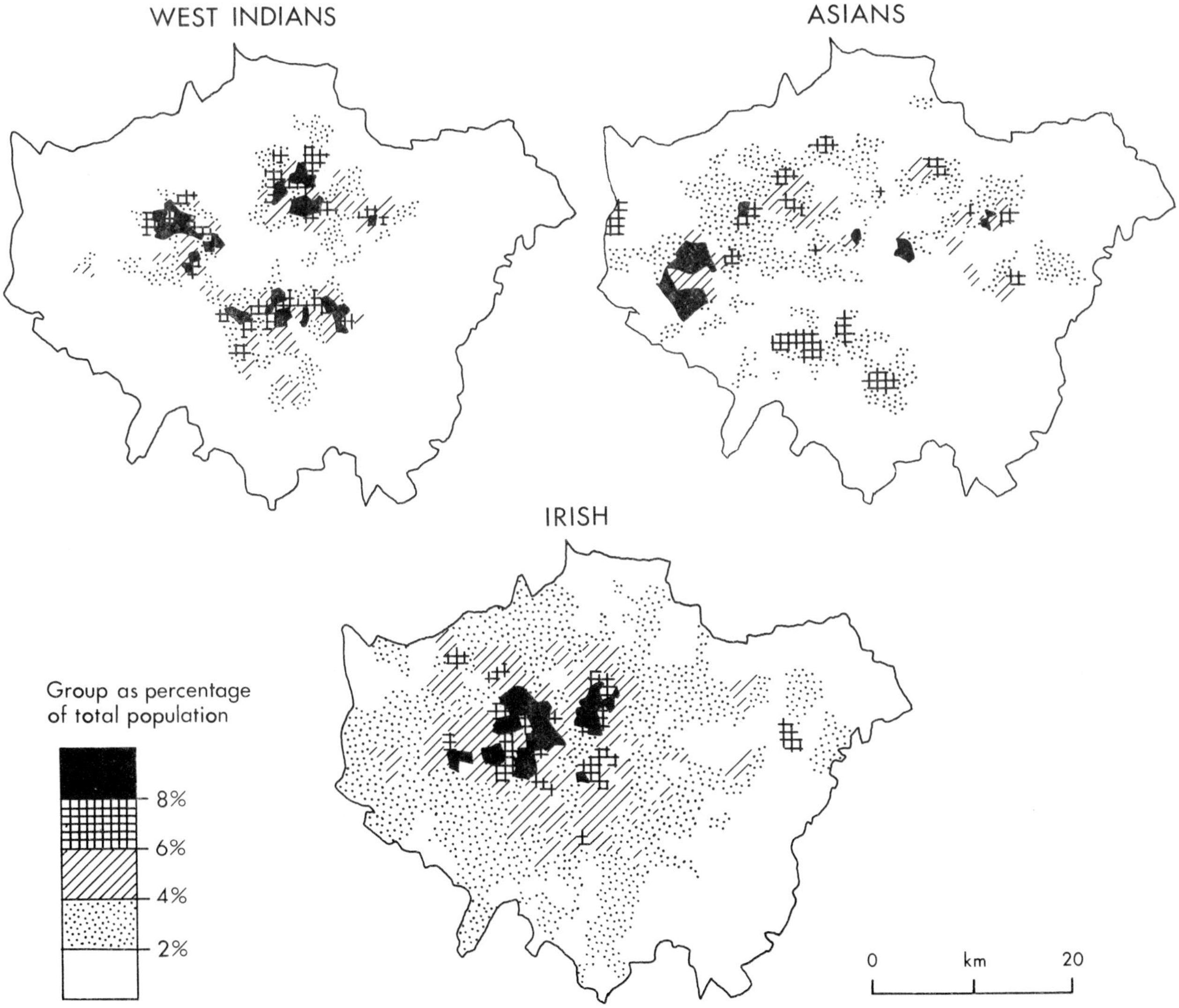

were less than for the city as a whole. Trends for the Irish born population were similar, with losses in inner London. These were heaviest in an arc from Islington to Hammersmith, where in 1961 a third of London's Irish population lived. Areas of increase tended to be to the north and west, reflecting some peripheral movement. As was seen above, the Asian born population did not show such a clear inner/outer borough contrast as the other two minority groups. Again, however, it was the areas of highest concentration in 1961 which had the biggest losses in the ensuing decade. Unlike West Indians and Irish, however, relative increases of Asians were more concentrated, with two areas standing out: Hounslow/ Ealing/Brent and Newham/Waltham Forest.

In summary, the period 1961–71 seems to have been one of change in the distributions of Irish and Asians, representing a relocation of areas of settlement rather than a trend towards ghetto-like intensification. For West Indians, the most concentrated group in both 1961 and 1971, there was a decline in their concentration as well as some redistribution. Rather than entrenchment of incipient ghettos, immigrants seem to have been leaving inner city areas faster than the indigenous population. In part, their distribution is becoming more widespread but also there is evidence, for Asians at least, of new concentrations forming in suburban areas. This out-migration of the immigrant population is almost certainly a response to the pressures exerted by the inner city on all its less-fortunate residents.

Summary and Conclusions

For London's population and employment the period since World War II has been one of change and current declines show no signs of halting. By 1991 London's population is projected to be only 5 700 000, according to *The Strategy for the South East, 1976 Review*. Decrease in population has been mainly because of a net fall in the number of UK born citizens living in the capital, especially in the inner boroughs. This has been partly compensated by a net increase in the proportion of London's population born overseas, especially in New Commonwealth countries. The overall pattern has thus been one of out-migration of indigenous population, in-migration from overseas.

Despite the dramatic fall in population numbers there does not seem to have been any great change in the capital's social composition. Evidence from the 1966 Census indicated a general tendency for all socio-economic groups to decentralize, although there was some counter-movement of white-collar workers. For the 1960s as a whole, however, the basic picture was of a relative gain in white-collar workers, and a loss of manual (especially skilled manual) workers. The seeming conflict in these findings may be resolved by factors other than migration, such as general upward social mobility in an urban economy that offered opportunities for white-collar employment to those who would formerly not have expected it. If London was showing a slight tendency during the 1960s to become more non-manual in its social composition, there does not seem to be an obvious trend towards social polarization of boroughs into 'rich' and 'poor'. This does not mean that rich and poor areas do not exist, simply that the dichotomy was not strengthened during the decade.

The role of immigration from overseas in ameliorating the trend for the nation's capital to lose population has been considerable. In the 1970s there are clearly recognizable concentrations of immigrant groups, especially in parts of inner London. However, the case for continuing ghetto creation is not proven and the immigrants seem to exhibit the same tendency as the indigenous population to leave overcrowded, decaying inner residential areas. Each of the three minority groups studied decentralized during the 1960s, though there is some evidence of new concentrations coming into existence beyond the inner areas of first settlement.

These changes in population have partly initiated and partly responded to the loss of employment from London, and especially from inner London. Losses of jobs, especially in manufacturing, have undoubtedly made more acute the unemployment problems of some areas but there is no clear positive correlation between areas facing redundancies and areas with high unemployment rates. It seems, in fact, that areas of high unemployment are frequently those of low cost private or council rented housing into which the lower paid and less skilled, often the most prone to unemployment, naturally gravitate. For example, it has been found that although in London the unemployment rates for Stepney and Poplar were high by national standards, unemployment rates among individual social groups living there were not all that different from the national average for those groups. In other words, unemployment rates in Stepney and Poplar were high because groups of people with high unemployment propensity tended to congregate there. The relationship between unemployment and low-cost housing, especially in the private rented sector, is not an absolute one though. Some of the areas of worst housing stress are in west London, while the unemployment rate is at its worst in east London. It is only in the southern inner area, especially in Lambeth and Southwark, that the worst housing problem areas are conterminous with those having the worst employment problems. This is the area of London's most difficult urban problem: acute housing stress in a locally stagnant labour market.

Falling population and employment and growing concern with problems of stress in urban areas have led to recent government initiatives in providing aid for the inner parts of cities. The success of this policy will be severely affected by the degree to which population and employment decline continues. At the moment it seems likely that falls will continue, reducing the city's economic base. This will make it harder for local government to find investment to aid the problem areas. If decline does continue, to the levels that have been projected, it is likely that at some stage fundamental changes will begin to take place in the social geography of the capital. What is not certain is how far population decline will continue. Clearly it cannot do so indefinitely, and perhaps the most important question for the city is what will be its new population equilibrium level?

Further Reading

Donnison, D. and Eversley, D. E. C. (eds.), *London: Urban Patterns, Problems and Policies* (Heinemann, London, 1973)

Lomas, G., *The Inner City* (London Council of Social Service, London, 1974)

3 Transport in the Capital

John Adams

Introduction

To most of us who travel in London, the city's transport system is bewilderingly large and complex. If we plan excursions which depart from our regular routes, we usually need to consult one of the various London maps or directories to find our way. We commonly find, especially if either end of our journey is close to the centre of the city, that we must choose from a number of possible routes and modes of travel. Our choice will be influenced by matters such as whether or not we have a car or a bicycle, the availability of a place to park, the length and cost of the journey, our knowledge of traffic conditions along the route and the weather.

For most of their journeys most people would probably describe their particular choice of route and mode of travel as the least of a number of possible evils. Traffic jams, fumes, noise and accidents afflict those who travel by road. Rail and Underground services are often dirty, unreliable and overcrowded. Traffic also makes life unpleasant in the residential neighbourhoods and high streets through which it passes.

To the people experiencing them, these problems have an air of permanence. Although there are occasional changes – road works, new schedules and altered services, new one-way systems and parking regulations—the great bulk of the physical network that carries the traffic and the institutions that administer it can seem solid and enduring. If we retreat, however, to a more detached perspective and contemplate London's transport over the span of the nineteenth century and the first three-quarters of the twentieth century the picture becomes one of dramatic change. Looking ahead to the end of this century the potential for change is equally impressive. The history of this change is intimately bound up with the story of the growth of London and the continuous efforts of the planners, operators and users of transport in the city to cope with a situation that has never been considered satisfactory. The future of London's transport will doubtless be shaped by a continuation of these same efforts.

The Past

The Nineteenth Century

> 'They knows its handy for a man's work' said one and all,
> 'and that's the reason why they imposes on a body'.
>
> from *Jacob's Island*, Henry Mayhew.

Jacob's Island, in Bermondsey in south-east London, was visited by Mayhew in 1849. The filth, overcrowding, hunger and disease described in his stomach-turning account of what he called 'a Venice of Drains', where the drains served also as the source of the area's drinking water, provoked an obvious question: how could people acquiesce in such an existence? Mayhew put this question to people living there. He encountered a remarkable stoicism in the inhabitants and an acute appreciation of the causes of their suffering. The reason why the landlords of Jacob's Island were able to impose so cruelly on them was that the area was convenient to the inhabitants' work. While this is obviously less than a complete explanation for the conditions Mayhew found, it does serve to illustrate what a powerful force the journey to work has been in shaping London. Of all the bustling to-ing and fro-ing in London's streets it was, and remains, the journeys to work which dominate the pattern of movement. These journeys, in turn, have been a dominant consideration in the myriad locational decisions which have produced London's land-use pattern.

The influence of the journey to work is strongest where people are poor and transport is expensive. The observations of Charles Pearson to the Royal Commission on Metropolitan Termini in 1846 are still relevant: 'A poor man is chained to the spot. He has not leisure to walk and he has not money to ride a distance from his work.' Pearson was convinced that cheap transport could play a vital role in breaking the chains that bound people to slums such as Jacob's Island. He was one of the most energetic of the promoters of the Metropolitan Line from Paddington to Moorgate, the world's first underground railway, and obtained an undertaking from its operators, the Great Western Railway, to carry workers from a proposed housing estate in the country, about 5 km west of London, to the City and back daily for one shilling a week.

Although the railway building of the nineteenth century was primarily spurred by other, less altruistic motives it did help to relieve the overcrowding of the urban poor. London experienced a six-fold growth in its population, from 1 110 000 at the beginning of the nineteenth century to over 8 600 000 by its peak in 1939, but experienced a more than seventy-fold growth in its area during the same period as it sprawled into the surrounding countryside. At the same time, the demand for land near the centre for industrial and commercial uses intensified. Thus, partly as a result of people being pushed out of the centre and partly as a result of the pull of the new suburbs the extreme residential densities at the centre began to decline. By 1961 when the number of people working in the City of London was close to its peak of 500 000 there were only 4771 people actually living there. Pearson's workers' estate however did not materialize. It was overwhelmingly the better off who took advantage of the opportunities afforded by the railways to live in the suburbs and work in the city.

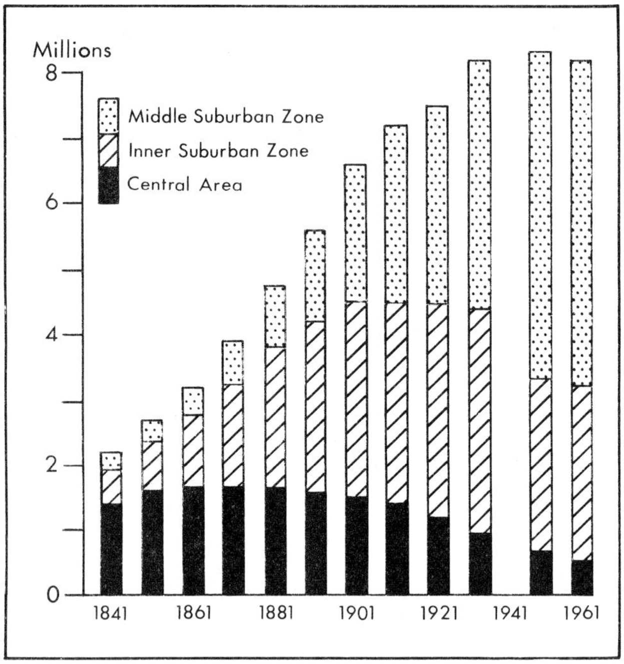

3·1 London's Population Growth, 1841–1961.

It is important to remember how malleable the terms 'suburb' and 'central city' have had to be. The underground Metropolitan Railway from Moorgate to Paddington, completed in 1865, was built to link the City with its north-western suburbs. It was also intended to relieve the severe congestion caused by the rapidly growing volume of horse-drawn traffic along London's northern perimeter road. Today, congestion is as bad as ever and both terminals of the railway as well as the 'perimeter road' (the present Marylebone and Euston Roads) are part of the modern transport planner's 'central city'. Figure 3·1 describes the suburbanization process from 1841 to 1961. The process of dispersal has continued to the present but after the peak reached on the graph in 1951 it spilled over into the outer metropolitan area so that population statistics for the GLC area alone are no longer sufficient to chart its progress.

The transformation of London's transport system in the nineteenth century was profound. Until London's first railway, from Spa Road to Deptford in south-east London, was opened in 1836 all travel over land in the city had to be on foot or in horse-drawn vehicles. The railways greatly improved London's links both with its immediate hinterland and with other major cities in the country but did not begin to play a major role in London's internal transport until the underground railways were built and the built up area grew to include the city's immediate hinterland. Within the central city horse-drawn omnibuses remained the principal form of public transport up to the end of the nineteenth century. The greater part of the railway system was completed before the end of that century and it is still the system by which most people get to work in central London. Over 70 % of the 1 075 000 people who arrived daily in central London between 07·00 hr and 10·00 hr during 1975 are estimated to have travelled by train or Underground.

The Twentieth Century While the nineteenth century witnessed great increases in the mobility of many Londoners, vehicular traffic, whether public or private, remained the prerogative of the well-to-do. Most people still lived within walking distance of their jobs, shops and schools and made use of public transport only on special occasions. In the early years of the twentieth century the pace of transport developments accelerated. In 1901 London's first electric tramway opened, from Shepherd's Bush to Acton, and within nine years the electrified tramway network was carrying almost 800 000 000 passengers a year. The electrification of the Underground was begun, greatly improving the quality of the air in the system, and motor buses started to force their horse-drawn competitors off the road. By 1939 public transport in London was carrying an estimated 3 783 000 000 passengers a year—on average more than one journey per day per head of the population. Almost 60 % of these passengers were carried in London Passenger Transport Board's buses, while trams, trolley buses and railways carried roughly equal shares of the remainder. Services were greatly disrupted during the war but recovered very quickly and by 1948 public transport in London was carrying an all time peak of 4 675 000 000 passengers a year.

It was a short-lived recovery. Since 1948 public transport has experienced a continuous decline in the numbers of passengers carried and a contraction of the services offered. What was once a highly profitable enterprise must now annually be rescued from collapse by government subsidies. The reason is

3·2 Zone to Zone Travel by Road, 1962 and 1981.

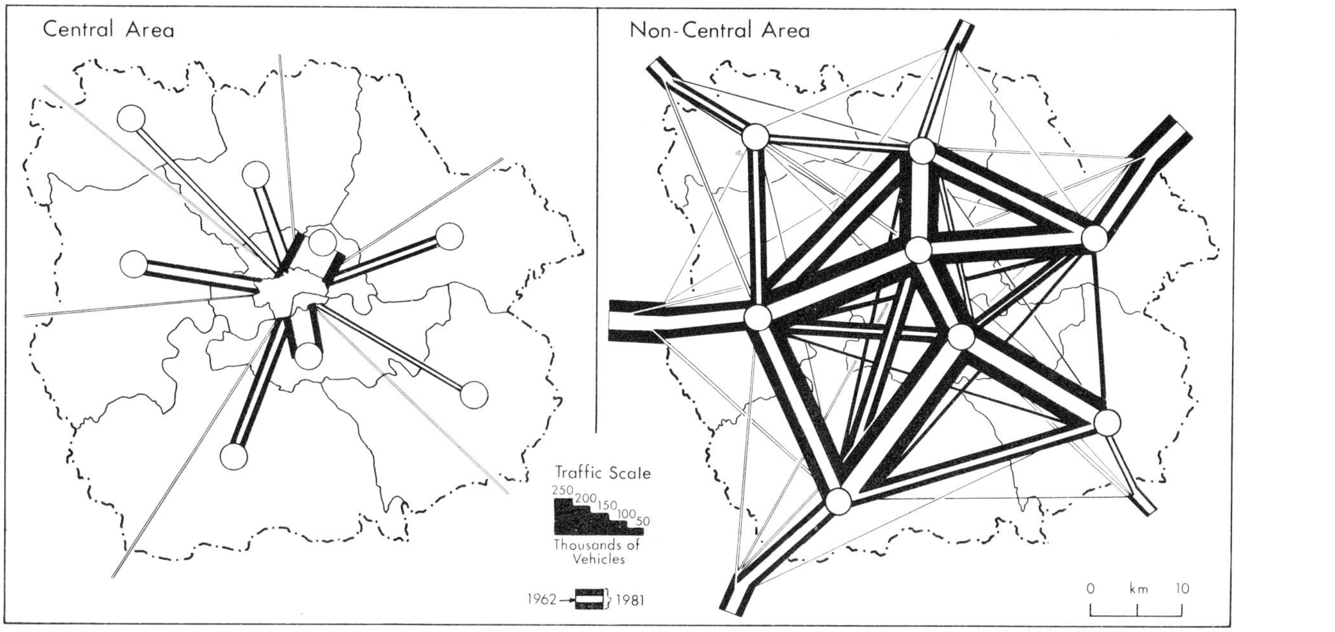

not hard to find. Large numbers of people have deserted public transport for cars.

The Car 'The motor vehicle is really demanding a radically new urban form.' This is the conclusion of the most influential transport planning document of the 1960s—the Buchanan Report, *Traffic in Towns*. It was published in 1963 and exemplifies post-war transport planning orthodoxy. The rapid growth in car ownership was seen as 'demanding' the provision of more road capacity to carry it.

In 1959 the Roads Campaign Council held a 'New Ways for London' competition for the best design of a long-term plan for highway development in the city. Buchanan was one of the panel of judges that awarded first prize to J. A. Proudlove's *Traffic Plan for London*. Proudlove noted that while road traffic was growing in Britain as a whole at a rate of 14 % per year, in London it was growing at only 2 % per year. This relatively slow growth of traffic in London was seen as the problem to be solved:

'The present slow increase in traffic will be hastened as changes take place to the structure which presently maintains this unnaturally low figure (of 2 %) namely the lack of road and parking space and the effective public transport system able to operate at rates cheaper than private travel.'

Proudlove's prize-winning scheme for solving this problem involved ambitious changes to London's road structure. Although his network of urban

3·3 Expected Traffic Patterns, 1981.

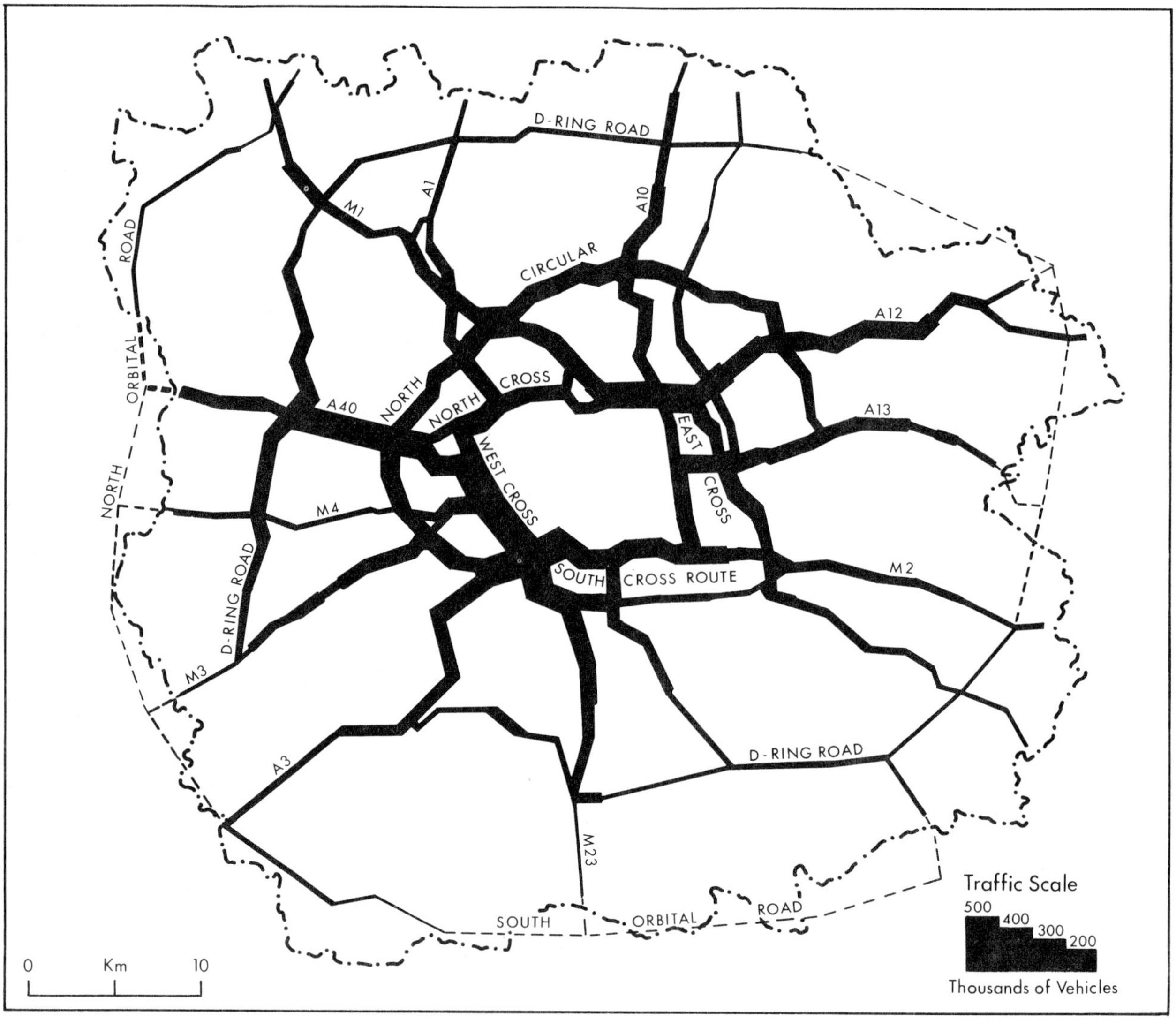

motorways was not adopted, its guiding principle, that the restraints on London's 'unnaturally' slow traffic growth should be removed, can be found in the Buchanan Report and in the major London traffic studies which were subsequently incorporated in the GLDP.

Transport planners frequently illustrate their problems with 'desire line' maps. These lines indicate the numbers of people estimated to travel between all pairs of zones in the study area. Figure 3·2, from the London Traffic Survey shows the pattern of zone to zone travel in London in 1962 and the growth anticipated, if traffic were not restrained by a lack of road space, by 1981. Figure 3·3 shows the pattern of traffic that was expected in 1981 if a system of ring and radial roads were to be built sufficient to carry the anticipated traffic.

As the desire lines of car travellers grew longer and wider during the 1950s, London's main road network, most of which was established before the invention of the car, came under increasing strain. As more and more Londoners flowed back and forth across the

3·4 Main Elements of Transportation in the South East.

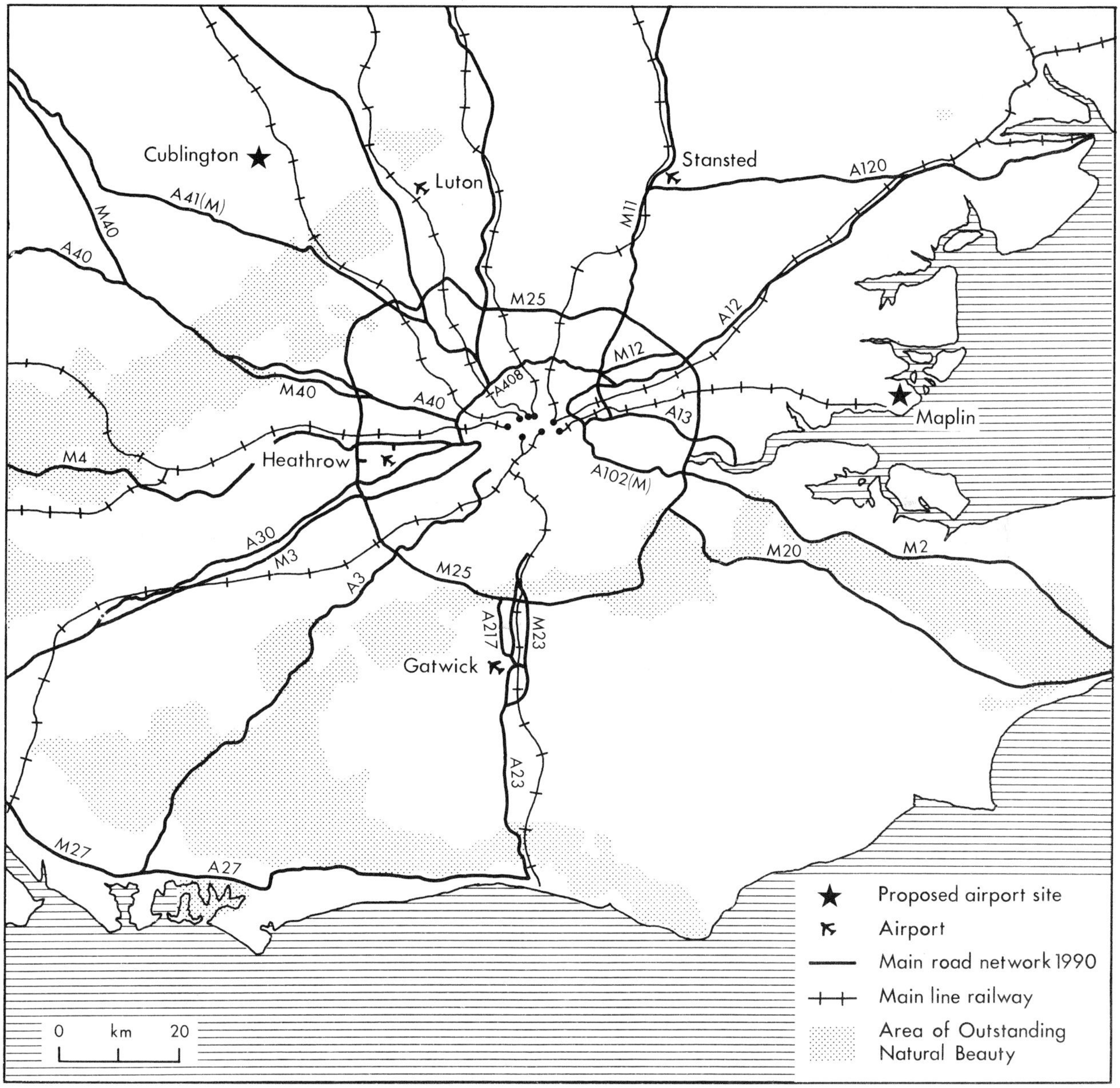

political and administrative boundaries laid down in less-mobile eras local traffic authorities found themselves vainly trying to cope with growing traffic of which an increasing proportion was just passing through their areas. This problem of traffic management was one important reason behind the creation of the GLC in 1965.

One of the first official acts of the new council was the announcement of plans to build the 'Motorway Box', the squarish inner ring on Fig. 3·3 to relieve the congested core of the city. Within a year it had unveiled the rest of its plans for the vast primary network of urban motorways which consisted of the additional ring and radial roads represented by the major flow lines on Fig. 3·3.

The plans were extraordinarily ambitious. The Motorway Box, to be built close to the congested, densely built-up centre of London, would have been one of the most expensive roads ever built anywhere. When first presented it was estimated to cost £15 000 000 per km. The whole of the proposed network was estimated to cost a total of around £2 000 000 000. Inflation quickly renders such monetary estimates useless as a standard of comparison. The whole scheme would have taken 2500 ha of some of the most expensive land in the world and would have involved knocking down and rebuilding housing occupied by 100 000 people. Its cost would have dwarfed that of other major transport projects under consideration at the time, such as Concorde, the Channel Tunnel or the new London airport.

The estimated costs of the scheme increased sharply towards the centre of the city. The land acquisition costs per km for the inner Motorway Box were estimated to be fifteen times higher than for the outer Ringway 3, and construction costs, because of more crowded working conditions in the inner area, were estimated to be five times greater.

The plans provoked fierce controversy and became one of the focal issues of the 1973 GLC elections. As an appreciation of the disruptive implications of the plans grew, especially in areas alongside the proposed new motorways, opposition began to organize. This opposition gathered momentum and in 1973 the GLC Labour Party, having initially proposed the Motorway Box, campaigned against it, and won the election. The new Labour controlled council continued to support construction of the outer ringway, mostly outside the GLC boundary, but within the GLC area it largely abandoned road building for a policy of restraining car traffic and promoting public transport. In its *Transport Policies and Programme 1977–82* it declared its intention to reduce peak hour traffic levels in central London by one-third below their 1974 levels.

The Aeroplane The building of the railway network in the nineteenth century and the motorway network in the twentieth century greatly increased London's accessibility to the rest of the country. As can be seen from Fig. 3·4 London is the focus of these networks. Since the war London has also become a major focus of international air travel. Figure 3·5 shows the growth of traffic through London's four airports up to the post-war peak of almost 30 000 000 in 1973. Heathrow to the west of London handled two-thirds

3·5 Traffic through London's Airports.

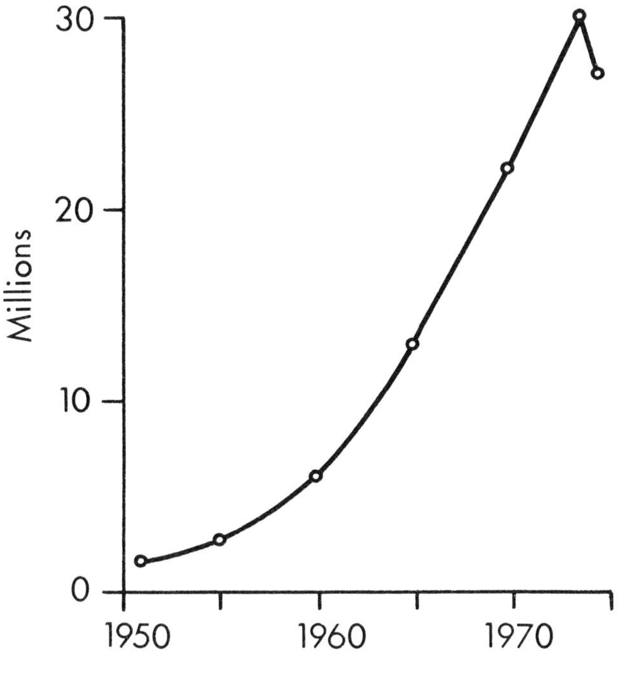

of this traffic, 20 300 000, Gatwick to the south took 5 700 000, Luton to the north-west, 3 200 000, and Stansted to the north-east (which is used primarily for private flying and test and training flights) 200 000. These four airports together account for over 80 % of Britain's international air traffic.

In 1974 there was a fall in air traffic for the first time since the war. This has been followed by a modest and uncertain recovery in 1975–6. The principal cause of this abrupt halt was the very large increase in the cost of aviation fuel in late 1973. Fuel now accounts for nearly one-quarter of total airline operating costs and future traffic trends will inevitably be strongly influenced by its price.

During the period of most rapid growth in the 1960s the air transport planners approached their job with a sense of urgency. Growing traffic was threatening to overwhelm the capacity of the airport system, and resentment was building up in the communities around the existing airports as the noise got steadily worse. The first proposal to deal with this situation was to expand greatly the airport at Stansted. This plan was abandoned in the face of strong local opposition and in 1968 the Roskill Commission was appointed to enquire into the siting of a major new London airport.

The Commission reported over two years later. It predicted that traffic would exceed the capacity of the existing airports by 1980 and recommended that a large new four-runway airport be built at Cublington near Aylesbury in Buckinghamshire.

The Commission attempted to balance the benefits of accessibility against the disadvantages of a major airport. Since London is the focus of south-east England's surface transport system, the most accessible site for a new London airport, from the point of view of its potential customers, would be central London itself. The airport was to perform a central London transport function for which there was no room in central London. The disadvantage of an airport that generally provokes the strongest public reaction is aircraft noise. Sites that would not inflict this on large numbers of people are only to be found at a considerable distance from the centre of the city. The site at Cublington represented the Roskill Commission's idea of a just compromise between centripetal and repelling forces. But its recommendation met strong opposition from the local inhabitants and the government rejected it and favoured a site on the less accessible and less densely populated Maplin Sands in south-east Essex. But again strong and vociferous opposition was encountered. The government announced a major review of its airport planning strategy and in July 1974 formally abandoned the Maplin project.

Having appeased the opposition at Stansted, Cublington and finally Maplin the government is now left facing the resentful residents of the areas in the noise shadows of Heathrow, Gatwick and Luton who are still clamouring for relief. Although it has increased substantially its estimates of the amount of traffic that the existing airports can handle, it still believes that traffic will exceed this capacity sometime before the end of the century. Stansted, ten years on, is once again a frequently nominated site for a major new airport.

The Present Debate about an Uncertain Future

Since the middle of the nineteenth century London has spread across an ever-widening area. While this dispersal has very largely been a consequence of improved transport, it has for most of the period had the blessing of government policy. The various promoters of the railways, the trams and the buses and most recently campaigners for roads have all extolled the benefits of the lower density living conditions that their mode of transport would facilitate. Air travel represents perhaps the ultimate stage of this dispersal, promoting international trade and tourism on an unprecedented scale.

These trends have been actively supported by both central government and the GLC. In recent years the GLC has been a willing participant in the exercise of 'decanting' large numbers of its residents into new towns beyond the Green Belt, and the Location of Offices Bureau continued to advertise the benefits to both employers and workers of migration from central London until its remit was changed in 1977.

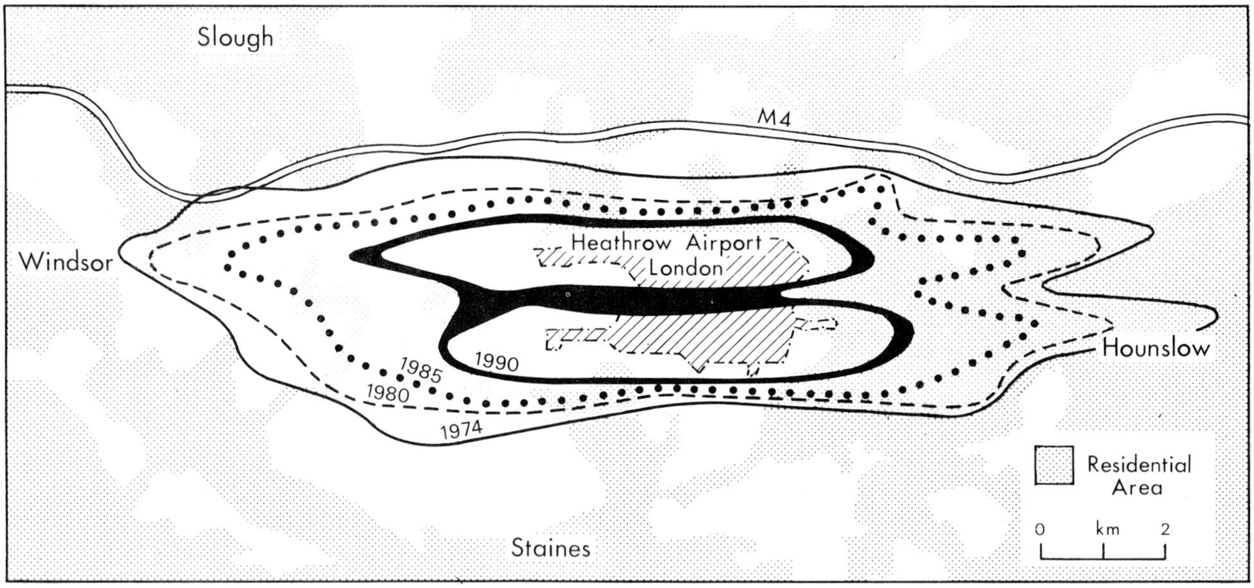

3·6 Aircraft Noise around Heathrow, 1974–90.

The trends have been considered not only desirable but virtually inevitable. Transport planners have consistently based their proposals for new roads and airports on 'unconstrained' traffic forecasts—that is on estimates of the rate at which traffic would grow if the forces that produced growth in the recent past were to continue into the future unconstrained by lack of road or airport capacity. The current official road traffic forecasts envisage almost twice as much traffic by the end of the century, and the most recent Department of Trade air traffic forecasts foretell a three- to four-fold increase in air traffic by 1990, with potential for considerably more growth by the end of the century.

The belief that such growth will, and should, occur is meeting a growing challenge. The sudden large increase in the price of fuel since 1973 which has confounded the trend forecasts is treated in the most recent government forecasts as a unique event which will not be repeated. These forecasts assume that there will be no further increase in the price of fuel this century. The impact of the 'energy crisis' is displayed as a pause on the graphs of future traffic which, after a brief period of readjustment, continue to rise as before.

Precisely how the price of fuel will behave for the rest of this century depends on unpredictable discoveries of new resources, on unforeseeable technological developments in both the production and use of energy, on changes in the relative power of energy producing and energy consuming nations, and on the unknowable psychology of a few key decision-makers. It is a realm of speculation beyond the scope of this chapter.

Suffice to say here that a number of speculators, including the authors of a Cabinet Office paper, *Future World Trends*, think that energy will become much more expensive in the future. If this speculation is proved right then a probable consequence is that many Londoners will become much less mobile than they are at present.

The desirability of achieving the forecast traffic growth is also contested. In the case of air travel, aircraft noise has tended to serve as the focus of the opposition to further growth. Figure 3·6 shows the location of the 55 Noise and Number Index Contour around Heathrow in 1974 when the airport was handling over 20 000 000 passengers. This contour embraces approximately 72 000 people who are considered to have a 'high annoyance rating'. The inner line shows the Department of Trade's estimate of the location of this line in 1990 when the airport is expected to be handling 53 000 000 passengers. This reduction in the number of people estimated to be in the 'highly annoyed' category is impressive but is based upon a contentious assumption: that the average aeroplane flying into Heathrow in 1990 will be very much quieter and very much larger. The assumed growth in aircraft size, up to a capacity of 800 passengers, is such that the increased traffic could be carried with no increase in the number of flights. The interpretation of the 55 NNI contour is also a vexing problem. Although this contour is intended to represent the outer boundary of the area of high annoyance, people in the author's household in Muswell Hill, 20 km beyond this boundary, have frequently been awakened by aircraft noise and have described their feelings in words which might be roughly translated as 'highly annoyed'.

However, even if developments in engine technology and air traffic control were to permit traffic to increase while noise decreased, there are other consequences of the forecast growth which provoke controversy. Prominent among these is the impact of the forecast five-fold increase in the number of foreign visitors coming to London. By 1976 the tourist influx was making a pronounced impression on central London; Selfridge's, a prominent Oxford Street department store, estimated that 40 % of its sales were to foreigners. Presumably five times as many foreigners would spend five times as much money in London's stores and need five times as many hotels to sleep in, restaurants to eat in and coaches to travel in. While the tourist industry contemplates such developments with apparent satisfaction there is far from unanimous agreement that the transformation of London that would follow should be described as an 'improvement'. Airports are major sources of direct employment and their attractiveness to related service industries and to businesses with foreign suppliers and customers makes them generators of considerable additional employment. Heathrow currently employs 52 000 people and the Department of Trade expects this number to increase to as much as 65 000 by 1990. For every job at the airport there is usually another in the immediate vicinity associated with hotels, catering, transport and air freight, as well as with the provision of goods and services for all these workers and their families. Beyond this there is the employment that is associated with internationally orientated businesses for whom access to an airport is important. In Heathrow's immediate journey-to-work area, employment directly and indirectly associated with the airport is approximately one-third of total employment. Since the residential population of this area is expected to continue to decrease, substantial growth in airport related employment must mean that many workers in the future will have to travel farther to work. Because the area is already one of labour shortage the most likely source of additional workers would be to the west of the airport; it is expected that Heathrow's commuting hinterland might grow to embrace Reading 40 km away. The combined impact of air travellers, commuters and commercial and industrial traffic places an increasingly heavy burden on the road network of west London. A recent government report observed that if air traffic grows as forecast both the roads and London Transport's Underground system serving the airport would become chronically overloaded without major additions to their capacity.

The present debate about cars is rather more complicated and confused. While a policy of traffic restraint in the city centre has been adopted by London, and while similar policies have been adopted or appear likely to be adopted in most other large cities, the Department of Transport is still pursuing policies to promote the growth of traffic on the roads outside these cities. On the radial roads leading out of the cities these growth and restraint policies collide head on. In 1958 Buchanan observed, 'the radials are, in fact, a nasty nagging problem to which there seems to be no satisfactory answer'. The problem of the radials in 1977 is more nasty and nagging than ever. At the time of writing, this problem was the focus of a public inquiry into the widening of the Archway Road, a stretch of the A1, one of the major northern radial roads leading out of London. The picture, Fig. 3·7, looking north up the Archway Road from the

Archway Bridge, illustrates the nature of the problem and demonstrates the difficulty of translating the expanded desire lines of the maps in Fig. 3·3 into actual road capacity. Extending the widened road through the terrace of shops and houses in the photograph for just one further 1·5 km, which is what the Department of Transport is proposing, would cost an estimated £11 000 000 and destroy the homes of 200 families.

The point where the road narrows is where it ceases to be a metropolitan road under the jurisdiction of the GLC and becomes a Department of Transport trunk road. It is ironic that the wide road belongs to the GLC who enlarged it to an urban motorway before it adopted its new policy of traffic restraint, while the narrow section is the responsibility of the Department of Transport which is still committed to building roads to accommodate anticipated large increases in traffic.

3·7 View Northwards along the Archway Road.

Estimates of how much traffic should be accommodated on the Archway Road have varied enormously. In 1962 the road carried 22 000 vehicles a day. In Fig. 3·2, the map showing the predicted unconstrained traffic flows for 1981, it is shown as carrying 180 000 vehicles a day—in 1966 when this estimate was made only one road in the world, the Harbor Freeway in Los Angeles, carried more traffic. By 1976 there had been virtually no increase above the 1962 level because the road and the adjoining road network were operating at close to their capacities. At the present inquiry the prediction has been revised by the Department to 75 000 vehicles a day by 1991. But it is not possible to reconcile even this greatly reduced estimate of traffic growth on a major London radial road with the GLC's resolve to reduce traffic in the centre. When confronted by this conflict at the enquiry the Department declared that the GLC's traffic restraint policies were 'unrealistic' and 'irresponsible'.

The Department and other supporters of the widening scheme argue much as Buchanan argued in 1958: 'to restrict movement on the radials would be to squeeze the life out of the town'. They cite evidence that this is already happening. Since the early 1960s not only has the dispersal of London's residents continued but it has been accompanied by a dispersal of jobs as well. Between 1961 and 1974 firms employing 396 000 people either moved out of town or simply went out of business. By 1975 there were 15 % fewer people entering central London during the morning rush hours than there were in 1960.

The opponents of the scheme point to the unfortunate example of many American cities, such as Detroit, whose ambitious urban road-building programmes have manifestly failed to arrest the decay of their centres. They also note that while the number of people commuting to work in central London has been declining, the proportion of commuters who come by car has been rising, from under 8 % in 1960 to over 15 % in 1975 (162 000 out of 1 075 000 in 1975). The loss from public transport has been such that if every car commuter in 1975 were to have travelled by public transport, public transport would still have carried 8 % fewer passengers than in 1960. It is further objected that the scheme is not accompanied by any plans to relieve the bottlenecks at either end of it, and that such plans, especially for the constrictions at the inner London end, are unlikely ever to materialize because they are now recognized to be prohibitively expensive.

Both sides to the dispute adduce compelling arguments. The much greater ease of moving about for both cars and lorries is undoubtedly one of the major attractive forces drawing people and firms out of London. But providing equally free ease of mobility within the core of the city could only be achieved by destroying a large part of it. London's transport problems cannot be treated in isolation from developments in the wider region of which it is the focus. The present GLC prescription, of private traffic restraint and public transport promotion, would seem to stand little chance of success so long as the Department of Transport is pursuing its converse policies in the wider region beyond the GLC's boundaries. London is likely to remain a congested island in a sea of unrestrained mobility. It will increasingly be seen by those who make the decisions about where to live and work as an island—like Venice—dependent on an obsolete transport system. As in Venice, the tourist trade might prosper, but most other sectors of the London economy and the people dependent on them, will feel themselves disadvantaged by their comparative immobility. The radials are likely to remain a nasty nagging problem until this policy conflict is resolved.

What the future holds, however, probably depends only in a small way on the transport policies of the GLC and the Department of Transport. Looming over the transport policymakers are forces beyond their power to influence. The process of change in London's transport that has been described in this chapter has been influenced only in minor, indirect and often unintended ways by government policies. If the trend of the past 150 years, for transport to become progressively cheaper, should be permanently arrested or reversed, then we can expect all the trends which derive from this underlying trend to have their directions altered radically. Today the lament of an increasing number of the least well off is no longer that they are 'chained to the spot' but that they are chained to a system of transport that they can no longer afford.

Further Reading

Barker, T. C. and Robbins, M., *A History of London Transport*, 2 vols, (George Allen and Unwin, London, 1975–6)

Buchanan, C. D., *Traffic in Towns* (Penguin, Harmondsworth, 1963)

White, H. P., *London Railway History* (David and Charles, Newton Abbot, 1971)

4 Industrial Changes in Inner London

Peter Wood

Introduction

By the mid-1960s a detailed understanding of the structure and geographical pattern of manufacturing industry in London had been built up, mainly through the work of Peter Hall and John Martin. It was recognized that industry in London was important, because it employed 20 % of the manufacturing workers of England and Wales, and was relatively prosperous. Expansion was directing industrial growth away from the inner areas towards the outer suburbs and surrounding areas of south-east England, but this was generally in line with an even faster outmovement of population. The variety of London's industry was remarkable, with only metal and textile manufacturing not significantly represented. Various distinctive zones of manufacturing were recognized which could be defined mainly in relation to characteristics inherited from the past. The geographical pattern of manufacturing in Greater London consisted of the Victorian Manufacturing Belt of Inner London; the Riverside Belt associated with the docks; the West London Belt, which had developed largely between the two world wars; and the Lee Valley Manufacturing Belt in north-east London (Fig. 4·1). In addition, beyond the boundaries of Greater London proper, the Outer Ring was the zone where most new manufacturing growth took place in the 1950s and 1960s.

In the late 1970s, the same broad characteristics of Greater London's manufacturing seem to survive although lack of statistics makes it difficult to trace local patterns of change. Visual inspection of the industrial belts often suggests stagnation and even decay, but the areas are still important and clearly identifiable components in the urban landscape. It would be surprising if the detailed pattern had undergone little change, if only because manufacturing employment in Greater London had been reduced to less than 1 000 000 in 1973, compared with 1 613 000 twelve years earlier. This chapter will investigate the character of inner London industry and the reasons for its decline, and will then examine some of the consequences. Concentration on inner London will allow some of the more acute problems associated with the changing role of manufacturing in London to be examined, but it should not be assumed that the same pressures do not work elsewhere in the capital. On the contrary, the problems that arise in inner London from obsolescent buildings, skilled labour shortage and transportation congestion have now become equally relevant to the future of many of the inter-war industrial areas of west London, including the largest at Park Royal. The Riverside Belt has also undergone a period of even more radical change, following the decline of dockland activities in the East End.

Keeble (1976) has recently declared that Greater London is 'by far the most dramatic industrial decline centre in the United Kingdom'. The principal question in response to this must be, 'Is this state of affairs undesirable?' It is certainly true that a recent acceleration in the decline has caused widespread alarm. Whereas between 1964 and 1969 industrial employment was falling at 2·5 % per annum the annual rate of decline between 1971 and 1973 was almost 6 %, a good deal more than the 3 % planned for by the GLC between 1966 and 1976. There has also been a rapid rise in unemployment in inner London during the recession of the mid-1970s, and it is popularly believed that the loss of manufacturing jobs has significantly added to the social and economic problems of the inner city, along with housing and social, educational and other deficiencies.

In fact, manufacturing decline has been by no means a dominant cause of the inner city problem in London. To some extent it is a *result* of the other trends. In the wake of the enormous concentration of jobs in the central city that accompanied the nineteenth century growth of London, and the widespread desire of people in the twentieth century to live in less-congested suburban and satellite settlements, a changing pattern of industrial location away from the inner areas of London has probably been both inevitable and socially desirable. Furthermore, out-of-date buildings and congested sites in old areas of the city are likely to be inefficient for many modern industries. As a result of these considerations, all plans for the improvement of London since the last war have assumed that manufacturing employment will fall in central London. The decline of industry in most of inner London began in 1939 and resumed in the 1950s. Only in outer London was decline a new trend in the 1960s.

4·1 Major Industrial Areas in Greater London. (After J. E. Martin).

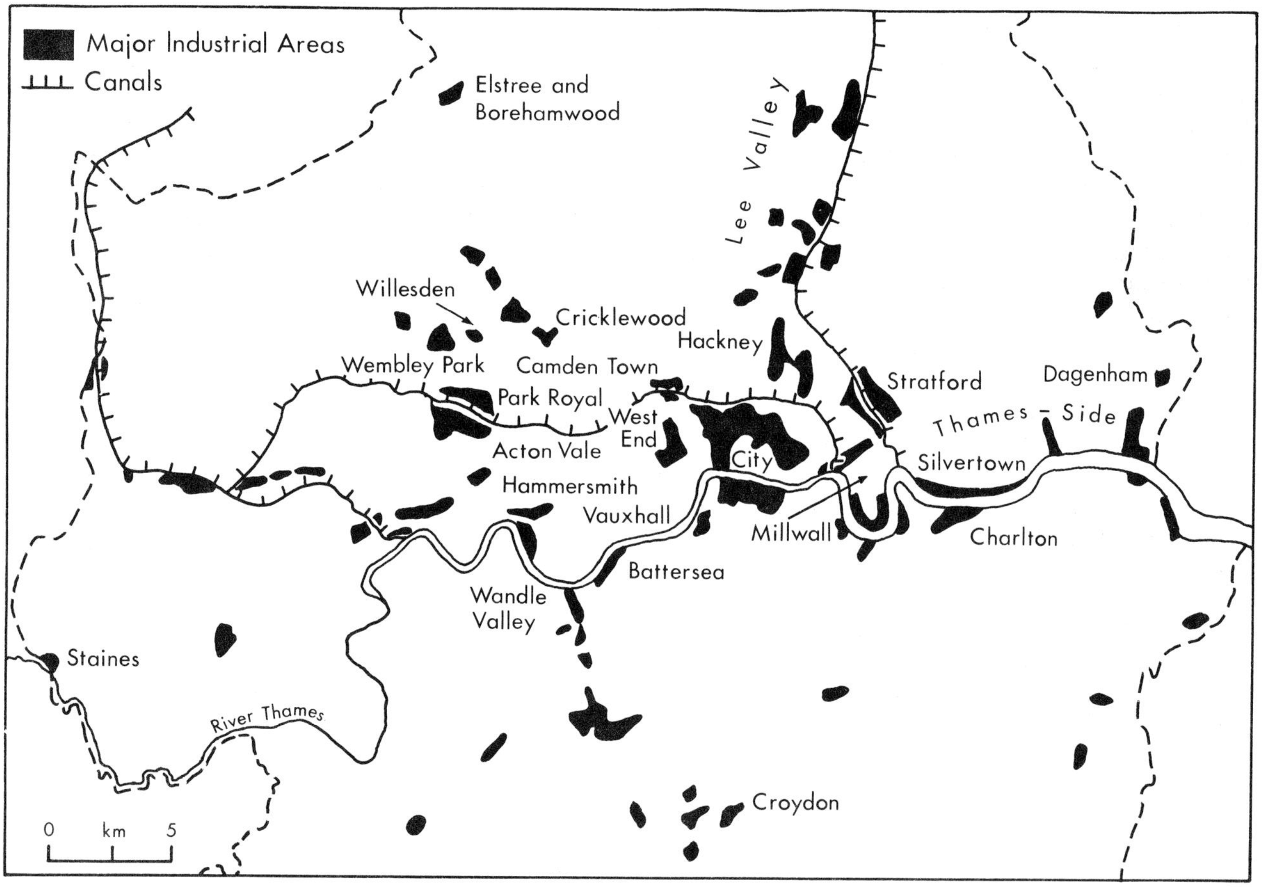

The Characteristics of Inner London Manufacturing

Although the statistics used later relate to inner London (defined as the London Boroughs of Hammersmith, all parts of Camden and Haringey, the City, Newham, Wandsworth, the whole of Lambeth and Southwark, and Lewisham) most of the discussion here will be directed towards the Victorian

Belt defined by Peter Hall. This lies in the London Boroughs of Islington, southern Camden, Kensington and Chelsea, Westminster, Hackney, Tower Hamlets and the northern parts of Lambeth and Southwark. The belt forms a crescent of industry around the north and east of central London, with an outlier south of the river. Projections of industrial activity extend north-westwards into Camden Town, Kentish Town and Holloway, largely associated with the Grand Union Canal and the railways, and north-eastwards along the Lee Valley to south Hackney and Stoke Newington. Although the belt is 'Victorian' in character, it was still the most important industrial area of London in the early 1960s, probably employing one-third of the industrial labour force of Greater London.

Three principal features are common to most industries of inner London: the predominance of small workshops; their organization into a complex system of interlinkage for the purposes of production (with each factory specializing upon a particular process or component); and extreme dependence of the various industries upon specialized local facilities. Broadly, the size and diversity of metropolitan demand has provided the base for inner London industrial growth, although many products ultimately have a much wider market.

These attributes help to explain the most distinctive geographical feature of the Victorian Belt: its subdivision into a number of specialized 'quarters', containing dense clusters of factories in particular trades. Martin's map for the mid-1950s remains the best guide to these quarters since, as has already been indicated, the general pattern survives to the present day (Fig. 4·2). The clothing industries of the West End (retail bespoke and ready-made) and the East End (wholesale ready-made) have grown during the past two decades because of the London fashion boom and their ability to attract new immigrant labour. The East End clothing quarter has therefore extended into surrounding areas, displacing other activities such as furniture-making and engineering. The Shoreditch furniture quarter has declined, but it remains clearly identifiable. Its survival in current circumstances is a tribute to the persistence of the

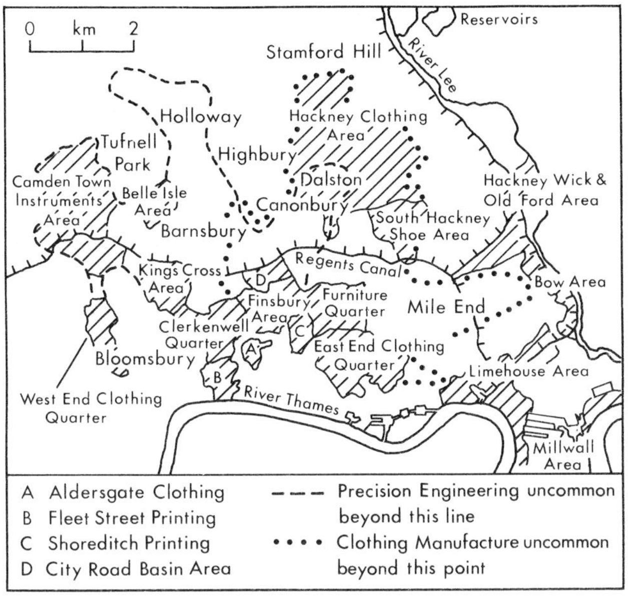

4·2 Industrial Areas in Inner North London. (After J. E. Martin).

traditional patterns of production in spite of a host of adverse forces.

The Clerkenwell quarter, which played a crucial role in the development of precision and electrical engineering in London, is also less distinctive than formerly, although Hatton Garden remains the centre of the jewellery trade. As with clothing manufacture, Clerkenwell was an important component in a wider zone of specialization. This zone of engineering, and metal and instrument manufacturing spread north and north-west into Kings Cross, Barnsbury, Holloway and Camden Town. It is difficult to trace the persistence of such a broad zone of specialization twenty years after Martin's survey, but manufacturing there has undoubtedly declined in recent years. Two printing quarters also survive more or less intact. The Fleet Street area has suffered from a fall in the number of newspapers printed in London. Some dispersal of production into nearby areas to the north around Holborn Circus and Gray's Inn Road has accompanied the rebuilding of congested sites by major companies. The Shoreditch printing quarter has prospered relatively through the specialized services that its firms provide to the advertising, periodical and commercial printing industries.

Other concentrations of more mixed manufacturing in the 1950s, in Finsbury, Kings Cross, Limehouse, Hackney Wick, Old Ford and Bow have suffered an appreciable contraction in their clothing, printing, food, engineering and other industries during the past two decades, although we have little clear information about the share taken by the various industries. Very commonly, other, less labour intensive uses, such as storage, warehousing, garaging, repair and maintenance depots and lorry parks have displaced manufacturing. In fact, with the rise of heavy lorry transport the whole emphasis of use in the inner zone around central London has moved from production towards storage and transhipment. Even where manufacturing is still active, trends towards more capital intensive production have displaced many workers during the past twenty years.

In spite of these trends, the traditional industries of the specialized quarters still persist in inner London, as they do in most western cities. Typically, the quarters are dominated by small firms often sharing the use of multi-storey, mid-nineteenth century workshops or even converted houses. The low rents and ready availability of these premises impose very low overhead costs, thus allowing firms to set up in business with relatively little capital outlay. The ready availability of second-hand machinery and specialized service and supply agents also keeps down the costs of starting a new firm. A rapid turnover of factory occupation is an integral feature of the quarters, with small firms regularly opening and closing, even in times of relative prosperity. Indeed, this turnover is one of the main mechanisms by which the industries are able to adapt themselves to changing market and technical demands. The close proximity of firms engaged in related and complementary processes of production allows individual firms to specialize in what they can do best. A finished garment or piece of reproduction antique furniture may thus result from the efforts of a number of firms, each adding their process to particular cloth or wood materials (vertical linkage) or making different items, such as buttons, belts, embroidery, pleating or millinery, to be assembled into a composite product (horizontal linkage). An important element in the organization of the quarters is the specialized merchant, providing a wide variety of materials, tools and equipment.

The emphasis of production has traditionally been placed on a skilled and adaptable labour force, rather than upon complex machinery which cannot so easily respond to the needs of changing fashion or taste. Machine-assisted batch production is the normal form of manufacture, for mass production usually takes place elsewhere, such as men's tailoring in Yorkshire, or modern furniture in High Wycombe. The importance of close links with other firms is not confined to the supply of materials for the production process. Access to metropolitan and wider markets is provided by specialist wholesalers and representatives through the 'contracting' system, although some larger firms maintain their own wholesaling and selling organizations.

In spite of their common characteristics the various industries display great diversity in the types of firm that operate in their quarters. A summary of the organization of the women's outerwear industry in the West and East Ends in the 1950s, is representative of the patterns found in other trades. It comprised four basic types of manufacturing firm: (i) Large self-contained firms with their own East End workshops, employing more than fifty workers. These tended to specialize in 'tailored' women's coats, jackets and skirts, often selling directly to retailers through West End showroom facilities. (ii) Firms, perhaps in the West End or in Finsbury, using 'outdoor' contractors in the East End to supplement their own indoor work. (iii) The outdoor contractors themselves, especially in Hackney, which were most important for the production of high fashion garments. These received orders mainly from 'principle firms', usually in the West End, which did not manufacture themselves but acted as wholesaling 'go-betweens', anticipating fluctuations in fashion and demand. (iv) Firms with their own small work-rooms, selling to wholesalers, often employing domestic outworkers and buying in proprietary supplies from local merchants.

The relative significance of these different types of organization has undoubtedly changed since the late 1950s. Another important change has been the influx of Asian immigrants, especially into the Spitalfields and Aldgate area, during the 1960s, which has shifted the emphasis from tailoring towards the production of lighter clothing and the merchanting of cloth. The role of Jewish enterprise in the East End therefore has become much less dominant.

In the eighteenth and nineteenth centuries, furniture-making also had a West End centre of production which migrated north from Covent Garden to the Tottenham Court Road area. In this century, manufacture has moved decisively towards mass-production, best applied in locations outside central London. The Shoreditch area became the chief centre in the East End around 1840. The pattern of production was again one of extreme specialization, with small firms turning, producing veneers, moulds, wire frames and springs, plywood shaping, glazing and so forth. Markets for the 'occasional furniture' that is commonly produced are found through major wholesalers and retailers in London. For the 1950s, Martin calculated that 400 plants were concentrated into about one square mile around Shoreditch. Total employment was about 3000 operatives at that time, and more than half of the firms employed fewer than five workers. In comparison, the square mile around Whitechapel contained about 800 clothing factories, with 15 000 operatives.

Causes for the Decline of Inner London Manufacturing

In the early 1960s, consumer demand was still expanding rapidly, particularly in specialized luxury markets which were benefiting from rising prosperity. In the 1970s economic prospects seem less optimistic and this must be counted as a fundamental reason for the recent decline of much inner London manufacturing. In itself, static or declining demand has had various effects on the industrial structure of the inner city. Most obvious has been the closure of small firms which have not been replaced by new enterprises. Larger firms may be able to weather such fluctuations without dismissing their whole labour force, but employment in a small-firm economy tends to react more sensitively to demand variations. A number of medium-sized factories may also have closed either through the failure of firms or as a result of decisions by multi-plant enterprises to close obsolete inner city plants and concentrate production in more profitable locations elsewhere. It is not clear how far the loss during the recession of the 1970s may be replaced if general economic conditions improve. Other longer-term trends have been exerting an influence, however, that makes full restoration of the employment levels of the mid-1960s extremely unlikely.

Amongst the various influences that contribute to this long-term decline, two are probably the most critical: the obsolescence of the buildings used by manufacturers; and the population and social trends of the city. Firms often have moved out of inner London because their existing premises have been unsuitable for modernization and too cramped for expansion. The most successful firms, often employing more skilled workers, are most vulnerable to such pressures . In searching for new factories they frequently look first in neighbouring areas and only consider longer distance moves when good sites at tolerable cost cannot be found in that vicinity.

More generally, the resources needed to reconstruct old factories in order to serve modern needs cannot by their very nature be generated by the industries themselves. In prosperous times they thrive on the low rent and low overhead environment provided in their own districts. In times of economic difficulty, of course, the firms are frequently no longer in business. Local authorities have done little to stimulate the factory rebuilding process, although a few 'unit factories' (*eg* at Long Street, Shoreditch) have been constructed to provide accommodation at rents that are low by modern standards, but even these are high compared with those in old buildings. More often, rebuilding has removed industrial premises from the scene altogether. Either public authorities have built housing and associated facilities or, in areas near to central London, private enterprise has developed office blocks or warehousing. In some inner areas, the sale value of land during the property boom of the early 1970s was so great that industrial firms sold off their sites to realize the capital asset, closing altogether or moving out of London. Thus neither public nor private resources have been directed towards renewing the industrial fabric of inner London. Each year the problem of physical obsolescence has become greater as the surviving nineteenth century factories decay still further.

As we have seen, since the last war, population in London has been leaving the inner areas even more rapidly than has industrial employment. The first obvious effect of this trend for industry was on the labour force, which increasingly had to be sought outside the local area. Inevitably, even workers whose skills might suit them to jobs in the old quarters have found more accessible employment in suburban or outer London. The numbers of skilled workers have been reduced most acutely by this process, since higher incomes have enabled them to lead the exodus. The female labour force, which is also important in many inner London trades, has also been disproportionately reduced by the decline of population, since women workers in manufacturing do not favour long journeys to work. Just as inner London manufacturing grew with an influx of people during the nineteenth century, so the reduction in population is contributing to the decline of industry today.

A further, more intangible aspect of the traditional small-firm economy of inner London is the 'social' environment that encouraged entrepreneurs in the past. This was based upon family businesses, working within closely defined areas, providing manual training and commercial knowhow from one generation to the next. The road to success for a skilled worker most frequently began with the setting up of his own firm, individually or in partnership. Today, not only have the social networks been dispersed by depopulation but many alternative opportunities are available to potential entrepreneurs.

The condition of both the physical and social fabric of inner London points to the inevitability of industrial decline. Other factors add their weight to the trend. Of special note, perhaps, is the fact that inner areas are no longer the most accessible parts of cities. Severe road congestion now imposes real costs on production that are not incurred in outer metropolitan areas. In addition, sources of materials and markets are much less confined to the inner urban area than they were at one time. The decline of port activities and of associated material processing and manufacturing has been another important factor in London. This reduction in the 'multiplier' provided by a major non-manufacturing activity has augmented the similar reduction in commercial opportunities following manufacturing decline itself. As inner London industry is reduced, so the stimuli of potential linkage with other firms, of cheaper supplies from merchants, or of well-organized market outlets are also reduced. As the disadvantages of operating in inner London grow, so the remaining special advantages are whittled away.

This perhaps depressing picture needs to be counterbalanced to some degree by more positive considerations. Generalizations about as diverse an activity as inner city manufacturing are bound to be proved inaccurate in their detailed implications. The first qualification has already been mentioned: the potential for regeneration that may produce a modest reversal of some of these trends when economic conditions improve. It is not likely, however, that such a reversal will be very significant for manufacturing as a whole. Secondly, some inner London trades are evidently capable of being successful and may certainly benefit from any economic upturn. This particularly applies, of course, to the clothing industry which, by specializing in fashion-related activities, is almost by definition proof against mass-produced competition. This trade has also maintained a source of labour and entrepreneurship as a result of the latest wave of Asian immigrants, following the Huguenots of the seventeenth century and the Jews of the nineteenth century. The jewellery trade also maintains its status, although more by trading than by manufacturing itself. In other industries, such as engineering or furniture making, the remaining scope for survival by specializing in high-skill processes is severely limited. A third perspective must take account of the evidence that exists about the total quantitative impact of the changes that have so far been described. In particular, what is the remaining importance of inner London industry? What have been the major components of change in recent years, and what does this tell us about the contribution of the various processes outlined above? Finally, how do manufacturing trends compare with other changes, particularly in the population of inner London—are they leading, or merely following, other changes?

The Extent of Recent Changes

The extent and composition of the decline of manufacturing activity in London has been investigated by the Economy Group of the planning team responsible for the Development of the Strategic Plan for the South East. The Group estimates that between 1966 and 1974 in Greater London manufacturing employment declined by 390 000 jobs, equivalent to about 30 % of the number counted in the 1966 Census. At that time, there were 608 000 manufacturing workers in inner London and 672 000 in outer London. Two-thirds of the loss had resulted from the closure of some 2600 factories with more than twenty workers, and only 12 900 jobs had been created to balance this by the opening of factories by new firms.

The most 'visible' cause of the decline has been the movement of firms out of London to the Assisted Areas of northern and western Britain and to the New and Expanding Towns. In fact, only 97 000 jobs seem to have been lost because of transfers of factories elsewhere and 41 % of these went as a result of closures by large multi-plant firms concentrating production on established factories outside London. Altogether, including 8200 jobs that were lost through the expansion of branch plants outside London without the actual closure of a London factory, only 27 % of the decline in London between 1966 and 1974 could be attributed to out-movement. This comprised 9 % to the Assisted Areas, 7 % to overspill centres, principally the New and Expanding Towns, and 11 % to other areas, mainly in the South East and East Anglia (Table 4).

If factory movement, whether encouraged by planners or on a voluntary basis, has made only a modest contribution to the recent decline of London manufacturing, the most crucial factor that emerges from a wide range of evidence has been the shutting down of firms, which has far outstripped the establishment of new businesses. The DSPSE Economy Group estimates that 183 000 jobs were lost through closures of factories with more than twenty workers in the

TABLE 4 The Composition of Industrial Decline in London 1966–74

	Greater London	*Inner London*	*as % of Greater London*
Movement to Assisted Areas	36 200	11 400	31·5
Movement to Overspill Towns	26 000	14 400	55·4
Movement elsewhere outside Great London	43 100	20 200	46·9
Total Net Loss due to movement to factories outside Greater London	105 300	46 000	43·6
Net Job Loss due to balance between openings and closures of firms employing more than twenty workers	170 300	88 200	51·8
Estimated decline in firms employing under twenty workers	26 000	N.D.	
Estimated decline of employees in surviving plants	88 500	N.D.	
Total decline in manufacturing employment in Greater London 1966–74	390 100		
Total manufacturing employment, 1966	1 280 400	608 300	47·5

nine years between 1966 and 1974, and only 12 900 jobs created by new firms. Thus no less than 44 % of the total decline was due to this process. If some allowance is made for the closure of smaller firms, at least another 26 000 manufacturing jobs can be added to the total. Finally, the net contraction of industrial plants in Greater London, without closure itself, withdrew an estimated 88 600 jobs, 23 % of the total decline. It is probable that a disproportionate share of this decline has been concentrated in inner London.

Examination of the evidence that exists for the closure of factories in inner London shows that those with more than twenty workers were responsible for the loss of around 24 % of inner London manufacturing jobs between 1966 and 1974, a rate that was not much greater than the 20 % in the outer boroughs. Two-thirds of the inner London change, however, was due to the total closure of firms and the remaining losses were dominated by relatively short-distance moves to other parts of the South East. Forty-two per cent of the job losses in outer London, on the other hand, were caused by moves and these were twice as likely to go outside the South East, to the Assisted Areas, than were moves from inner London.

A wide variety of local conditions was revealed in a supporting calculation of job losses due to factory closure within individual London boroughs. South-east London, for example, seems to have been worst hit by closures, with Greenwich losing 43 % of its 1966 manufacturing employment by 1974, followed by Southwark (38 %), Lambeth (28 %) and Lewisham (25 %). The East End also fared badly, with a 30 % loss in Newham, 26 % in Tower Hamlets and 31 % in Hackney. As already mentioned, however, outer London boroughs were not exempt, since Merton saw a loss of 29 % of its 1966 manufacturing employment through closures, Hounslow 28 % and Bexley 25 %. The impression given by these data, of course, may be misleading, since the figures do not account for the establishment of new firms to replace the losses. In Greenwich, for example, the closure of the AEI factory in the late 1960s has probably had a disturbing effect on other manufacturing in the area but it has also provided a pool of industrial land that is being occupied by a wide range of new industries, some moving from other parts of inner London.

This evidence of trends in inner London manufacturing during what has clearly been a crucial period of employment decline leaves many important questions unanswered. For example, the closure of small firms has probably been particularly significant there but we have no satisfactory count of its net impact. The Department of Industry's estimate of a 26 000 decline in London as a whole is probably an underestimate, but if it was assumed that 15–20 000 of these had been lost in inner London, another 3 % would be added to the loss of manufacturing employment since 1966. Similarly, the contraction of employment in surviving plants would also be expected to hit inner London hardest, so that at least 50 000 of the Greater London loss of 88 500 might be estimated to have occurred there. This would comprise another 8 % of the 1966 employment in inner London, producing a total decline of around 35 % in nine years—200 000 jobs.

Other evidence about the impact of trends in inner London is more diverse, but generally confirms the scale and composition of change outlined by the DSPSE Economy Group. For example, the Group itself investigated the distinctive features of what they called the 'London Factor', creating a more rapid decline than national trends would suggest in individual industries. Between 1966 and 1974, jobs in the clothing and footwear industries had fallen by 38 %, compared with a national decline of only 10 %. The reduction in engineering and electrical goods jobs was 25 % at a time when national employment was virtually static. Food and drink employment in London fell by 28 %, and paper, printing and publishing by 24 %, when national changes would have suggested a growth of 2–3 %.

Martin and Seaman (1975) provided more information in their analysis of the fate of industrial sites and buildings. They calculated that, between 1954 and 1968, the number of large factories (with more than 100 workers) in the ILEA area fell from 784 to 443. This represents a 44 % decline, compared with an estimate of 17 % for outer London, and suggests that, however comparable have been the rate of closure between inner and outer London since 1966, over the longer time period inner London has declined more rapidly. Looking more closely at clothing factories with more than eleven workers in 1954 in five outer and four inner north London boroughs, it was calculated that by 1968 their numbers fell by 40% in the inner boroughs and 19% in the outer boroughs. A similar study of electrical engineering factories with more than six workers showed that the numbers had fallen by 53% and 21% respectively.

The same authors made an investigation in the Boroughs of Ealing and Southwark into what had happened by 1974 to factory sites with more than 200 workers in 1954. Forty-two per cent of the Ealing factories were still in use by the same firms, compared with 22% in Southwark. Seventeen per cent of the Southwark plants (12% in Ealing) were occupied by different manufacturing firms. In both boroughs, a few large factory sites had been subdivided for use as smaller factories and warehouses. This subdivision has occurred more often on outer London sites. No significant difference emerged between the boroughs in their proportions of sites put to completely different uses, but 20% of the Southwark sites were vacant in 1974, compared with only 9% in Ealing. In addition, 11% of the factories in Southwark had been or were being demolished, so that over 30% of this borough's stock of major industrial sites were in various states of disuse. The comparable figure for Ealing was 14%.

Another type of evidence comes from such local surveys as have been carried out by the Canning Town Community Development Project which was able to identify the closure of factories as the cause of 64% of the gross loss of 10 500 jobs in this dockland area between 1966 and 1972. The net decline had been 8800, 37% of the manufacturing employment at the beginning of the period, since 1700 jobs had been created by new firms and by the limited growth of established firms. This study demonstrates the local impact both of the widespread closure of firms and of the persistence of some growth even against a tide of rapid decline.

The Consequences of Manufacturing Decline in Inner London

As was pointed out at the beginning of this chapter, there has been a recent tendency to regard the rate of manufacturing decline in inner London as a near disaster. Certainly, for a number of reasons that have already been discussed, it has accelerated to a degree that is unprecedented, and may be especially damaging to such local areas as Canning Town, where the rate of job loss between 1966 and 1971 was twice the decline of the resident workforce. The key to the change has been the rate of firm closures and the contraction of surviving firms, with out-movement as a subsidiary influence. The main cause for alarm has been the clear growth of unemployment in inner London in recent years. Unfortunately, the part played by manufacturing in any policy designed to relieve this problem is much less clear. An examination of the basis for and character of the unemployment will help to demonstrate the difficulty.

During the 1960s, the reduction in jobs in London was associated with an even faster decline in the resident labour force. The result has been a growing level of in-commuting (by 80 000 between 1966 and 1971) especially to central and outer London. In

TABLE 5 Changing Distribution of Employment and the Resident Labour Force in London, 1966–71

	Percentage 1971	Changes 1966–71 (000's)	Changes 1966–71 (%)
A. Employment			
Conurbation Centre	30·6	−54	−4·2
Rest of Inner London	26·5	−156	−12·6
Outer London	42·8	−33	−1·9
Greater London		−244	−5·6
B. Resident Labour Force			
Conurbation Centre	3·2	−18	−13·7
Rest of Inner London	38·0	−217	−13·5
Outer London	58·8	−91	−4·1
Greater London		−327	−8·2

1971, inner London contained 57% of the jobs in Greater London and only 41% of the workforce (Table 5). Thirty per cent of London's jobs, however, are compressed into the central areas, where only 3% of the working population lives, so that the remaining parts of inner London possessed 38% of the workforce and only 27% of the jobs. More significant than these aggregate shares, of course, has been the trend of change in recent years. Unfortunately, 1971 is the last date for which comprehensive data are available but the census of that year showed that jobs in inner London outside the centre had fallen by 12·6% since 1966, while the workforce has declined by 13·5%. Thus a state of near balance prevailed. Of course, if central London is included with inner London, the decline of jobs was only 8·3%. In general, therefore, the cause of unemployment in inner London is not one of quantitative insufficiency. On the contrary, against the background of a general fall in population and employment in the capital, and of an increased mobility of workers, in-commuting of tertiary workers continues to grow. The explanation of unemployment lies more with shifts in the structure of labour supply and demand.

Basically, manufacturing jobs are declining while service jobs are becoming relatively even more important. At the same time the supply of skilled manual workers has fallen faster than the inner London demand for them. Unskilled workers, therefore, dominate the unemployment scene. One important feature of the labour market of inner London that is not always discerned beneath the daily flow of commuters between central London and the outer suburbs, is its relatively self-contained character. In spite of a general tendency towards higher worker mobility, 69% of the 1 082 000 people who worked in inner London outside the central area in 1971 also lived in that zone (Table 6). Those groups that were most dependent upon jobs in their local boroughs (more than half of them working locally) were the unskilled and semi-skilled manual workers and manual workers on their own account. These are the groups, therefore, that are most severely affected by local employment decline. The next question therefore is how far has manufacturing decline contributed to unemployment growth there?

The DSPSE Economy Group pursued this in 1972 with a detailed survey of long-term, male unemployment in Poplar, Deptford and Brixton. Most of the unemployment in these areas was amongst unskilled men and of relatively short duration, with a high rate of turnover. Such occupations as cleaners,

TABLE 6 Area of Residence of Greater London Workforce, 1966–71

Workplace		*Percentage of Workforce living in—* *Centre of Conurbation*	*Rest of Inner London*	*Outer London*	*Other Areas*	*Total Workforce (000's)*
Centre of Conurbation	1966	8·6	41·0	33·4	17·1	1304
	1971	7·8	37·8	33·5	20·8	1250
Rest of Inner London	1966	1·3	71·7	21·5	5·3	1238
	1971	1·3	69·4	23·0	6·2	1082
Outer London	1966	0·2	8·9	81·3	9·6	1780
	1971	0·2	8·1	79·5	12·1	1748
Greater London	1966	3·0	36·6	49·7	10·6	4322
	1971	2·8	33·5	50·5	13·2	4080

porters, general clerks, construction labourers and light vehicle drivers were typical. The main conclusion of the study was that the unemployed generally had not lost jobs in manufacturing but in construction, transportation and distribution. In fact, between 1969 and 1973, vacancies in manufacturing in London actually grew by 27 %, and had grown even more than this in inner London, where the competition of the large and growing service sector was most acute. The DSPSE report also cites evidence that this phenomenon of high vacancy rates in manufacturing along with high unemployment has been found in inner Manchester, Merseyside and Tyneside.

This evidence clearly demonstrates how any evaluation of the consequences of the decline in manufacturing in inner London must be placed in the context of other trends in the metropolis. No doubt, it is contributing to the problems of the area, but these problems themselves have created an environment that is inimical to successful industrial activity. Inadequate premises and shifting patterns of labour supply have been identified in this chapter as the main factors over which industrialists have little control. In seeking solutions to the problems of inner London, particularly those of unemployment, it seems clear that the stimulation of manufacturing activity can only help if it can employ the unskilled labour left by the long-term decline of the transportation sector (including the docks) and of construction and distribution. It is unlikely that the traditional industries of inner London can provide these opportunities and, in fact, the shortage of skilled labour will probably continue to contribute to their decline.

Alternative policies will have to be employed; the stimulation of construction and of the basic service economy, perhaps the attraction of industries that require less-skilled labour to sites made available at prices realistic for manufacturing, training schemes to allow the unskilled to learn the trades that are still needed by firms in inner London, or improving the mobility of the unemployed by providing better access to those parts of London where jobs can more easily be made available. Another component of any strategy to reduce unemployment might involve more active attempts to enable the unemployed, who cannot at present escape from the inner city because of housing difficulties, to move to areas where job opportunities are better.

The DSPSE Review came to the conclusion that there was little to be done, nor was there a particularly strong case for attempting to halt the decline of industry in London.On the other hand, some slowing of the recent rate of decline would probably be broadly beneficial, if only to preserve as varied an economy as possible in inner London. Apart from ensuring a better supply of skilled labour, something clearly needs to be done about the inadequacy of industrial premises in inner London and the lack of space for redevelopment. More particularly, the mechanisms that might bring either private or public funds to bear on this problem need to be reviewed. In similar vein, the process of speculation that freezes land from job-creating industrial investment by demanding high prices even on vacant or derelict sites needs to be controlled. Nevertheless, in exploiting what modest potential there may be to reverse recent trends, the conclusion of the DSPSE Group must still be kept in mind. They saw no clear evidence that people are suffering as a result of industrial decline in inner London—the changes are primarily the result of necessary adjustments in an outdated urban fabric.

Further Reading

Economy Group of the DSPSE Team, *Strategy for the South-East: 1976 Review* (Department of the Environment, London, 1976)

Keeble, D. E., *Industrial Location and Planning in the UK* (Methuen, London, 1976)

Martin, J. E., *Greater London: an Industrial Geography* (Bell, London, 1966)

Martin, J. E. and Seaman, J. M., 'The fate of the London factory: twenty years of change', *Town and Country Planning*, 1975, **43**, pp. 492–5.

Hall, P. G., *The Industries of Greater London since 1861* (Hutchinson, London, 1962)

5 Central London

Hugh Clout and Jacquie Burgess

The Depopulation of Central London

Among the striking features of city growth in Britain over the past 150 years have been the increasing distances that separate place of work from place of residence and the greater specialization of land uses in inner city areas. City centres contain very high densities of people during the working day but are virtually depopulated at nights and weekends except for caretakers and cats. For more than a century, successive redevelopment schemes in central London have been replacing housing by specially designed business premises. Some inner housing areas have escaped demolition but have been converted to accommodate work activities rather than homes. This trend towards specialization of function and floor space began in the 'square mile' of the City of London and now covers a much larger zone that extends out to the capital's main line railway termini. This will be referred to as 'central London'.

In 1801 129 000 people had their homes in the City of London and fifty years later the figure had fallen by only 1000. By then a small, but unrecorded, additional number of people were coming on foot or by horsebus to work in the City each day. Commercial buildings already occupied much of the southern and central parts of the City but whole areas along its northern boundary were given over to housing and contained shops, churches and schools that were in active use. In another fifty years much of this changed. In 1901 only 27 000 people lived in the City but 305 000 workers moved in each day. The life of the City had been transformed and this trend towards functional specialization has continued almost without exception to the present day.

Victorian London was the capital not only of the most important industrial nation in the world but also of a far-flung ocean empire. In the 1850s half of the nation's overseas trade was passing through the Port of London. The City's long-established banking, insurance and trading institutions were of crucial importance in this expansionist phase of Britain's history. At the same time the City housed a wide range of craft industries, including publishing and printing, and the manufacture of clothing, furniture, precision instruments and jewellery. All these activities competed for space and property prices rose substantially in the second half of the nineteenth century as a result.

During the same period London's public transport system was gradually enhanced by surface railways, tramcars, underground railways and omnibuses which permitted the growth of suburbs by allowing suburbanites to travel to work each day in central London. Areas of slum housing, old industrial premises, churches and historic buildings were swept away, as railway termini were built, new roads and markets laid out and commercial buildings constructed. Many sites in the City and in neighbouring districts like Holborn and Westminster were cleared and redeveloped with Victorian and Edwardian office blocks. Similar transformations continued up to World War II. The City's residential population fell to

10 000 in 1935 when almost 500 000 people were travelling to work there each day. This kind of trend was also underway in the West End but in a less dramatic way.

Central London experienced enormous damage during World War II. About one-third of the City was destroyed, with areas of warehousing along the Thames and in a north/south band between St. Paul's Cathedral and the Bank of England suffering the most. Destruction on this scale and the reconstruction that followed served to accentuate earlier trends of functional specialization. For example, in 1939 the City had contained 2 007 000 m^2 of warehousing but only 927 000 m^2 ten years later. The figure has not increased since then. The 900 000 m^2 of industrial premises in 1939 fell to half that amount. Housing, shops and public houses had covered 567 000 m^2 in 1939 but in 1949 had fallen by one-third and reached only 441 000 m^2 in 1968. Office space declined from 3 384 000 m^2 in 1939 to 2 835 000 m^2 in 1949 but, unlike every other form of floor space, it then expanded to reach 4 320 000 m^2 twenty years later.

At the end of the war only 5000 people were living in the City and that figure declined further until the Barbican scheme began to bring residents back in the late 1960s. Now just under 10 000 people have their homes in the City. In 1966 about 360 000 people travelled to work there each day and over two-thirds were involved in office work. Apart from printing and publishing around Fleet Street there were hardly any large manufacturing concerns left in the City but over 100 small concerns survived, producing electrical and engineering goods (Fleet Street/Smithfield) and clothing and furs (Houndsditch/Billingsgate). Perhaps as many as 20 000 people were engaged in manufacturing. Other City jobs involved shop assistants, catering workers, maintenance men, and the employees of wholesale markets such as Billingsgate (fish) and Smithfield (meat).

The picture is similar in the West End where comparable labour-intensive activities are still to be found tucked behind offices, shops and department stores along such thoroughfares as Tottenham Court Road and the eastern section of Oxford Street. But these industries are pale shadows of what they were at the beginning of the century or even on the eve of World War II well before the offices and hotels of the recent 'property boom' swept across central London, changing its skyline and contributing to the further depopulation of the West End. In the short period between 1961 and 1975 the City of Westminster's population fell from 272 000 to 214 000 and in neighbouring Kensington and Chelsea numbers declined from 219 000 to 162 000.

The Property Boom

London's commercial economy revived at the end of the war and the offices that have been constructed since then have produced enormous visual changes throughout the central area. Some 4 500 000 m^2 have been added to the capital's office accommodation in the past thirty years, amounting to over five times the amount destroyed by bombing. The office property boom reached its peak by 1962, with the LCC approving about 400 000 m^2 of new office construction in each of the preceding five years. In November 1964 the new Labour government announced its intention to control office development in the capital. Each proposed scheme involving more than 270 m^2 required an office development permit as well as usual planning permission. The Location of Offices Bureau provided information on the advantages that were to be gained by firms moving out of central London. Rents soared towards the end of the 1960s as office floorspace in the inner area increased much more slowly than before. But by 1973–4 the property market had entered a depressed state and many freshly completed blocks were short of tenants. Central London's skyline has been transformed by the insertion of high-rise office buildings of varying architectural merit. Along Victoria Street a jumble of nineteenth-century shops, hotels and dwellings of varied height and scale, but that was unmistakably part of London, has been swept away. In its place a collection of slabs and towers of concrete and glass has been built with the common purpose of providing office space. The new buildings of Victoria Street are indistinguishable from new blocks anywhere else. Major redevelopment schemes under way in the City of

London in the 1960s included the National Westminster tower in Drapers Gardens, the new Stock Exchange with its tower, and lower rise blocks along and to the south of Lombard Street. Since 1970 developments on a more massive scale have occurred on either side of Bishopsgate.

As well as attracting a vast daily workforce, central London receives large numbers of foreign visitors each year, 95 % of tourists come to London and 75 % stay in the central area. With tourism being Britain's fourth largest export activity and growing fast during the 1960s, the Labour government introduced the Development of Tourism Act in 1969 which provided grants to help increase hotel accommodation. Up to £1000 per bedroom was allocated for new hotels and for extending existing premises. In order to qualify for a grant work had to begin between March 1968 and April 1971 and be completed by April 1973. Well over half of the new rooms that have been built with grant aid have been constructed in London and in particular in the West End and in Kensington. The giant Tower Hotel at St. Katharines Dock is the only example of a new hotel of any size in East London. Even during the years 1968–73 there was a progressive westward shift in hotel building away from the Strand and Bloomsbury to the West End proper (W1 postal district), Kensington and Heathrow Airport (Fig. 5·1). With the Cromwell Road air terminal, Kensington functioned as the key point for tourist entry into central London. Land was cheaper than in the West End proper and areas of Victorian housing off the Cromwell Road were considered ripe for redevelopment. In fact some new hotels have gone bankrupt or have been seriously under-occupied. Other proposals obtained planning permission but were never constructed. By 1974 the hotel building boom was over but not before it had produced a crop of large and often undistinguished buildings and made a further contribution to the westward shift of central city functions that had been apparent since the beginning of the century.

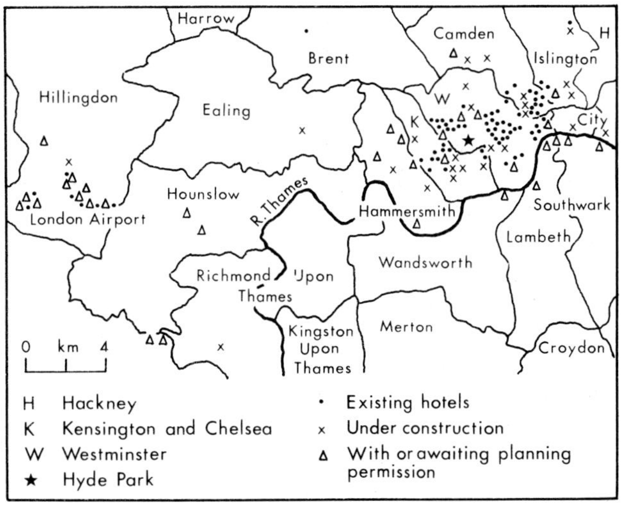

5·1 Hotels with over Two Hundred Rooms, 1973.

Central London's new hotels and office buildings have come under fire from many quarters. Some critics lament the disappearance of old buildings of varying age, style, height and function and their replacement by slabs of concrete and glass, either pointing in the sky or laid on their side. Others indicate the continuing loss of residential population in central London to which redevelopment schemes have undoubtedly contributed. Property developers made great profits from their new buildings in the heady years of the 1960s but inner London still contains vast numbers of poor dwellings and inadequately-housed people. The Centre Point affair highlighted the contrast between profitmaking and social need. The high rise office block at the intersection of Oxford Street and Tottenham Court Road remained empty for years while the number of homeless Londoners grew alarmingly. In the 1970s the case for conservation rather than demolition and for rehabilitation rather than redevelopment has been voiced loudly. This has certainly been so in the long and complicated debate on what should happen to the Covent Garden area when the wholesale market had been moved south of the Thames to Nine Elms (Vauxhall). In any case, the collapse of London's property market and Britain's declining economic health in the 1970s have combined to bring expensive redevelopment projects to a halt for the time being.

New Homes in the Barbican

As early as 1956 an ambitious project was announced to build new homes in the City of London. The Corporation of the City wanted to reverse the long-established trend of depopulation and Mr. Duncan Sandys, the Minister of Housing, recommended that a 14 ha bomb site in the Barbican district north of St. Pauls should be reconstructed as 'a genuine residential neighbourhood incorporating schools, shops, open spaces and other amenities, even if this means foregoing a more remunerative return on the land'—in other words, not building offices. A plan was duly prepared and implemented to provide accommodation for 6500 people. The dominant features are three triangular towers of flats, each over forty storeys high and rising more than 125 m above ground level. They are the highest blocks of flats in Europe. Additional accommodation is located in a hostel for young City workers and in terrace blocks that surround gardens and courtyards. Residential densities are high (575 persons/ha) but there are 9·3 ha of amenity open space and 3·2 ha of gardens and water surfaces. Pedestrians and vehicles move on separate levels, with roads, service bays and parking space for 2500 cars located out of sight beneath courtyards and walkways. Because their position was known, sections of the city wall of Roman and medieval London have been conserved and may be viewed by the public. The ancient church of St. Giles has also been incorporated in this massive new development. Residential parts of the Barbican are almost complete. The Museum of London has already been sited there. In addition, an Arts Centre is being built and will contain a theatre for the Royal Shakespeare Company, a 2000 seat concert hall for the London Symphony Orchestra, and a new home for the Guildhall School of Music and Drama. These activities will attract more people and more life into the area.

Strictly speaking, the Barbican is a municipal housing scheme, since it has been undertaken by the City Corporation, but its inhabitants are very different from those on the average council estate. Barbican residents comprise young professional people without children and older people who are approaching retirement age and in some cases have already bought retirement homes which they visit at weekends. By virtue of its social uniformity the Barbican has been described as a 'voluntary ghetto'. A survey by its Residents' Association in 1973 showed that most flats were either the sole or the principal homes of their occupants, rather than just *pieds-à-terre* for weektime use by businessmen with mansions in the country. Residents are charged 'economic rents' that are by no means cheap but are reasonable by the standards of central London. However, they are high by comparison with mortgage repayments on suburban property. To start with flats in the Barbican were let on five-year leases, but when these began to expire in 1973 the Corporation replaced them with three-year tenancy agreements. Higher rents and changes in leasing have created a sense of insecurity among tenants and some moved away as their leases became due for renewal. Rapid inflation and present tax arrangements (which favour mortgage-paying owner-occupiers) do not encourage younger middle-income couples to move to the Barbican or to stay there once their initial leases have expired. Under present economic circumstances it seems unlikely that the Barbican will survive much longer as a collection of first homes for professional people. It may well be transformed into a mass of *pieds-à-terre* that are occupied by businessmen for four nights each week. This is not what had been intended twenty years ago when the Barbican was conceived to provide homes for Londoners in the middle and lower-middle income brackets. It has proved to be an architecturally exciting but highly expensive piece of urban design that has failed (at least in part) as far as social objectives are concerned. It is unlikely that such a grandiose scheme could be attempted again in central London.

Coping with Cars: Conservation or Demolition ?

Planned vertical segregation in the Barbican allowed motor cars to be kept below ground and conflicting demands on road space between pedestrians and vehicles to be resolved. A similar approach was proposed in 1962 in the comprehensive redevelopment plan for Piccadilly Circus but this failed to come to fruition. Two other ways of reducing the conflict have been adopted in other parts of central London. These are the creation of pedestrian streets from which vehicles are banned (except for night-time deliveries) and the exclusion of particular types of traffic from specified streets.

Oxford Street is the best-known example of the second approach. It extends for 2 km from Marble Arch to St. Giles Circus and is London's leading shopping street, lined by a wide range of shops, department stores, cinemas, restaurants and offices. Mayfair adjoins it to the south and exclusive residential streets and squares are found to the north. Oxford Circus, mid-way along Oxford Street, is the busiest station on the Underground system. By the early 1970s congestion of traffic and pedestrians had made conditions intolerable along Oxford Street which had the highest accident rate of any street in Britain. In 1972 an experimental scheme was introduced along the western half of the street and only buses, taxis and service vehicles were allowed to enter. The scheme has since been extended over the whole length of Oxford Street between 07·00 and 19·00 hours Monday to Saturday inclusive. Cars and lorries have been diverted to parallel streets and some sections of pavement in Oxford Street have been widened. Fewer vehicles have allowed buses and taxis to move at higher speeds and accident rates have not fallen as significantly as had been hoped. But air pollution from car exhausts has decreased substantially and most shoppers, pedestrians, and shop and hotel managers along Oxford Street have expressed satisfaction with this scheme. Unfortunately, conditions have deteriorated in neighbouring streets into which car and lorry traffic has had to be displaced.

Central London also has a number of old-established pedestrian streets and ways. In the City many of these reflect the ancient street plan dating from before the Great Fire of 1666. They are well developed in the area between Lombard Street and Cornhill. New pedestrian precincts have been created at Tower Place on the western side of Tower Hill, and on bombed sites in the Barbican, and at Paternoster Square immediately north of St. Pauls where office blocks and shops have been arranged around inter-linked paved surfaces. These are 2 m above the original ground level and accommodate a car park below. Most pedestrian streets in the West End have been designated and closed to traffic in only recent years. As well as earning a world-wide reputation for its fashions, Carnaby Street was converted into a pedestrian street in 1972. It has since been repaved to form a precinct and is closed to all traffic between 11·00 and 20·00 hours Monday to Saturday. Many more pedestrians now use the street and three out of four shop managers believe that the scheme is a good idea and have adapted their delivery system satisfactorily. To the south of Oxford Street, South Molton Street has been closed to traffic between 11·00 and 17·30 hours Monday to Saturday. The street is lined with small shops in early eighteenth-century buildings and forms an exceptionally attractive pedestrian scheme that might well be emulated in other parts of central London. In 1975 an experimental scheme closed sections of Leicester Square to traffic at weekends. Now the sections are closed throughout the week and pavements have been widened and landscaping provided to enhance the environmental quality of the Square. These examples are just part of a much more ambitious programme that is underway to make walking in the West End a more pleasant and less hazardous activity.

By contrast with these examples of controlling the use of cars, central London has experienced savage demolition programmes to provide more space for them. One of the most devastating examples involves Upper and Lower Thames Streets between Blackfriars and the Tower of London. The space between these narrow streets and the River Thames was packed with quays, wharves and warehouses, intersected by narrow lanes and alleys leading down to public landing places (or 'stairs'). This area no longer handles water-borne goods and many buildings of historic interest have been demolished in recent years to make way for redevelopment and road widening. These include the Victorian Coal Exchange that was constructed between 1847 and 1849 on the corner of

Lower Thames Street and St. Dunstan's Hill. It was an elegant iron-framed building, with galleries, a dome, and the remains of a Roman bath house preserved in the basement. In spite of strong opposition from conservation groups the Exchange was demolished in 1962. Many old warehouses and commercial buildings have also been flattened and replaced by undistinguished office blocks and multi-storey car parks. However there are a few examples of wise conservation and new construction. One warehouse has been converted successfully into a restaurant and a new office block has been designed to harmonize with what remains of the old alleys, wharves and warehouses. Extensive demolition works have also provided the opportunity to conduct 'rescue digs' to excavate the remains of Baynard's Castle, dating from Tudor times, and an unexpected stretch of Roman wall alongside the river. But Thames Street has now become a broad characterless highway and the remaining old buildings that are found around Billingsgate Market are extremely vulnerable to redevelopment schemes.

Thames Street is a harsh but not solitary example of an historic urban environment being swept away for road 'improvement' in central London. It is to be hoped that the sacrifice of these areas may enable other historic quarters to be conserved, but maybe that is just wishful thinking. In 1967 the Civic Amenities Act laid a duty on local authorities to designate conservation areas that are of special architectural or historic interest and whose character or appearance is worthy of being preserved or enhanced. This extended the concept of urban conservation from individual buildings to whole streets and neighbourhoods. The first conservation area in London involved the surroundings of the Royal Naval College in Greenwich (1968). By the beginning of 1976 over 300 had been designated in Greater London. Some include just a handful of houses, others are as large as the whole of Belgravia. One-third of the City of Westminster and half of Kensington and Chelsea have conservation area status (Fig. 5·2). In addition, there are eight conservation areas in the City of London. No particular planning procedures are attached to them but by the early 1970s planners were using their existence as a reason for refusing permission for redevelopment or for imposing particularly rigorous conditions. Tremendous scope exists for conserving and rehabilitating parts of central London. A group of urban conservationists urge that we should now take advantage of the economic situation, and the consequent lull in new projects, to make a re-assessment of how future developments should respect and improve the City's unique character. But conservation schemes are expensive—and money is short. They offer much less

5·2 Conservation Areas in Central London.

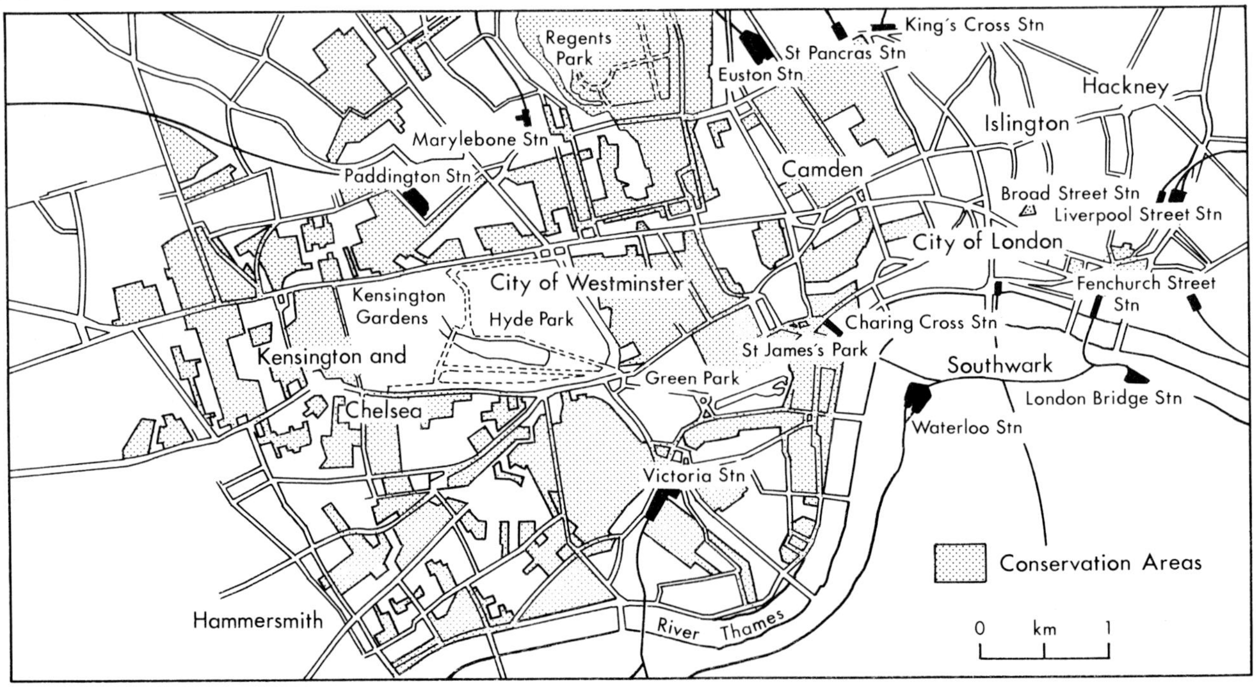

by way of financial return than more blatantly commercial brands of redevelopment.

Covent Garden: Community, Conservation and Conflict

The area designated as Covent Garden lies in the heart of the West End and is bounded by five major routeways (Kingsway, High Holborn, Shaftesbury Avenue, Charing Cross and the Strand). In all, about 38 ha of streets and buildings make up the Garden which is famous for the fruit, vegetable and flower market that occupied its central area for over 300 years. Covent Garden is also well known for its theatres and the Royal Opera House. The area has a unique visual and social character which comes from its great number of old buildings, the mixture of housing with business land uses, and its tangle of small streets.

Life in Covent Garden used to be described as a chaos of 'ballerinas and bananas cheek by jowl'. The area had a unique overlap of late night and early morning activities. Lorries full of market produce would start arriving as the last opera and theatregoers wandered home. Trading would begin about 05·00 h and finish by 11·00 h. In 1970, 250 businesses traded in the market; approximately 5000 buyers used it each day and the annual turnover reached £75 000 000.

Change in Covent Garden has been forced by the decision to move the market out of the area. The traders were experiencing considerable difficulties in carrying on their businesses. Traffic congestion grew more troublesome as larger container lorries, having battled first to get through the West End, attempted to gain access to the narrow streets of the Garden. The market premises were insecure and pilfering went on at an alarming rate. Additionally, the quality of life for local residents was deteriorating with increased noise and congestion. Either the market site would have to be redeveloped, or the market itself would have to be moved somewhere else. Redevelopment of the site would not solve problems with the existing road network and access through central London, and any large-scale redevelopment would involve the loss of historic and protected buildings associated with the market. The decision to move south of the Thames to a new, purpose-built site at Nine Elms was made in 1966. Construction of the new market building began in 1971. The Nine Elms market has easy access, extensive parking space and secure warehousing for the traders. The market moved out of Covent Garden on 12 November 1974, leaving the planning authorities with a problem on a scale analogous to the devastation caused by the bombing in World War II. Over 6 ha of buildings had been exclusively in market use, their removal raised questions about the future of the whole area.

Differing opinions about the future of Covent Garden resulted in heated debate between the planning authorities, government and the public. The major issues exemplify many of the planning problems that have faced other parts of central London; issues about the acceptable balance between the demolition or rehabilitation of buildings; the conservation of the physical and social environments of areas within the city; and the acceptable level of public participation in planning decisions. The future of Covent Garden rested on two proposals. A draft plan was put forward in 1968. Public reaction to the scale of the changes envisaged in the plan, combined with certain crucial changes in the political and financial climate led to the development of a new plan. This was published in 1974.

Two questions are raised by the changes in Covent Garden. How can the planners protect and conserve historic buildings and an outworn physical fabric without adequate financial resources? The conflict lies between large scale, high cost redevelopment programmes which entail the destruction of the existing environment, and rehabilitation schemes for buildings that cost less but offer nothing like the same return on capital investment. The change in commitment from redevelopment to conservation and rehabilitation is the most striking difference between the two proposals.

The second dilemma concerns the social community itself. How can the public and the planners work together to preserve and enhance the local community? The presence of the market in Covent

Garden until 1974 fossilized both physical and social environments, protecting them from changes occurring in other parts of London. The predominantly working-class community of the Garden, stranded by these changes, is totally unable to afford the 'economic' rents charged for accommodation in the remainder of central London. The authorities need to provide accommodation for the community at low rents, and to attract light industries back into the heart of the city to provide employment. Such

5·3 Covent Garden Area Draft Plan, 1968.

employment would encourage new growth among the traditional population. This requires new housing in face of increasing competition from professional and middle classes with greater financial resources. How far can and should the local authorities protect and subsidize the existing community in Covent Garden from the realities of such competition?

The 1968 and 1974 Draft Plans Very few people doubted the necessity to move the market but the future of Covent Garden and the market site was a pressing problem. In 1968 a draft plan was published by the three planning authorities involved with the area: the GLC, the City of Westminster and the London Borough of Camden. The scale of the change in the physical and social fabric of Covent Garden envisaged in the plan stimulated a great public outcry. In response to the volume of protest, the chairman of the committee resigned in 1972. She felt unable to support proposals that were so out of tune with public opinion. The Secretary of State for the Environment intervened in 1973. Covent Garden was designated as a comprehensive development area which gave the authorities powers of compulsory purchase and effectively halted any large-scale, private development. A new plan was drawn up in 1974 and modified through extensive consultation with the local community. Final approval for the 1974–6 proposals was granted in 1977.

Two themes run through the 1968 proposals. First, to increase dramatically the residential population of the Garden and second, to expand the entertainment facilities and hotel accommodation of the area. The draft planning team set themselves seven objectives in 1968. These were to retain the mixed land-use character of Covent Garden; to increase residential accommodation; to provide new public open space; to ease traffic congestion and separate vehicles from pedestrians. The final objectives of this proposal were to conserve a number of buildings of historic and architectural interest; and to ensure that the new development should be integrated into the existing character of the Garden. The draft plan, in fact, met neither of these crucial objectives.

The objectives of the new plan appear to be similar, particularly in their commitment to retain a mixture of types of land use. However they have a greatly reduced scale of change and a different political sentiment. The 1974 plan is to increase the residential community and to improve existing housing; to improve local services; and to strengthen the economic vitality of the Garden through new and traditional industrial enterprises.

The outline changes for the area in 1968 and 1974 are shown in Figs. 5·3 and 5·4. The most striking contrast between the two proposals is the scale of redevelopment considered to be necessary. In 1968, redevelopment of 22 out of the 38 ha of the Garden was proposed. Justification for the scale of demolition was obtained through the very real evidence of planning blight in Covent Garden. The failure to take any decisions about the future of the area had frozen new development and renovation of properties for several years, and this, in the words of the 1968 proposal had left the area ‘ripe for redevelopment’.

The major change saw a broad band of new development running north and parallel to the Strand, connecting Drury Lane to Leicester Square. Within this belt would be an expanded Opera House, a new theatre complex, an international conference centre, a large tourist hotel and a multiplicity of shops and light entertainment. These new buildings were almost totally dependent upon the capital and investment from private developers. The costs of the proposals at the time left a bill of £103 000 000 with private developers and £29 000 000 with the public authorities. Speculation was taking place in Covent Garden by the middle 1960s. Individuals began to speculate with the high land values of the area and the possibility of new developments. The planning authorities were gratified at the growth in financial interest since their draft proposal was so dependent upon private finance.

Everything about the 1968 plan was on a large scale: grandiose schemes that reflect the architectural and planning values of the period. Dramatic changes occurred in the following few years in both the economic and political climates. The tenor of the 1974–6 plan reflect these changes. Based on ‘realistic, small scale proposals’, the 1976 local plan is committed to the preservation and enhancement of existing conditions. The estimates for the new proposals include private investment of £25 000 000, a public investment of £30 000 000 and a contribution of £11 000 000 from other government agencies.

The change in attitude towards the conservation of buildings in Covent Garden is a striking feature. The two proposals show a major extension of the main conservation area around Covent Garden Square and the designation of a completely new conservation area around Seven Dials (Monmouth Street). Over 85 % of the buildings in Covent Garden are over fifty years old. In 1968, a decidedly cavalier attitude existed towards the historic buildings. The planning team argued that the buildings, apart from exceptional cases, should be judged in relation to their setting in any new development and that the new proposals should come before the preservation of buildings. In 1974, the team argued that conservation of the present buildings would 'largely establish the contexts and constraints of the planning objectives'.

In 1968, about forty individual buildings were listed. Listing protects them from wholesale demolition or change. These forty formed the basis of the limited conservation area. They included three very important or grade 1 buildings—St. Paul's Church in the Piazza, the Theatre Royal in Drury Lane and the Royal Opera House. The remainder included the central market building, eight theatres and twenty-six houses. In 1973, the Secretary of State sanctioned the listing of another 250 buildings. The designation of two conservation areas in Covent Garden and the listing of such a large number of buildings effectively halted any movement towards private development, and large-scale change. It ushered in schemes for the rehabilitation of the whole urban environment that included renovation of buildings, tree planting and the paving and pedestrianization of streets. The 1974 proposal is thus committed to the rehabilitation of buildings. Private developers are usually unwilling to engage in rehabilitation because the expense incurred does not justify the financial return. Rehabilitation thus remains the responsibility of the local authorities in Covent Garden who are committed to the maintenance of the visual character of the area. One possible solution to the problems incurred in rehabilitation programmes is through a policy of mixed use for buildings. Mixed use encourages light industrial, retail or commercial units at ground level with residential accommodation above. It also allows for changes in the function of buildings without changing their physical appearance; so the Floral Hall in the market, for example, is to become the National Theatre Museum.

The major change, therefore, has been to increase protection for the physical environment of Covent Garden. Similar trends have occurred in the implementation of housing proposals and the protection of the local community. The residents of the area (just under 3000 at present) are a distinctive and perhaps unique group. In comparison with other areas of central London, the residents are considerably older, more are retired people (over 30 % over 60). The majority of the residents live in low rental housing trust developments, unmodernized local authority housing and private, unfurnished accommodation with protected rents. The community is made up of a greater proportion of skilled and unskilled manual workers than elsewhere in the city. Over 43 % of the residents have lived in the Garden for more than twenty years and the majority feel a strong sense of identity with each other and the area.

The 1968 plan proposed to demolish over half the existing housing stock: over 6 ha of housing were considered to be in urgent need of redevelopment. Not because the houses could be classed as statutory slums but because residential densities were considered to be too high and many residents were sharing basic facilities such as bathrooms. An increased number of residential units were to be provided in new, high rise blocks of flats. The majority of these flats were to be let at rents similar to those in other parts of central London.

The housing proposals have also changed dramatically. The 1976 plan seeks to maintain the local community in the centre of London when much of the remainder is either a museum piece or it dies at 17·00 h. The new planning team encountered tremendous resistance from the local population to any suggestion of demolition and high-rise blocks. Only a very small proportion of the housing stock has been demolished: the great majority will be rehabilitated over two or three years. The team is committed to maintaining and enhancing the existing social networks by moving people back into their flats once they have been improved.

Again the question arises from this change in policy; why was it considered necessary to demolish buildings in 1968 and not in 1974? The rationale for demolition was that residential densities were too high. But, as the 1976 report acknowledges, residential density is a question of the perceptions of the residents themselves and cannot be used as an objective planning criterion. Covent Garden residents have a long tradition of living in the centre of the city and

5·4 Covent Garden Local Plan, 1974.

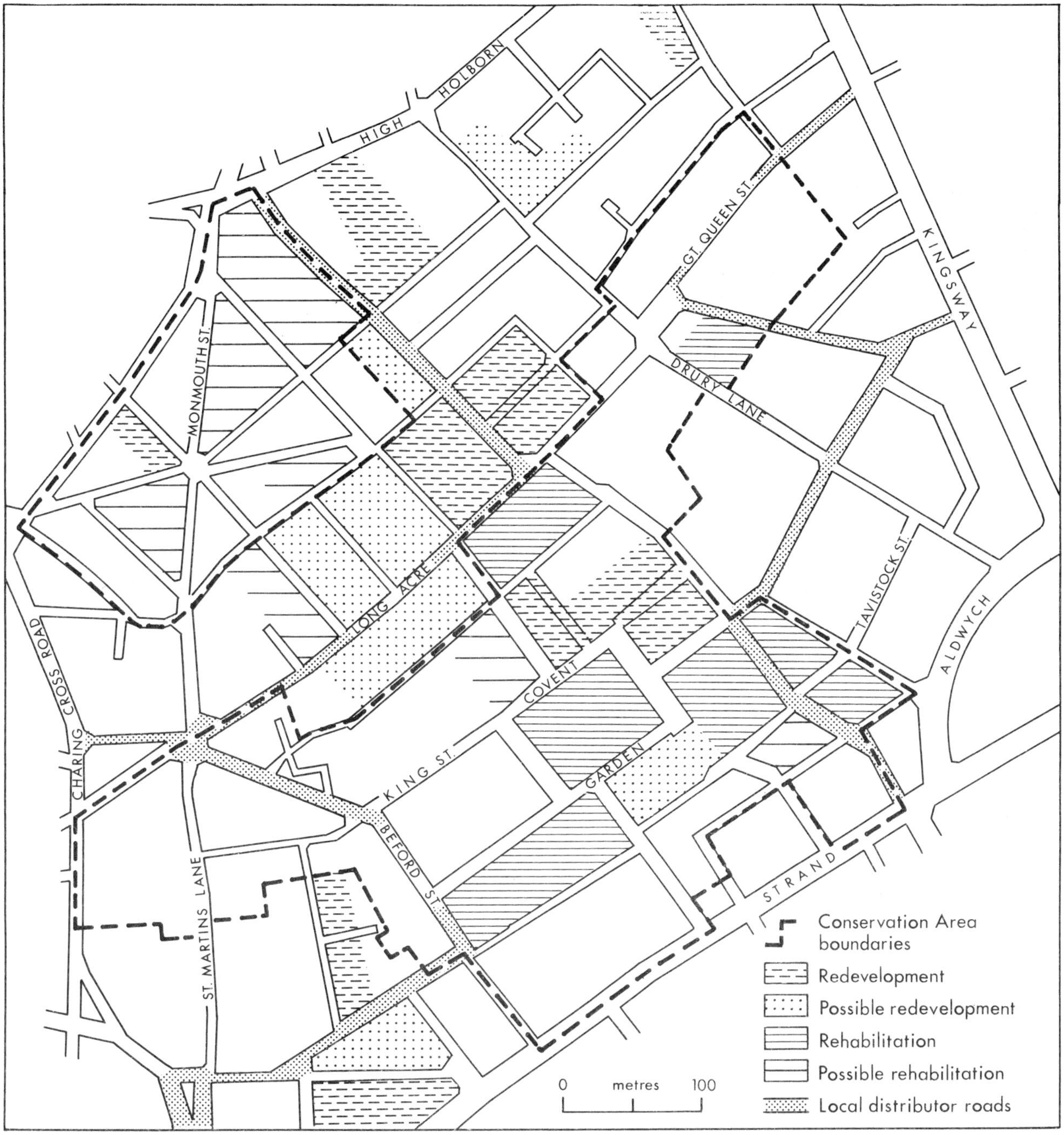

their perceptions of acceptable densities are not the same of those of the planners.

A major requirement for the maintenance and expansion of the traditional community is to attract light industry and commerce back into the area. Some movement is taking place; small firms are reopening and many have traditional links with the Garden such as costumiers, theatrical scenery and photography. Many employ less than five people.

The Community and Change Community protest to the 1968 proposals was crucial in the decision to reconsider the future of Covent Garden. A pressure group called the Covent Garden Community Association formed in 1971 to organize all sections of the community. Their success was far greater than they probably expected themselves. This was for two reasons. First, the dramatic change in the financial climate which effectively halted most of the speculative development, and a change in the politics of planning. Since the Skeffington Report in 1969, all local and structure plans have to be put to public enquiry before they can be implemented. The public have to be consulted, informed and allowed to register their reactions and opinions.

It was largely in reaction to this local pressure that the Secretary of State for the Environment requested that the three councils involved in Covent Garden should prepare a new informal plan with full public participation. He felt that the scale of any new development found to be necessary should be related to the existing character of the area, and that the people who live and work in the Garden should determine their level of participation. A forum of local representatives has liased with the planning team. Since 1974 meetings take place every three weeks to put the views of the local residents. The new plan is a result of extensive consultation and compromise between planners and the public.

The compromise has been costly for Covent Garden. The indecision since 1968 has meant that many more buildings have fallen into disrepair and people, uncertain about the future, have been unwilling to make any improvements. Although the private speculators have been denied access to the Garden, a more insidious change is taking place. Local shops are of great importance for the maintenance of the local community, particularly for the elderly and less mobile. Between 1968 and 1975, a fall of 30% in retailing establishments took place, with the greatest decline in the number of food shops. Many other shops are changing to meet the needs of workers at lunchtime. Increased tourist interest in Covent Garden has encouraged growth in new, fashionable craft shops, health food shops and florists. These are not particularly appropriate for the needs of the local residents. As tenants die, private owners are renovating their accommodation to let at much higher rents to people who can afford to pay for accommodation in the centre of London. The local authorities can do little to stop this change. Instead of instant destruction envisaged by the 1968 plan, a slow but steady erosion of character is taking place in the face of such competition.

Further Reading

Booker, C. and Green, C. L., *Goodbye London* (Fontana, London, 1975)

Burke, G., *Townscapes* (Penguin, Harmondsworth, 1976)

Dunning, J. H. and Morgan, E. V. (eds.), *An Economic Study of the City of London* (George Allen and Unwin, London, 1971)

Gardiner, G., *The Changing Life of London* (Stacey, London, 1973)

Jenkins, S., *Landlords to London: the story of a capital and its growth* (Constable, London, 1975)

6 The Dockland Dilemma

Hugh Clout

East and West

The internal balance of cities changes through time. For centuries 'London' was the City of London but by the seventeenth century a functional separation had begun to take place as wealthy Londoners chose to build homes around the royal residences of Westminster in preference to the crowded City. The western side of the capital became fashionable and desirable, but downstream from London Bridge the banks of the Thames retained their distinct advantages for ocean going trade and allied industries. In the present century, however, the balance of economic strength has also tipped in favour of West London. The central business district has shifted progressively westwards from the heart of the City. Main roads, motorways and London Airport have attracted modern, dynamic industries to the western side of the capital. Visitors flock to the shops, cinemas, theatres and museums of the West End and stay in its hotels. Why should they venture to the East End that has missed out in the economic and technological 'revolutions' of the present century?

The fact that East has lagged behind West in terms of wealth and living conditions has been demonstrated in social and economic surveys for more than a century, but not until the past couple of decades have the weaknesses of Dockland been revealed fully. Closure has affected docks and factories alike and in the 1970s the whole *raison d'être* of Dockland has come into question. In the heady days before July 1974, when Maplin was still being considered as a location for a third airport for London, there was hope that the imbalance between West and East might be adjusted, with East London receiving new forms of transport and a share in the 'spread effects' of future economic growth. But even then the chances of Dockland benefiting were only slight. Maplin proved to be no more than an expensive day-dream. The hard times of the 1970s offer little hope of solving Dockland's problems which fit into the same category with those of mining and heavy industry.

The Building of Dockland

Tower Bridge is more than the most easterly bridge across the Thames. For visitors and for many Londoners it forms a boundary on their 'mental map' of the capital and also the eastern limit of their field of exploration. The City, Westminster and the West End are all upstream whilst the unknown territory of Dockland stretches downriver. Five peninsulas are fringed by the great meanders of the Thames between the Tower of London and Barking Creek. This low-lying, marshy terrain was ideal for excavating docks to complement the busy mooring places in the Thames and its tributaries. Two wet docks had been built at Blackwall and Rotherhithe as early as the seventeenth century but it was not until 1799 that a Royal Commission reported in favour of creating more. The London Docks were opened six years later and were followed by eight other dock systems during the nineteenth century, with the George V Dock being completed as recently as 1921. The docks offered a number of advantages. By accommodating vessels away from London's busy river they helped reduce congestion. Water levels could be controlled inside the docks and this made loading and unloading much easier than along the river bank where the tidal range was about 6 m. Each dock system was surrounded by high walls so that the serious problem of theft might be reduced.

Building the docks required a large labour force and this contributed to the great increases in population that Dockland underwent during the nineteenth century. For example, 2–3000 labourers were employed in building the Royal Albert Docks during the 1870s. Workers came not only from the Home Counties but from all parts of the British Isles. The years surrounding the great Irish Famine of 1847–8 brought many Irish to East London where they helped construct the capital's docks, warehouses, bridges and tunnels. Those who were not involved in building found work as costermongers, street sweepers or scavengers—or simply begged. By mid-century the Irish brogue and ways of life dominated many streets and courtyards in the East End. The dockers had to live close to the dockgates in order to be near at hand whenever ships came in. Many streets of cheap housing were put up in such areas as Custom House and Canning Town to provide accommodation for this casual and poorly paid labour force.

Industrial development provided another stimulus for the growth of Dockland. In some cases industry arrived before the wet docks were built. Noxious industries, such as the manufacture of glass, lead and paint, had been installed on riverside land in Stepney before 1800. Farther downstream, the marshy Isle of Dogs was still undeveloped in 1800 but by the 1840s the riverside had become lined with timber wharves, sawmills and ironworks to supply the shipbuilding industry among others. The Millwall Docks at the heart of the 'island' were not to be opened for a further twenty years. As the years went by, industrial development expanded downstream. Sites beyond the river Lee in Essex were particularly 'attractive' since by-laws that affected house building and health were even less demanding than in Stepney and Poplar. By the end of the nineteenth century the banks of the Thames as far east as Barking Creek were lined with factories, gasworks and sewage works. Dockland was the manufacturing annexe of Britain's ocean empire and on the margins of Dockland industries such as the building and repairing of locomotives (Stratford) and the manufacture of clothing and furniture contributed to the importance of the East End. But not every branch of industry flourished. The Thames shipbuilding trade survived the transition from sail to steam but could not withstand competition from northern estuaries and fell into decline in the second half of the century.

Early in the nineteenth century settlements such as Wapping and Limehouse underwent a phase of rapid growth but rates of increase slackened after 1850 and fifty years later the numbers of residents had begun to decline. In Poplar peak rates of growth occurred at mid-century and West Ham developed even later. From a mere 19 000 residents in 1851 the borough's population grew to 267 000 in 1901 and a peak of 300 000 in 1921. By that time West Ham was the eighth largest 'town' in England and Wales. The quality of housing was poor in Dockland as it was in much of the East End. Overcrowding was widespread, health conditions were bad, and water supply and mains drainage were inadequate during the greater part of the nineteenth century. Those who could afford to do so moved out to East Ham or beyond but their place was taken by other Londoners, displaced by slum clearance schemes or by public works, such as the demolition work associated with building the approaches to Blackwall Tunnel in the 1890s. In addition, new waves of immigrants settled in the East End including 50–60 000 Jews who arrived between 1880 and 1914.

The port of London functioned as Britain's vital trading contact with the rest of the world but, in dramatic contrast, the everyday world of the dockworker was remarkably local. While improving facilities for shipping, the construction of dock systems had reduced accessibility by land for the riverside settlements. Roads had to skirt around the dock basins and their warehousing premises. Swing bridges over access channels to the docks hindered movement by road. The main highways and railways of East London had been built away from the fragmented terrain of Dockland but spur lines provided connections for carrying merchandise to and from the newer docks. Opportunities for dockers to move out and find work in other parts of London were few and far between.

By the eve of World War I two features had already emerged in Dockland that were to become particularly disturbing half a century later. First, the balance of the port had shifted progressively eastward as large docks were needed for new vessels. The detached dock system opened at Tilbury was well downstream from the five peninsulas. Second, some branches of port-based manufacturing, such as shipbuilding, were already dead. As early as the 1880s the Isle of Dogs had a share of empty cottages that had been deserted by shipbuilders who had moved to Clydeside. The conjunction of these two trends gave cause for concern as early as 1913 but by the late 1960s they had taken on a much bigger dimension. The traditional economic base of Dockland had been reduced to a shadow of its former importance.

In the inter-war years new legislation for improving housing came into force and local authorities in East London began programmes of slum clearance. Rehousing was cheaper and easier on greenfield sites and the LCC made use of the District Line as an 'escape route' in their project for building an out-county estate at Becontree, where over 2000 families from Stepney alone were rehoused during the mid-1930s. However some rehousing did take place in Dockland with, for example, the Borough of Poplar building 'garden suburb' houses in East Ferry Road on the Isle of Dogs. West Ham Council built 1200 houses as part of slum clearance schemes and 600 homes that were built by the Ministry of Transport as part of the Silvertown Way road-improvement project (1932–4) were transferred to the Council.

Devastation and Reconstruction

Dockland formed a prime target for nearly 1000 high explosive bombs and thousands of incendiaries during World War II. As a result of the raid on the East End of 7 September 1940 the city was lit up for three days by great fires in Wapping and Rotherhithe. The blitz destroyed one-third of the enormous warehouse area of the port and half of its storage accommodation. Goods had to be stored under tarpaulins and in makeshift huts amidst the ruined warehouses. Much equipment was destroyed or taken away for use in other ports at home and abroad. Vast residential areas were also devastated. By the end of the war 11 000 houses in Stepney (one-third of the total) had been demolished or were uninhabitable and in West Ham some 14 000 homes (over a quarter of the borough's total) had been destroyed. The Luftwaffe had made a start on slum clearance schemes that might have been delayed for years. Bombing and evacuation reduced the population of the boroughs that contained Dockland by no less than 520 000 (50 %) between 1939 and 1941. At the end of the war the East End was a desert of desolate streets, derelict buildings and quiet weed-covered waste ground.

Here was a chance to remedy the ills of the past through bold and imaginative reconstruction. To the immediate north of the upstream docks the Stepney–Poplar Comprehensive Development Area was designated in 1947, covering over 600 ha that were to be rebuilt at much lower densities than before. Eleven (later thirteen) neighbourhood units would be constructed with appropriate new housing, schools, community buildings and open spaces. Upon completion the resident population of the CDA was planned to be less than half of that on the eve of the war. In fact, progress has been slow. By 1970 only half of the CDA had been completed, with redeveloped areas jostling with decayed housing, industrial buildings and old, but expensive, premises that front on to main roads. Located between the East India Dock Road and the Limehouse Cut, the Lansbury neighbourhood (50 ha) is the most attractive and benefited from being chosen for reconstruction as part of the 'live architecture' exhibition of the Festival of Britain (1951). A small CDA was defined in Bermondsey–Rotherhithe on the south bank of the Thames.

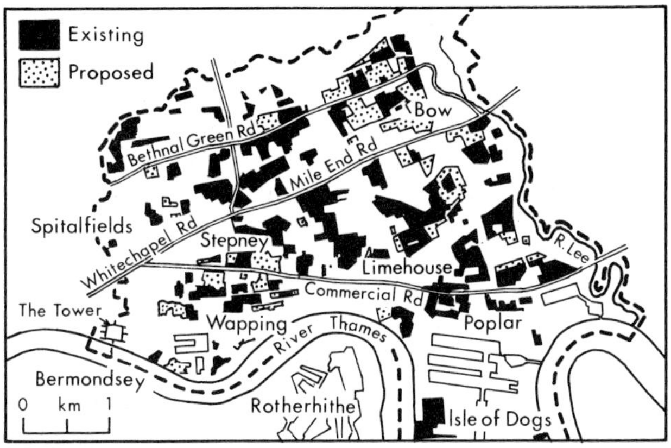

6·1 Post-war Council Housing in Tower Hamlets.

No such comprehensive scheme was drawn up for Dockland proper. Each local authority undertook its own reconstruction programme with new estates replacing damaged housing. For example, 500 new homes were built at North Woolwich (East Ham) involving small 'town squares' and a shopping precinct dominated by five eight-storey blocks of flats as well as smaller blocks. In neighbouring West Ham the local authority built over 8000 permanent dwellings from 1945 to 1965, with the largest development at the Keir Hardie estate north of the Royal Victoria Dock. Replacing war damage gradually gave way to slum clearance once again. Between 1965 and 1970 the new London Borough of Tower Hamlets rehoused 7700 families in tower blocks, many up to twenty-four storeys high. Public hostility to high-rise blocks was reinforced by the Ronan Point gas explosion in 1968. Tower Hamlets turned its attention to ten- to twelve-storey blocks instead. In 1970 only twenty-three private homes were built in the borough, compared with 1691 local authority dwellings. Tower Hamlets is in danger of becoming a municipal ghetto of streets in the sky (Fig. 6·1). Survey after survey has shown that the single family home with a garden remains the Londoner's ideal.

Closure of the Upstream Docks

By the mid-1960s it was clear that all was not well in the small upstream docks. The Port of London Authority had to concentrate on activities that were viable and could accommodate new trends in bulk handling such as containerization, roll on/roll off, and bulk transfer of grain and timber. That meant developing facilities downstream, where there was room to expand, and closing small installations that were making a loss. New handling facilities permit shorter turn-round times for ships and this further reduces berth requirements. In 1967 the PLA closed the East India Dock, after a life of 161 years during which it had berthed the tea clippers such as the *Cutty Sark*. Prior to closure it had handled coasters and ships on short sea runs but was not viable. The St. Katharine and London Docks were closed in 1968 and 1969 respectively, following a recommendation in 1965 after it had been learned that both were running at a loss. Some facilities, such as the London Dock bulk wine berth (1963), had been completed only recently, but for many years both docks had functioned as warehousing points for goods discharged downstream and brought upriver in smaller ships. In 1970 the last ship left the Surrey Commercial Docks and timber handling was transferred to Tilbury. For the same year the PLA announced that further closures and rationalization of berths in the enclosed docks were imminent, with more of the Port's activities being concentrated at Tilbury. By 1977 the Millwall and West India Docks had received a reprieve but further closures were envisaged for the 1980s. The Port of London was having to face fierce competition from East Coast container ports, such as Felixstowe, that are well located for trade with the EEC. In as short a time as 1970–5 the Port of London's share of UK foreign trade fell from 25 to 14% of exports and from 19 to 11% of imports. Tonnage handled fell from a record 60 000 000 tonnes in 1968 to 45 000 000 tonnes in 1975 (partly because of a strike over stuffing and stripping containers) and the Port of London's workforce fell from 26 000 to 9500.

The Dockland Environment

Faced with the early phases of such enormous

changes, the Secretary of State for the Environment announced in 1971 that a comprehensive study of Dockland should be made by consultants and that a number of costed alternative approaches for redevelopment should be proposed. The area under investigation extended for 12 km east from St. Katharine Dock, involved parts of five boroughs, and covered 2250 ha, which included 214 ha of enclosed docks (Fig. 6·2). The boundaries of Dockland were drawn to exclude the Royal Naval College at Greenwich on the south bank. Large organizations owned over three-quarters of the area, with the PLA holding 825 ha, the GLC 340 ha and British Gas 279 ha. With land held by the London Boroughs, the Central Electricity Generating Board and British Rail added in, the total rose to 1757 ha. The former marshland is flat and low lying, although material excavated for the docks was used to raise surrounding areas. Among the highest points are the 'Beckton Alps' and the 'Limmo' (Bow Creek), made up of waste from gas production and spoil from roadworks. Apart from a few small parks and churchyards, the area is treeless. However, naturalists noted that wildlife was returning to some of the abandoned docks, with over ninety bird species being observed in the deserted Surrey Docks, of which twenty-eight had been breeding in the locality.

Some 55 000 people lived in the area in 1966. Their age structure was rather younger than that for the five boroughs or for the whole GLC. Only 3 % were born outside the British Isles (compared with 7 % for the GLC) and there were high populations of semi-skilled and unskilled workers living in this strongly working-class area. Purpose-built flats rented from local

6·2 The Dockland Environment.

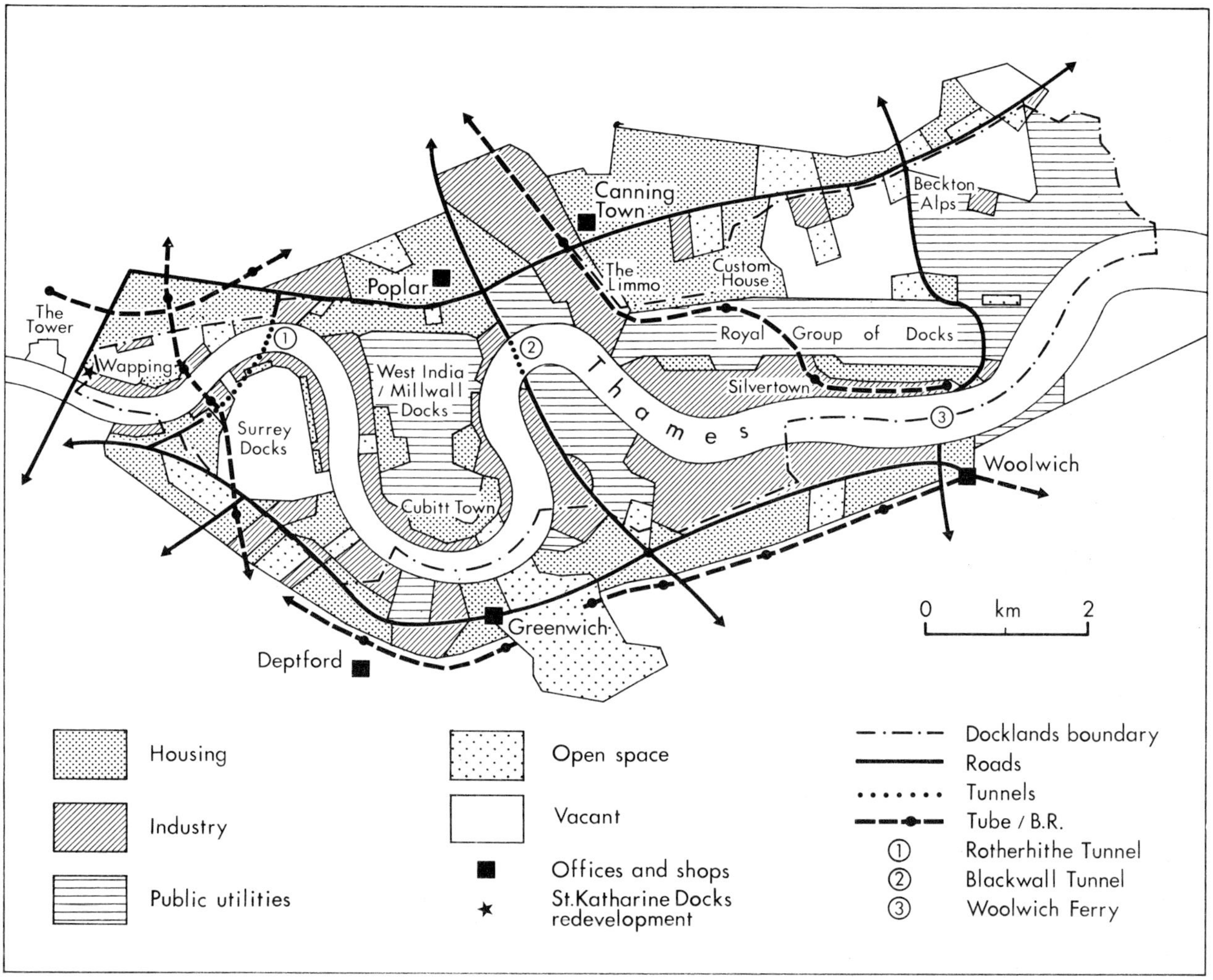

authorities made up two-thirds of the total accommodation, compared with a quarter for the GLC. Only 8% of households were owner occupied, compared with 37% for the GLC. Half of the 17 000 houses were built after 1945 to replace war-damaged property or slums. Many of the new flats were in tower blocks. As had been the case earlier in the century, a series of highly integrated neighbourhoods were still to be found in Dockland. For example, a Home Office community development project in Canning Town noted that 'for three or four generations, people have lived and worked in the same locality ... there are few, if any, similar areas anywhere else in London outside the East End where the pattern of living and working in one place still pervades'. But such a pattern was highly vulnerable to disruption when traditional forms of employment began to disappear and adequate numbers of suitable jobs were not available for school-leavers or for those made redundant.

About 58 000 people worked in Dockland in 1971, of whom only 24 000 lived there. Nearly half of the workforce was employed in a wide range of manufacturing and about a quarter in transport activities associated with the docks. In the preceding five years over 15 000 jobs had been lost in the Docklands. Unemployment rates were high and the majority of men out of work were looking for jobs in manufacturing, transport or warehousing. In 1971 the PLA was the largest single employer (6000) but since then the number of jobs in the port, the gas industry and many branches of old-established manufacturing have contracted substantially. Successive policies for controlling industrial growth in London and steering it away to the regions have not helped Dockland over the past decade. In any case the present condition of the area is hardly conducive for new factories and offices to move in.

Dock excavation has isolated housing areas from each other and from adjoining parts of London. Public transport is poorer in Dockland than in surrounding areas. The East London branch of the Metropolitan line serves the extreme west of the area and there is an infrequent British Rail service between North Woolwich and Stratford. In each case a change has to be made to take a train into central London, since the Central, District and Metropolitan lines and suburban British Rail services run well to the north of Dockland. South of the Thames the North Kent railway fringes the southern edge of Dockland and gives a direct link to central London. The main form of public transport is by bus, but there are no direct services to central London. By public transport virtually all of the area is more than fifty minutes away from central London's shops. Traffic congestion on the A13 and A200 slows down movement out of the area and dock entrances at Limehouse, Poplar and North Woolwich cause further complications on the roads. The banks of the Thames are linked by the Woolwich ferry and by five tunnels, two for pedestrians (Greenwich and Woolwich), two for vehicles (Rotherhithe and the dualled Blackwall Tunnel), and one for the Metropolitan line's East London branch. Poor accessibility is a particularly serious problem in the Isle of Dogs and, together with outdated schools, lack of doctors, dock rationalization and dereliction, formed one of the reasons for the Island to make a 'unilateral declaration of independence' in March 1970.

Dockland is poorly provided with shopping facilities, some 400 shops, betting shops and launderettes were in operation in 1972 and others were boarded up. Dockland contains no major shopping centre (nor indeed does the whole of Tower Hamlets LB) and there is no easily accessible small centre that is ripe for expansion. A small legacy of attractive old buildings has survived the onslaught of bombing raids and slum clearance schemes but, in the words of the Dockland Report ... 'the appearance of many parts of Dockland is drab and uncared for. Dwellings and shops are boarded up; temporary open spaces are used for rubbish; roads are poorly maintained; there are few play areas. Even recent housing areas have little landscaping and lack a sense of well being'.

Five Dreams of the Future

In order to remedy these problems and to take advantage of the area's potential for redevelopment, a number of planning schemes were prepared and costed. Five were presented in detail.

In the 'Waterside' plan housing would form the leading use of land and would be arranged around 100 ha of water parks that would follow the pattern of the old docks. A further 74 000 people might live in the area by 1991, of whom three-quarters would be in private housing. New office jobs would need to be created in Dockland. Two north/south roads were proposed to improve access to shopping centres beyond the area.

Wooded parks covering 300 ha on the Isle of Dogs, the site of the Surrey Docks and at Beckton formed the leading feature of the 'Thames Park' plan. Fifty thousand more people might live in new housing that would be built in equal shares by local authorities and private developers. Office construction would be encouraged in the western part of the area. Once again, two new north/south roads were included.

The 'East End Consolidated' plan would provide accommodation for an extra 92 000 people, of whom three-quarters would live in council housing. Office centres would be built at Wapping and Surrey Docks, with a medium-sized shopping centre at Beckton. Industry would be encouraged and transport improved by three new river bridges, a new east/west main road (linking Surrey Docks, the Isle of Dogs, the Greenwich Peninsula and Canning Town), and extended bus services.

The 'Europa' plan would include an extra 92 000 residents, two-thirds of whom would be owner/occupiers. Two new north/south roads would be supplemented by an east/west minitram to serve new office and shopping centres. Considerable amounts of manufacturing industry would have to be relocated.

Finally, the 'City New Town' plan would house 106 000 extra people in accommodation that would be split equally between the private and public sectors. A major 'town centre', with offices, shops and entertainment facilities would be built on the Isle of Dogs and would be served by a minitram and new east/west and north/south roads.

Rejection and Uncertainty

The consultants' report that included these plans appeared in March 1973 and was greeted by opposition from local authorities and action groups and was rejected by the newly elected GLC which had a Labour majority. Not only had proposals favoured commercial and middle-class intrusions into a strongly working-class industrial area but their capital cost ranged from £666 000 000 to £948 000 000 (at 1971 prices). The engineering work that would be required to fill the dock basins and put down foundation piles in soft ground would make the cost of each new Dockland dwelling at least 50–60 % higher than each new home in a greenfield new town. The report was quietly forgotten. In 1974 a Docklands Joint Committee brought together the GLC and five local boroughs (Tower Hamlets, Southwark, Lewisham, Greenwich, Newham) to prepare a strategy for Dockland. In April 1976 a draft plan was put forward for public consultation (Fig. 6·3). It proposed a doubling of population in the area in order to relieve housing pressure in other parts of inner London. Manufacturing was to be encouraged at three main industrial areas. An east/west Underground line was proposed to extend the Fleet line from Fenchurch Street to Thamesmead, with new roads and river crossings included.

However the future of Dockland is uncertain in the extreme. Public spending cuts may well prevent any 'grand designs' being started and a number of specific projects have already been suspended. For example, a £3 000 000 Trade Mart scheme proposed by an American company for the Surrey Docks has been deferred until the investment climate improves and an office scheme in the London Docks is not to start until there is more visible demand for new office space. Problems become bigger and prospects dimmer the farther one moves downstream between Tower Bridge and Barking Creek.

A Controversial Example of Redevelopment

St. Katharine Dock, immediately east of Tower Bridge, was excluded from the abortive 'Dockland' study since a scheme combining redevelopment and conservation had already been started there. London merchants promoted the St. Katharine Dock

Company Bill in 1824 because they wanted a dock as close as possible to the City. In the following year the Bill became law and clearing the 10 ha site began. Unlike the location of future docks, the site of St. Katharine's was already built up and contained an ancient hospital, a distillery and over 1000 crowded houses. These were demolished and the excavated soil was taken by barge to reclaim riverside land at Chelsea and Pimlico. The dock was opened in 1828 and continued to function until 1969.

All the dock's warehouses that backed on to East Smithfield were destroyed or badly damaged in the blitz of September 1940. Some were razed to the ground. Even before the war had ended there were proposals for using part of the riverside for a tree-lined promenade along the blitzed line of Wapping High Street to King Edward Memorial Park overlying the northern approaches to Rotherhithe Tunnel. In 1969 the GLC purchased the dock from the PLA and invited applications from developers to produce a plan that would include 300 units of local authority housing and a primary school and would retain the historic warehouses and the 4 ha of water as a yacht basin.

As well as the features already mentioned, the successful scheme included proposals for a major hotel, 378 private dwellings, shops, restaurants and a British (later World) Trade Centre. In 1973 the new labour-dominated GLC and action groups in Tower Hamlets expressed concern about the inclusion of office space and luxury accommodation in the scheme. The PLA was roundly criticized for having disposed of the dock for a relatively small amount (£1 500 000) and for associating itself with private developers. The East End Dockland Action Group made its position clear:

'We demand a massive increase in industrial jobs to replace the thousands that have been lost in recent years. We will fight the myth that the Docks are finished. We will not commute to work outside London while office blocks are built in our backyard for other people to work here. We have the chance now to catch up with basic amenities enjoyed by the

6·3 Docklands Joint Committee Proposals, 1976.

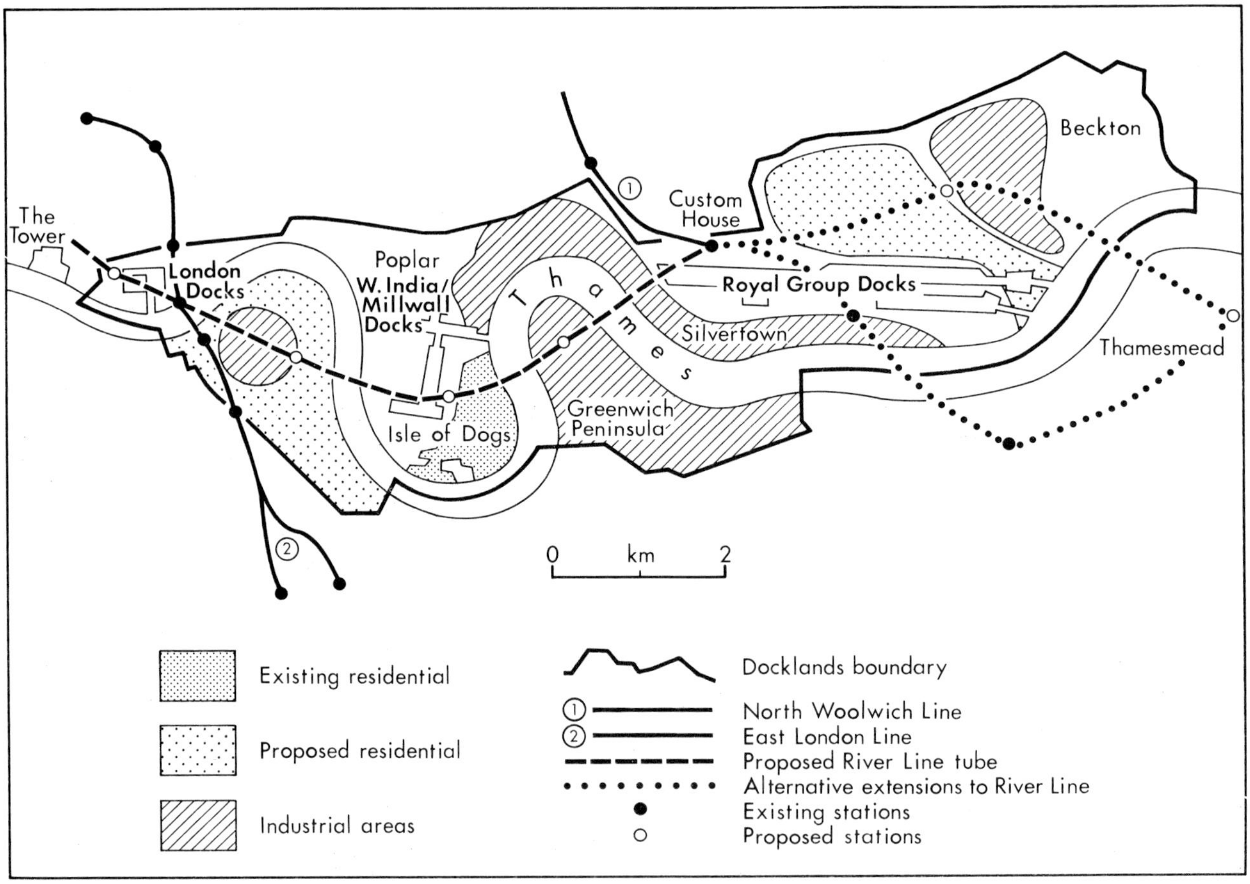

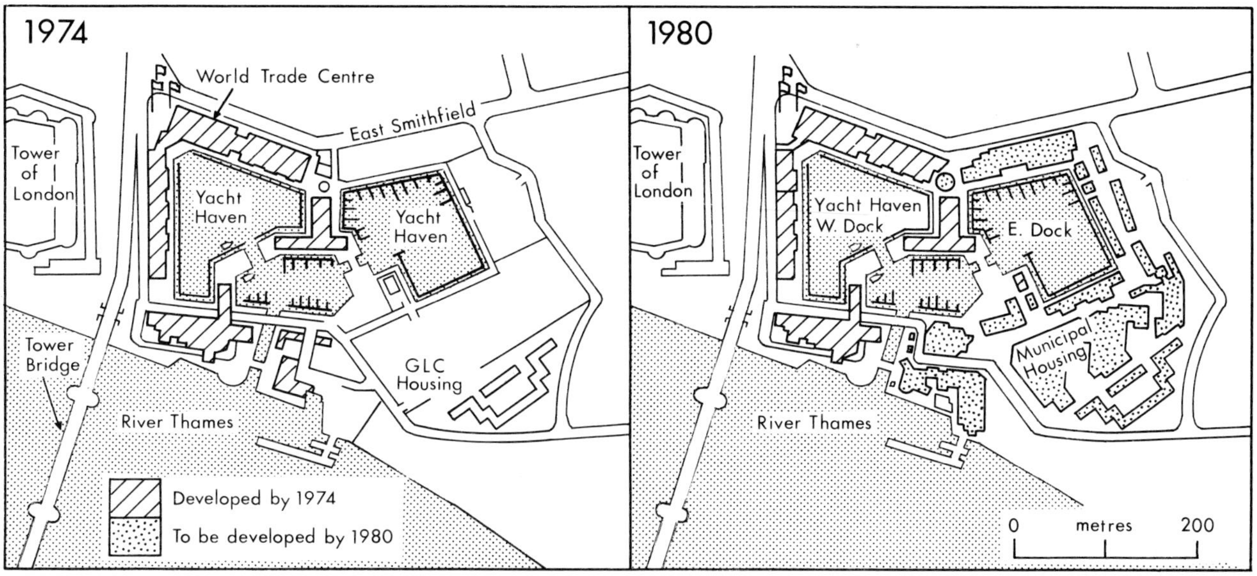

6·4 Redevelopment of St. Katharine Dock, 1974 and 1980.

rest of London. We want play space for our kids, better schools, better shopping centres, decent public transport and community facilities for the people of the East End. We want the riverside to be enjoyed by all the people—not to be parcelled off for sale to the rich. We have no use for yachting marinas and luxury hotels. Local people must decide what is to happen to their area'.

By the mid-1970s the 826-room Tower Hotel (built when Tower Hamlets had 6000 people on its waiting list for homes) had introduced some startling new architecture alongside Tower Bridge; Europe House offered 11 250 m² of office space, with facilities for conferences and exhibitions; and part of the restoration of the Ivory House had been completed (Fig. 6·4). The building had been constructed in Italianate style in 1854 and was used for storing tusks. New functions have been found for it, with the three upper floors being converted into luxury flats and the ground floor being used for shops and exhibition purposes. Conservation will not be complete until 1985. The dockmaster's house near the Thames has been restored and an interesting conservation project is underway for 'G' warehouse. In the early stages of demolition what looked like a small brick warehouse was discovered to be a mid-eighteenth century timber-framed building. It has been stripped of its brick covering and has been moved 100 m on to a new site where it will be restored and used as a restaurant. The school and local authority housing will be built to the south-east of the dock, backing on to existing blocks of GLC flats, while private accommodation will be constructed around the eastern and north-eastern sections of the dock. But, unlike the hotel and World Trade Centre, these are things for the future.

Further Reading

London Dockland Study Team, *Docklands Redevelopment Proposals for East London*, 2 vols, (Greater London Council, London, 1973)

Pudney, J., *London's Docks* (Thames and Hudson, London, 1975)

7 Thamesmead

Hugh Clout

A Challenging Environment

The shortage of land for housing and rehousing the population of Greater London poses severe problems for the city's planners. Few unused sites remain that are not protected by law. New construction can normally take place only when existing development has been cleared away. In the late 1950s the major redevelopment areas that had been designated for rebuilding the war-damaged East End were well underway and the LCC searched for other sites where large housing schemes might be constructed. All surplus or undeveloped land was scrutinized. For south-east London the reserve land surrounding Crossness sewage works on Erith marshes had originally been needed for extending the works but after they had been rebuilt during the 1950s about half of the reserve land was found to be surplus to requirements. In the 1960s additional areas of land at Plumstead were freed, which had been used in part for storing and testing explosives for Woolwich Arsenal nearby. A total area of 650 ha of marshland became available for development, bounded on the north by the river Thames and to the south by steep ground rising up to Bostock Heath and Abbey Woods.

The marshland fringes of London's river had been defended by walls and floodbanks for many centuries but were still subject to flooding by exceptionally high water, as in 1953 when the river wall was breached downstream from Erith. Schemes for draining Plumstead and Erith marshes were begun in the sixteenth century but they met with little initial success. In the reign of Elizabeth I 800ha were reported to be entirely under water in the great loop of land between Woolwich and Erith. Settlement was restricted to a few villages on higher ground inland, with the marshes being used as good grazing land (Fig. 7·1). During the nineteenth and especially twentieth centuries suburbia covered most of the higher parts of Thames-side but the marshland is still readily discernible in the land-use pattern, even though sections have been taken for docks (easily excavated from soft alluvial deposits), for public utilities (gas-works, thermal power stations and sewage works), and for large industrial works needing broad stretches of relatively cheap land. The Ford car plant, at Dagenham on the north bank, provides the best example and Woolwich Arsenal, with its marshy experimental zone, may be seen as an earlier case on the south bank.

The origin of the idea for a housing project on the Plumstead–Erith marshes goes back as far as 1952 when it was stated that Woolwich Arsenal held excess land and that activities might be concentrated in the western section, with 47 ha to be released to the LCC. The 1957 Defence White Paper led to a contraction of military forces and equipment so that the arsenal's very survival was threatened. By 1963 its closure was determined, in spite of strong local opposition since the arsenal had been an important source of employment. In April 1967 the land was handed over to the GLC. Consideration had been given to what might be done with the marshland ever since it appeared likely that it might become available. In 1963 a proposal was made for housing 25 000 people on Erith Marshes. A mixture of thirty-one storey towers and clusters of lower blocks built on decks above car parking and servicing areas was proposed. The scheme was shelved since negotiations were underway for the land at Woolwich and Plumstead.

The Master Plan

For March 1966 the GLC announced its draft Master Plan, with a revised version appearing a year later, for a scheme that would house 60 000 people and would be completed by the early 1980s. (In fact, the total was later scaled down to 45–48 000, to allow some

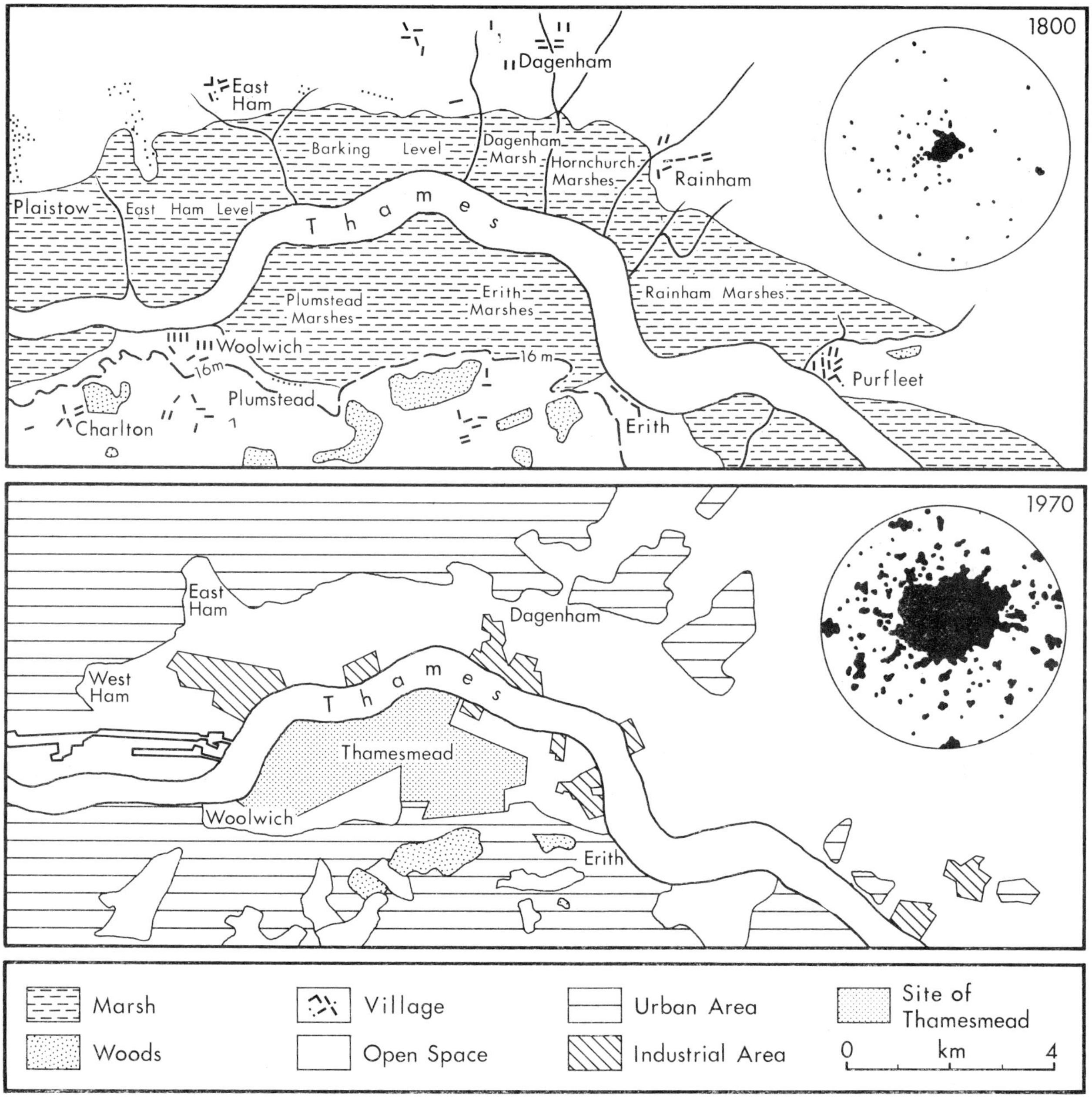

7·1 The Environment of Thamesmead, 1800 and 1970.

areas to be developed at lower densities, with a revised completion date of 1988.) The scheme was to be known as Thamesmead.

A project of this size was a truly massive operation and GLC planners were anxious to improve on conditions in old residential areas and to learn from the mistakes of earlier council estates and post-war new towns in order to design a better kind of environment for living. Accordingly, a number of guiding principles were devised (Fig. 7·2).

First, on such a large site, involving an open featureless stretch of riverside, it was necessary to produce an imaginative development on a grand scale.

Second, unlike the majority of housing estates, Thamesmead was not to be simply a dormitory area. It was to be planned to be truly town-like and provide a range of schools, shops, community activities, recreation facilities and local employment. This latter point would ensure that as few people as possible would have to make use of the already overloaded North Kent railway into central London.

Third, pedestrian routes and vehicle routes would be kept separate in Thamesmead in order to provide a safe and convenient environment for residents and for motorists. In an age of rising rates of car ownership it was important to avoid the mistakes of earlier estates and so one garage (or parking space) would be allocated for each dwelling. The needs of the car-less were not to be forgotten and it was stressed that adequate public transport from Thamesmead to both central London and surrounding suburbs was essential. There should be a bus route within 400 m of every new home.

Fourth, the site was to be developed on the 'neighbourhood' principle, with each neighbourhood having its own schools, community facilities and shops for meeting day-to-day needs. This decision reflected research that had been carried out for the proposed new town at Hook in Hampshire. In addition, a town centre would include a range of shops and department stores, medical services, higher education, recreation facilities and office employment to serve the whole of Thamesmead. Close to the town centre a yacht basin would be created that would be capable of mooring sea-going yachts.

Fifth, Thamesmead was not to be a 'one class town' and hence 35 % of the dwellings would be built by developers other than the local authority and would be for sale, whilst the remainder would be local authority houses and flats for rent. The town centre

7·2 Thamesmead Master Plan.

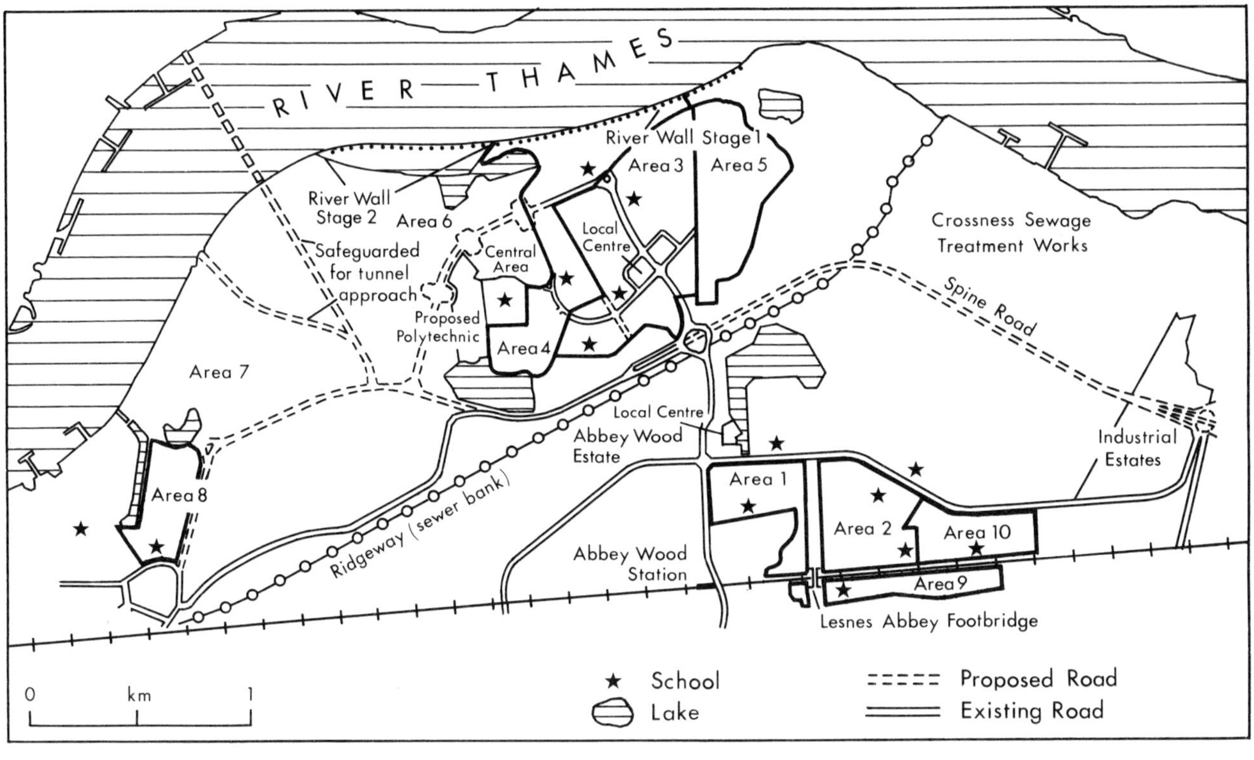

would generate a range of managerial and professional jobs which might in part be held by residents of the private housing.

Sixth, particular attention would be paid to the broad problem of building design, landscaping and the provision of open space in order to produce as attractive an environment as possible. Housing would be built at a relatively high density with extensive areas of surrounding open space. Emphasis was to be placed on linear development, rather than isolated point blocks. Industrial building methods would be used widely, involving assembly of concrete slabs that had been produced on site.

Developing the Thamesmead site would demand a high level of technical and architectural ingenuity if the scheme were to be a success. The marshland was flat, treeless and with a high water table. With the exception of a small area in the extreme west, it was appreciably lower than normal high tide levels and was subject to flooding during periods of heavy rainfall. The site formed a receptacle for water draining by gravity from higher land to the south and through ditches and sluices into the Thames. Because of the difference in level between the river and the marshes, discharge was possible for only a short period to either side of low tide. Water was stored in the ditches and spilled across sections of marshland in the intervening hours. Such a system of drainage would be totally unsatisfactory for a residential development and a new approach was necessary. The ground surface was of a poor load-bearing capacity, being made up of 1·5 m of silty clay, overlying 5·0–7·0 m of peat and alluvium. At the base of the alluvium, water-bearing gravel overlies Thanet Sand on Chalk. All buildings, mains drains and other structures at Thamesmead would require piling down to the gravel layer to provide firm foundations.

This area of marshland, surrounded by water on three sides and exposed to wind blowing off the Thames, faced the additional environmental problem of air pollution emanating from nearby power stations and large industrial works, as well as from London's remaining domestic hearths. On the north bank of the Thames there is Barking power station (which can be heard from Thamesmead), a sewage works, the Ford car plant and a chemical factory. On the south bank there is the Belvedere power station, factories around Abbey Wood, and the Crossness sewage treatment works which shares the marshland site with Thamesmead and bisects it with a 6 m high embankment containing sewage outfall pipes. According to the GLC's Thames-side Environmental Assessment, this stretch of the river largely comprised 'areas of negative environmental significance'. A truly imaginative urban design would be needed to minimize these disadvantages and capitalize on the grandeur and openness of this section of the river.

The plan that was produced for Thamesmead has a line of tall buildings running roughly parallel to the river frontage to provide shelter for less densely developed areas behind. This line swings away from the Thames at Tripock Point where a major riverside open space is planned and also preserves the sight lines for the navigation light on the Point. A further line of high-density development will run from Abbey Wood station northwards to the Thamesmead central area with its yacht basin.

The pattern of internal communications consists of completely independent networks of roads and footpaths. Pedestrian routes will run through open space, over and under roads, and at an upper level through high-density development. They will serve schools, shops and playing fields. Main distributor roads will run from an east/west spine road toward areas of high density housing, with secondary distributor roads and culs-de-sac giving access to the houses and flats. The spine road was planned to feed on to the proposed 'C-ring motorway' with a river crossing in the form of either a bridge or a tunnel.

Five lakes and a connecting network of canals (32 ha in all) have been designed to provide watercourses and storage for the existing runoff and for additional surface water from Thamesmead. The lakes and channels have an important amenity value, as well as being vital for this difficult site to be used effectively.

The whole Thamesmead scheme will provide about 13 600 dwellings, grouped in neighbourhoods which will vary in size from 1500 to 2000 homes. In general, these neighbourhoods have been designed with tall buildings on their edges, to afford protection from noise and wind, and lower buildings within. Each will contain its own primary school and a local centre with shops, churches and a pub. Beyond these neighbourhood units, school playing fields and public open spaces will separate housing from the spine road.

The First Three Areas

The south-eastern sections of the Thamesmead site are the most readily accessible from existing built-up areas and were selected for the first phase of construction. In these three 'areas', involving 4159 dwellings, it is possible to examine how the plan worked in practice. A local by-law in force during the design period of Areas I and II prohibited building habitable rooms within 2·5 m of the ground as a precaution against flooding from the river at Crossness. Houses were therefore designed specially to meet this requirement. The river defences have since been improved and this by-law is no longer in force. Work is underway along the whole 5·2 km of river frontage to raise the banks up to a level of 7·2 m OD (Newlyn), that is up to 1·8 m above the existing levels. A continuous riverside walkway is being prepared. Surveys indicate that air pollution from the north bank can reach objectionable intensities at heights of 40–60 m over the Thamesmead site, depending upon distance from the source and the direction and velocity of the wind. Building heights have been limited accordingly.

Area I, to the north-east of Abbey Wood station, contains a dozen thirteen-storey point blocks which are built with pedestrian decks at first floor level covering extensive areas of garage space at ground level. Perhaps the most distinctive feature is the three- to five-storey linear block which follows Harrow Manor Way for almost 1 km and forms the western edge of the area. It contains maisonettes and old people's flats. In the lee of the linear block low-rise terrace houses, with individual gardens, are grouped around small courtyards. Two special blocks of flats for old people have been built but accommodation for old people is available elsewhere in the Area. Vehicle access is by way of culs-de-sac which approach the fringes of the low-rise housing zones which are completely traffic-free. A 10 ha lake, the South Mere, is vital for surface drainage and also forms an important recreational focus. Nine shops, together with a launderette, bank and police station, have been opened in the local shopping centre which is located on a deck above a ground-level car park. Community facilities include two primary schools, a clubroom, medical centre, library, church and public house. Throughout Areas I and II the ground floors of all housing blocks are given over to garages, services, access and storage space.

By the time Area II was constructed Ministry of Housing restraints on expenditure for local authority housing were in operation and hence economies had to be made. For example, the linear block in Area II is a drastically simplified version of that in Area I. Nine point blocks, low-rise housing and old people's blocks complete the accommodation of Area II. A supermarket, post-office, church, clubrooms and three schools have also been opened. A 60 m elevated strip of landscaped open space separates the two Areas and gives access to the wooded area of Lesnes Park to the south. Area III (A and D) is located north of the Ridgeway. A wider range of housing types is available, with none rising more than nine storeys high. Roughly half of the dwellings are built by industrialized building techniques (as all of those in Areas I and II) and the remainder are brick built. Shops, schools and community facilities have been constructed.

By the spring of 1976 11 500 people were living in the first 3350 dwellings to be completed in Thamesmead. Monitoring of the first 1000 families to arrive showed that half had lived previously in local authority housing. A quarter of all Thamesmead families actually came from other GLC estates. A major incentive for this group to move must have been the offer of a house since most had been living in flats. The remaining half had their names on lists for local authority housing in individual London boroughs.

The average size of incoming family was 3·45 people, compared with the GLC average of 2·72. As is usual in new developments, the Thamesmead population was a young one, with 38 % being under 15 years of age, by contrast with the GLC average of

20%. Thamesmead was catering for established families (parents with one or more children) rather than newlyweds. In fact, 60% of Thamesmead heads of household were aged 35 years or more. The principal socio-economic group comprised skilled manual workers who formed 46% of household heads. This working-class dominance was linked to the fact that only local authority housing was available to the first 1000 families. Undoubtedly the pattern has changed since then as private housing has been occupied. In view of the fact that there is a high proportion of primary and pre-school children the female employment rate is low.

Problems of Settling In

The social problems that were faced in the first few years of Thamesmead's existence were very similar to those experienced in post-war new towns. The earliest months were probably the most difficult, before shops, schools, churches, clubs and the pub had been built. New residents had to establish a sense of identity with Thamesmead. They had to get used to new housing conditions, new shops, rents that were higher than they had been used to, and perhaps new jobs and journeys to work. The greater share of residents had come from local authority housing in many different parts of London where they had been accustomed to a variety of family linkages (visiting parents), social activities (friends, clubs, pubs) and general facilities (corner shops, football teams). The move to Thamesmead probably meant that such ties would have to be cut or else continued in greatly modified form, often involving considerable transport costs. Difficulties arose inevitably when trying to maintain contact over lengthy distances that needed a bus ride, a train journey or a trip by car. New bus routes had to be got used to in Thamesmead, new friends had to be made, and new clubs and associations had to be formed. The great challenge was that all the residents of Thamesmead, to some degree, were in the same situation. They were all newcomers. It was not just a question of new arrivals integrating themselves into the community, for the community still had to be created. Families that moved into the first flats and houses faced added problems of living in a very unfinished environment, being surrounded by buildings that were still under construction, shops and social facilities still to be installed, landscaping and tree-planting operations that were still in progress, and only temporary play spaces for the children.

These problems diminished with the passage of time as more of Thamesmead's facilities were installed and as social life developed. But the newcomers continue to arrive and to pull up roots from one's old home to move elsewhere always involves a 'wrench'. Thamesmead's houses and flats, with their constant hot water and background heating from the district heating plant, have met most of the residents' expectations, but inevitably complaints have arisen. These tended to focus on the issue of rent levels, which are higher at Thamesmead than on other GLC estates. Rebates are not available as readily as is sometimes thought. In a report to the GLC Della Nevitt noted that the tenants interviewed insisted that 'they had nothing against Thamesmead itself; they were full of praise for the architects and for their own individual flats. They are basically very proud to be living in a place with a world-wide architectural reputation; but they see no reason why they should have to pay more rent simply because of architectural merit'.

Specific complaints included inadequate drainage of walkways and pavements, inadequate cleaning of public space, and the 'dog problem'. Thamesmead has a lot of public areas and unless such space is kept well cleaned the whole quality of the district will be reduced. With the exception of laundry areas and low-level lights, there was little sign of vandalism, but high-density living inevitably gave rise to 'incidents' such as carelessness in parking which caused damage to surrounding cars. The very location of Thamesmead, with industries on the north bank and a normally odourless sewage works as nearest neighbour on the south bank, also gave rise to complaints.

Residents regretted the lack of colour to break up the overall impression of concrete in the linear and point blocks of Area I. People moving into flats for the first time missed individual gardens and the element of 'outdoor privacy' that they may have had in their old homes. Many Thamesmead residents with gardens have built trellis-work and introduced other decorations to make each garden distinctive. For those without gardens, the layout of housing units means that children at play cannot be watched by mothers from their kitchen windows as may have been the case before. Problems also arose from noise during construction work and parents worried that other children might stray into building sites. But in general, residents have welcomed the better housing conditions that Thamesmead offers, whilst realizing that settling into a new environment takes time and involves financial readjustments.

An Uncertain Future

The first three areas of Thamesmead have been constructed and the range of houses, shops, schools and other facilities has been installed according to plan. Local activities have proliferated as the months have passed so that newcomers may detect a community to which they may belong. But few local jobs have been created and the closure of the pre-cast concrete works (for individual building parts) has reduced the total. Even before the impact of Thamesmead had been felt, southern Thames-side had emerged as something of an industrially depressed district, with jobs being lost at Woolwich Arsenal, at Associated Electrical Industries, Woolwich (5500 employees) and Parsons at Erith (2000 workers). The problem was intensified by its effect on local sub-contractors and other linked activities. The North Kent rail service has been improved but British Rail has been unable to go ahead with reconstructing Abbey Wood station, where the former level crossing has been replaced by an overpass.

A number of major uncertainties surround the projected town centre and the remainder of the Thamesmead project. Motorway construction has been deferred and there is indecision about the proposed river crossing. It now seems unlikely that Thamesmead will be served by a new Underground line as had once been hoped. Finance has not been forthcoming for the planned polytechnic and student housing that would be vital components in the town centre. In any case, Thamesmead's central shopping area will certainly be smaller than was proposed originally in response to opposition from the accessible and already established shopping centres of Erith and Woolwich. Sections of the Thamesmead road programme have been deferred, even the principal traffic route that will be vital to the development of the central area. But the Thamesmead Annual Report for 1975–6 stresses . . . 'with the population of Thamesmead expected to exceed 23 000 by the end of 1980, it is becoming increasingly obvious that there will be a pressing need for a central area offering a variety of shops and entertainments, opportunities for employment and major health facilities'. Already Maurice Ash (1972) has delivered a harsh judgement on Thamesmead, with respect to . . . 'its siting, its lack of relationship to employment, its inadequate transport links and social isolation . . . At worst, the place could become merely an in-town out-county estate'. Just what will materialize only time—and the health of the national economy—will tell.

8 Changes in the Northern Suburbs

Hugh Clout

Views on Suburbia

Some writers use the word 'suburbia' almost pejoratively to refer to a tide of bricks and mortar that has washed across the inner part of the London Basin, coating it with a drab cover of housing interspersed with occasional shopping centres, schools and municipal parks. Alan Jackson (1973) captures something of this mood as he describes 'the sudden, wide-ranging onslaught of the private builder across outer London in the 1920s and through the 1930s ... little affected by the pitifully inadequate planning measures ... Both the waste of opportunity and the resultant ugly monotony are appalling to contemplate'. But at the same time, the growth of suburbia around London brought unquestionable benefits to its new residents. 'Finding a new house within their financial reach, many thousands had their living standards transformed; in a few short years, the sum of human happiness was immeasurably increased' (Jackson). In any case, virtually all Londoners are suburbanites as far as residence is concerned and the great majority work, shop, attend school, go to church, and find their entertainment in the suburbs rather than in central London.

A closer look at suburbia reveals that it has not simply sprawled outwards with the passage of time and in response to innovations in transportation, from the earliest railways to the most recent motorways. Instead, it has been inserted into the pre-urban pattern of land ownership, as country estates, whole farms, individual fields and even modest plots of land were purchased (and sometimes consolidated) before development took place and suburban homes were built. The earlier structure of settlement and land ownership is reflected not only by fragments of old villages and market towns but also by variations in the style and age of suburban housing that has engulfed them.

Since the last war the further spread of London's continuously built-up suburbia in general terms has been halted by the designation of the Green Belt and the operation of planning controls. Suburban London is straitjacketed, hence the changes that are discussed in this chapter are concerned almost exclusively with the task of remodelling housing areas and service centres that had been laid out over the past 150 years. Open sites that are not conserved by law are few and far between and the term *redevelopment* offers a reasonable summary for many recent changes. Sometimes this involves replacing old housing by new, but in other instances the land-use category is changed, as in the case of the new housing built on the former aerodrome at Hendon (Grahame Park) and on the site of the old Metropolitan Market between Camden Road and Caledonian Road.

Selected aspects of redevelopment in the London Boroughs of Barnet, Camden, Enfield, Haringey and Islington are examined in this chapter. Defined in this way, the 'northern suburbs' include old market towns (*eg* Enfield), coaching settlements along important routeways (*eg* Hampstead, Chipping Barnet,

Whetstone), districts that were built up as early as the 1820s and 1830s (*eg* Barnsbury), as well as a wide range of more recent residential areas designed for virtually all sorts and conditions of Londoners. Broad sections of Green Belt are found in Barnet and Enfield, whilst Hampstead Heath forms a valuable expanse of recreational land at the heart of the northern suburbs.

Many types of Londoners live in the five boroughs which form a wedge cut out of the class pattern for the whole of Greater London that has been depicted by Willmott and Young (1973). A working-class 'cross' runs from east to west (parallel to the Thames) and from north to south (following the valleys of the Lee and Wandle). The eastern and southern parts of the 'northern suburbs' form part of that working-class 'cross', but the remainder comprises more favoured residential areas, including Hampstead, Highgate, Southgate and Totteridge.

8·1 Population Change in the GLC 1961-71 (by ward).

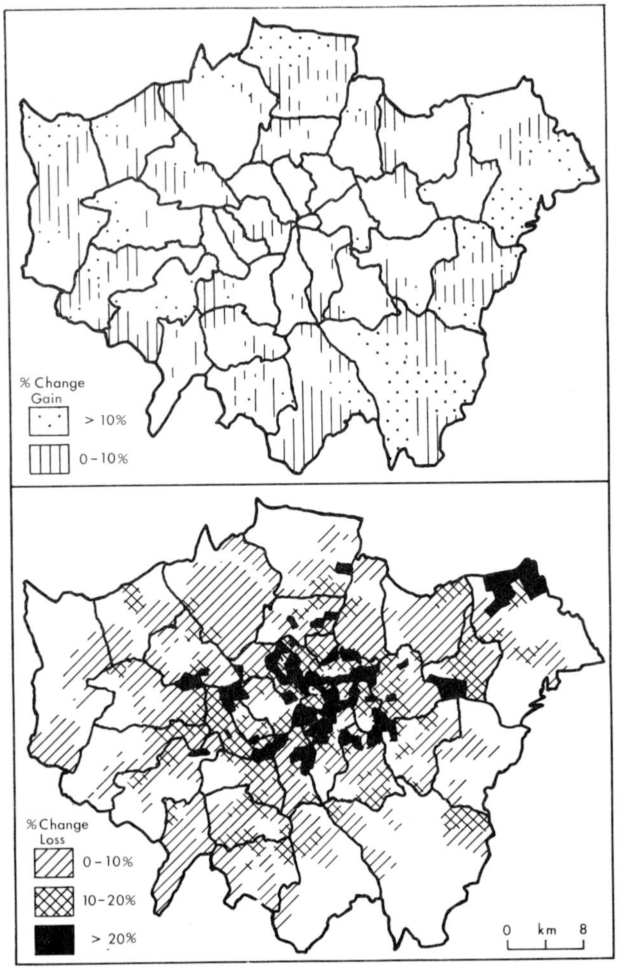

Recent censuses have recorded substantial losses in population from the inner and intermediate wards of all London's suburbs (Fig. 8·1). The five boroughs were no exception, with the number of residents falling from 1 386 000 in 1961 to an estimated 1 201 000 in 1975 (−13·3 %), at a rate faster than that of the GLC area as a whole (−11·1 %). Areas of population growth in the GLC have been confined to the inner fringes of the Green Belt. Slum clearance and redevelopment have contributed to population loss in the inner suburbs as many north Londoners have been rehoused in council properties located farther out. In the private housing sector social advancement is usually associated with 'moving out' to more respectable suburbs. But many complex changes are occurring as well as the decline of inner suburbs and the flight to outer areas. For example, professional people have rediscovered some working-class districts in inner suburbia and have moved in to produce a process of 'gentrification' in recent years. In spite of the general tendency for their population to decline, the inner suburbs still function as reception areas for newcomers to the capital. In the past quarter century migrants from other parts of the British Isles have been joined by newcomers from Cyprus, the West Indies, Africa and the Indian subcontinent, as the proliferation of 'ethnic' stores, restaurants and places of worship bears ample witness across northern suburbia.

Housing Problems

The ageing and obsolescence of sections of the housing stock form a major problem in many parts of suburban London. Such areas are not just found in inner boroughs like Camden and Islington but also in outer boroughs where early nodes of housing for City workers were constructed around railway stations.

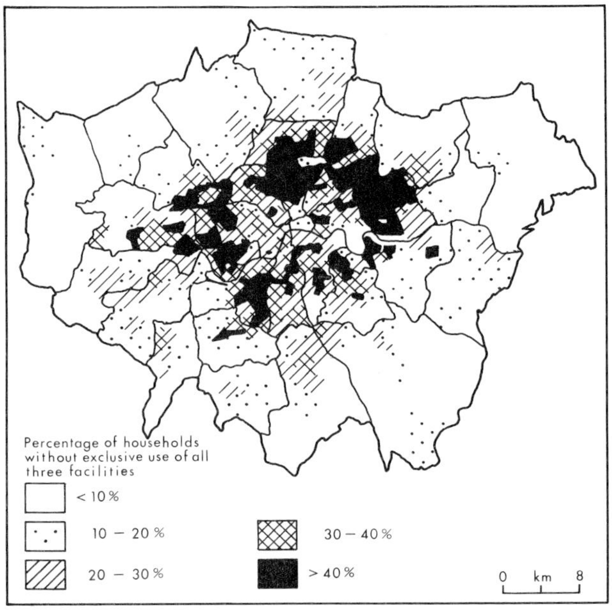

8·2 Households without Exclusive Use of Hot Water, Bath and Inside WC, 1971 (by ward).

The classic example is provided by the growth of parts of Tottenham and Edmonton after 1870 following the introduction of cheap workmen's services by the Great Eastern Railway in compensation for houses demolished in inner London as the railway was built into Liverpool Street.

But age alone is not an adequate index of poor housing. Much depends on the quality of materials and workmanship and the way in which properties have been maintained. No fewer than 293 000 households (11 % of the GLC total) were living in overcrowded 'zones of housing stress' in 1967, and many homes were without inside toilets, baths and hot water supplies (Fig. 8·2). On the basis of these deficiencies four 'housing problem areas' (HPAs) were recognized in the Greater London Development Plan (1969). Three were north of the Thames. They contained no fewer than 340 000 dwellings. Sixteen per cent had been built before 1875 and 69 % before 1921 (GLC averages 7 and 43 % respectively). Sixteen per cent of dwellings in the HPAs were 'poor or unfit', 23 % had no inside toilet and 25 % lacked baths (Fig. 8·3). However, there were important differences between the HPAs. Those in the north and west had a higher proportion of young adults than in London as a whole. Young single people (often newcomers to London) move in, marry, and some will move away when more living space is needed as children start to arrive. Their place is taken by other single migrants and the cycle begins again. Some do not move on. They are caught in the web of poverty and social deprivation that surrounds the HPAs, especially those in the north and west which have a large supply of privately rented furnished dwellings. By contrast, HPAs in the east and south have large amounts of council housing and their population is rather less transitory (Fig. 8·4).

In fact, the problems of HPAs do not just relate to housing but to the whole environment. School buildings are poor, play facilities for children are often lacking, and social facilities for adults are poorly provided. Social problems, such as poverty, ill-health, unemployment and educational deprivation, often reach serious dimensions. The HPAs and smaller pockets of deficient housing have been prime targets

8·3 Poor Dwellings, 1971 (by ward).

for slum clearance and redevelopment in the past twenty years. Major changes have occurred in some parts of the HPAs but only a start has been made. As fast as one area is redeveloped the housing problem redefines itself in other districts since property deteriorates with every week that passes. Unless widespread rehabilitation is carried out beforehand the avenues of inter-war suburbia may well have become HPAs by the twenty-first century.

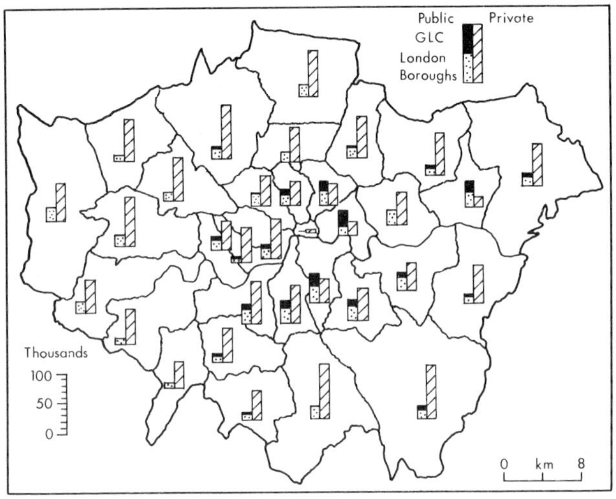

8·4 Housing Stock in the GLC, 1971 (by London Borough).

Redevelopment

Rehabilitation has already begun to take place in a piecemeal way throughout London. Bathrooms and toilets have been built on to many Victorian and Edwardian houses that are still structurally sound. In addition, redevelopment schemes have brought striking changes in the townscape as obsolescent dwellings have been demolished and replaced by blocks of council flats or rows of maisonettes. For example, the area between Hornsey Rise and Archway Road in northernmost Islington was described by Jon Rowland (1973) as 'a community in decay'. The majority of people living there were unskilled manual workers, many of whom had been unemployed for long periods of time. Now the whole area has been flattened and rebuilding is in progress. To the west of Archway Road the redevelopment area between Highgate cemetery and Dartmouth Park Hill in North Camden involves not only demolition and rebuilding but also rehabilitation of stretches of sound housing.

Extensive redevelopment schemes in the outer boroughs have swept away the earliest areas of railway suburbia. New Southgate (Enfield LB) was built up in the 1850s and 1860s following the construction in 1850 of a railway station at Colney Hatch which served the Middlesex county asylum and opened the way for land on the other side of the tracks to be studded with villas and ribbed with terraces. These dwellings and the shops that once served them have been swept away in the past twenty years and replaced by council flats and premises for light industry. In 1965 a more grandiose scheme was approved for 24 ha at Edmonton Green, in the south-east of the borough, where building had started when the station was opened in 1849. The first stage of redevelopment was completed by 1970 when a shopping precinct, swimming pool, entertainment centre and blocks containing 376 flats were opened. More shops and accommodation were finished in the mid-1970s. Many other patches of redevelopment have been inserted into the townscapes of the western Lee Valley in the boroughs of Enfield and Haringey. One of the largest stretches east from High Cross (Tottenham High Road) to Tottenham Hale. Redevelopment in another part of Haringey has replaced many early suburban dwellings by council housing in the angle between Wood Green High Road and Bounds Green Road. Parts of this detached 'island' of 1870s suburbia still survive but many Victorian villas have been demolished over the past fifteen years and have been replaced in a piecemeal fashion by privately developed blocks of low-rise flats that have been inserted into areas once occupied by neighbouring villas and spacious gardens. Similar changes have taken place in areas of large Victorian and Edwardian houses close to Underground stations in many parts of northern London. Particularly clear examples are found around Highgate and East Finchley (Northern line) and Bounds Green (Piccadilly line).

Rehabilitation and Gentrification

Other sections of the northern suburbs have undergone important rehabilitation in recent years. Often this has been paralleled by significant social changes, as middle-class families have moved into predominantly working-class inner areas in preference to living in outer suburbs or commuter settlements. 'Gentrification' has occurred in many inner suburbs, but perhaps nowhere more clearly than in the Barnsbury district to the north-west of the Angel Islington.

The landed estates of Barnsbury were developed in the first half of the nineteenth century in a variety of styles in order to provide accommodation for the families of the City clerks, managers and local merchants. The Stonefield estate was laid out in the 1870s, being focused on Holy Trinity Church (a miniature version of Kings College Chapel, Cambridge) in Cloudesley Square. Lonsdale Square and Barnsbury Square were developed in the 1830s and 1840s. Construction on the Thornhill estate spread between 1820 and 1850; and on Thomas Milner Gibson's estate the elegantly classical Gibson Square was built in 1832 and the less appealing Milner Square in 1841. Many of the three- or four-storey town houses in these squares were endowed with attractive façades and were set in spacious surroundings. Their construction in Barnsbury and in neighbouring districts contributed to the growth of Islington's population from a mere 37 000 in 1831 to 155 000 thirty years later. By the 1880s, however, the social composition of Barnsbury had begun to change as middle-class suburbanites moved out to new villas. Their place was taken by manual workers and their families who occupied the newly subdivided town houses of Islington. This social transformation, as well as the building of new houses, was reflected by a rapid growth of the borough's population which reached a peak of 335 000 in 1901. Rented houses gradually fell into disrepair and manufacturing invaded empty halls, churches and other buildings in Barnsbury.

In spite of such disfigurements, the district still contained streets and squares of fine scale and buildings of architectural interest. Barnsbury was only a couple of kilometres from central London and offered good and potentially attractive homes for professional families at much cheaper prices than those being asked in select residential districts such as South Kensington, Chelsea and Hampstead. 'Gentrification' had begun in Barnsbury in the 1950s and gathered pace in the late 1960s and the 1970s. Already the proportion of 'professional' and 'management' households had risen from 4 to 8% of the Barnsbury total between 1961 and 1966. Provisions under the 1969 Housing Act assisted this trend by making finance available for renovating existing housing stock. Standard improvement grants were available for installing toilets, baths and hot water systems (up to £1000 per dwelling for improvement and £1200 for complete conversion) and there were discretionary grants as well. But all these grants had to be matched pound for pound by money from the potential recipients and were therefore more accessible to developers and relatively affluent newcomers than to the district's working-class residents. Very real profits were undoubtedly to be made by those who received 'no strings' grants and then resold their renovated property.

The middle-class newcomers had founded the Barnsbury Association as early as 1964 with the objective of promoting the management of the district in ways that paid regard to its architectural quality. The Association opposed the GLC's attempt to compulsorily purchase and demolish Regency property in Bewdley Street and then turned to the difficult problem of helping to devise a traffic management scheme for heavy lorries that moved through the district *en route* for Kings Cross and the City. An official scheme was announced in 1970 to channel through traffic along fewer roads and keep it out of some parts of Barnsbury. Protests against the scheme came not only from residents of streets that were carrying more traffic but also from shopkeepers along streets that were carrying less, on the grounds that their passing trade was suffering. Others complained that the scheme hampered access for emergency service vehicles and was socially discriminatory, since it diverted lorries away from Thornhill Road and Cloudesley Road (where many of the middle-class newcomers lived) to a couple of other thoroughfares

(Liverpool Road and Copenhagen Street) which remained strongly working class. Another local group (the Barnsbury Action Group) campaigned to get the scheme withdrawn and expressed serious concern about tenants being harassed by landlords who wanted to get possession of their property before renovating it or selling it to newcomers. Reports quoted enticements of £400–£800 being offered to encourage tenants to leave. Builders' lorries, cement mixers and demolition skips confirm that rehabilitation and gentrification of the squares and terraces of Barnsbury and surrounding districts are still actively in progress in the second half of the 1970s.

Terms as strong as 'class warfare' and 'the geography of conflict' have been used to describe what has occurred in Islington and these would not be inappropriate for the case of Tolmers Square (Camden). The Square and its surrounding Georgian and Victorian streets had housed no fewer than 5200 people in 1871. By 1965 the number had fallen to 1500, comprising old-established working-class residents, immigrants, students and professionals, with small industries, shops and restaurants in the midst of housing. But land in the area, immediately north of Euston Road underpass and adjacent to the Euston Centre, was being bought up piece by piece by a major property development company in the hope of carrying out a large programme of office building. Housing was allowed to fall into disrepair and part of the area owned by the developers was cleared and used for car parking until redevelopment was to begin. In 1973 the company almost obtained planning permission to go ahead but was stopped at the last minute. By then one-third of the habitable rooms in the Tolmers area were empty, many businesses had closed and the numbers of residents had dwindled to 650. Public opinion was roused by the imminent sacrifice of another housing area for more office construction. Squatters moved in and voiced the case for defending Tolmers Square, rehabilitating its housing and enhancing its environment. After years of conflict—and the collapse of the property market in 1974—the developers sold their pieces of land to Camden Council. The debate continues as to what should happen to the area and what kind of compromise may be reached between rehabilitation and redevelopment.

Conservation and Development of Shopping Centres

Over and above issues associated with housing, local authorities are faced by the need to plan shopping centres for use by car-owning suburbanites. The remarkably complicated problems that affect the management of these focal points of suburban life are being tackled in a variety of ways. At Enfield Town, for example, urban redevelopment has been complemented by the designation of a conservation area nearby. Modern office blocks, such as Tower Point and the Civic Centre Tower, have been installed in the eastern part of the 'town' which is served by a one-way traffic system. By contrast, the northern and western parts of the town still have a remarkable number of old buildings, walled gardens and leafy walks. At the western end of the main shopping street, the New River, Gentleman's Row and Chase Green Gardens form a collection of houses, cottages and footpaths which recall what Enfield must have been like in the late eighteenth and early nineteenth centuries. Not surprisingly, this area forms the nucleus of an official conservation area.

Conservation rather than change has long been the watchword for Hampstead's shop-lined streets in defiance of ever-growing traffic congestion. As early as 1871, the Hampstead Heath Act had authorized London's Metropolitan Board of Works to purchase the manorial rights of the nearby heath and ensure that it should always remain unenclosed and free from building for the enjoyment of Londoners. The limits of this conserved open space were extended substantially by later land transactions. Increasing attention is being paid to protecting the environment in and around other attractive old town centres such as Chipping Barnet, which is complemented by the protected open space of Monken Hadley nearby.

Other suburban boroughs have adopted a more developmental approach toward planning the future of their shopping centres. This certainly has been the case in Haringey which contains north London's

8·5 The New Haringey Central Area at Wood Green.

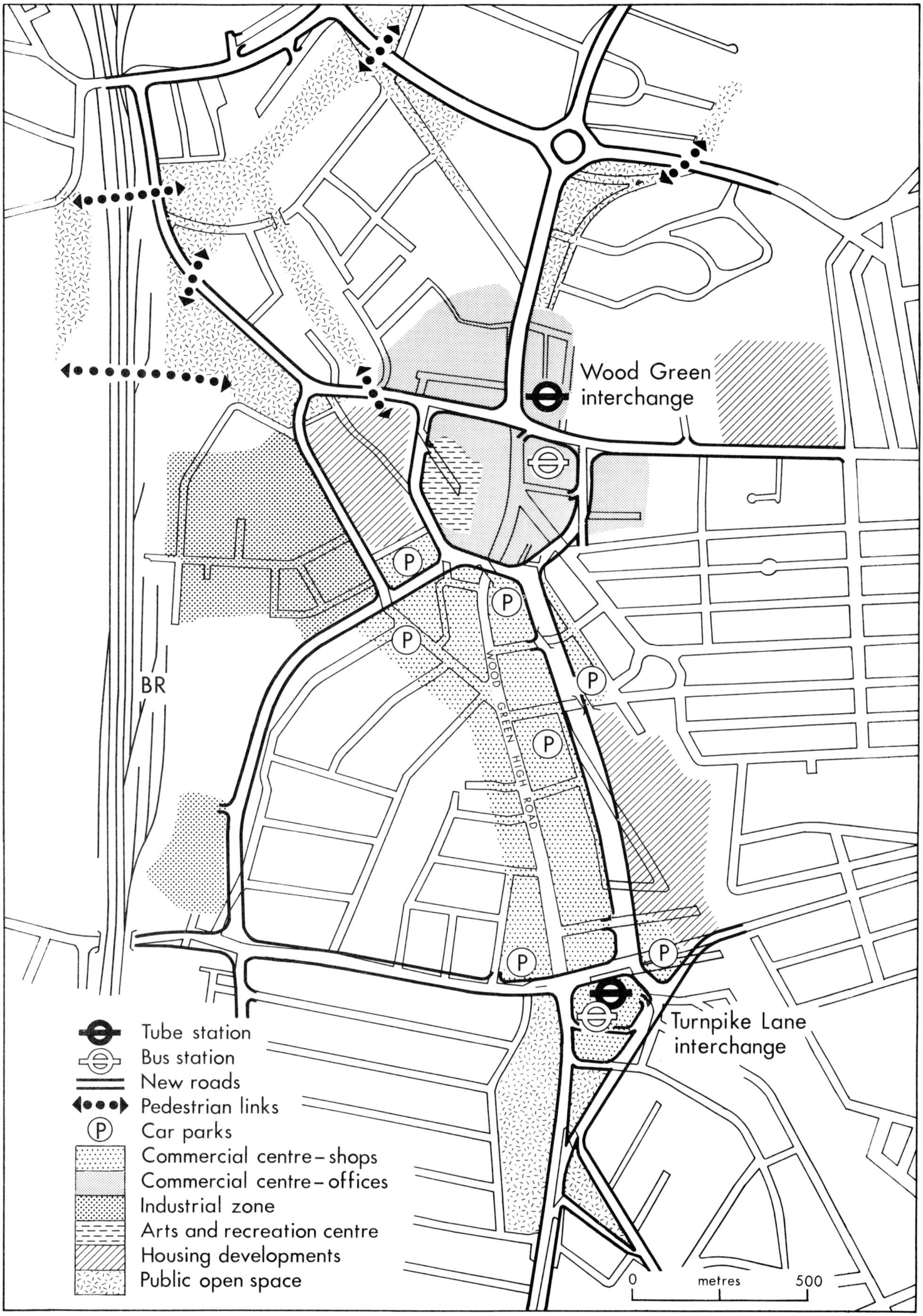
Wood Green interchange
Turnpike Lane interchange
BR
WOOD GREEN HIGH ROAD
Tube station
Bus station
New roads
Pedestrian links
Car parks
Commercial centre – shops
Commercial centre – offices
Industrial zone
Arts and recreation centre
Housing developments
Public open space
0 metres 500

major shopping centre at Wood Green, with an annual retail turnover that rose from £10 000 000 in 1961 to nearly £15 000 000 in 1966. By virtue of its location, existing facilities and bus and Underground services, Wood Green (along with Croydon, Ealing, Ilford, Kingston and Lewisham) was recognized as a 'major strategic town centre' in the Greater London Development Plan. As such it was to be equipped to function as a service centre for more than 750 000 North Londoners. As well as important advantages, Wood Green also had deficiencies such as traffic congestion on the main shopping street, growing obsolescence of surrounding housing, industrial premises and of some of the shops themselves, a lack of space for large shops to be built, as well as unseen problems like inadequate mains drainage. The shopping centre was entirely in the old Borough of Wood Green but neighbouring streets were in Hornsey and Tottenham. Not until local government reorganization in 1965, when all three boroughs were combined to form Haringey, was it possible to examine the shopping centre and its environs in an integrated way. A further stimulus for redevelopment was the closure in 1962 of the Palace Gates railway line which crossed the northern end of the shopping centre and ran parallel to its central and southern part. The railway had been opened in 1878 and had been followed by the now rehabilitated 40 ha estate at Noel Park (1883–1902) to house the families of higher artisans and clerks. Closure of the line and its goods yards released sizeable amounts of land which provided vital elbow room for redevelopment.

Between 1965 and 1968 the new Borough of Haringey investigated the land use, shopping facilities, traffic and parking problems of Wood Green before producing a comprehensive plan (Fig. 8·5). The first objective was to strengthen Wood Green's role as a centre for shopping, commerce and entertainment. Many existing shops were to be retained in the plan, but new ones were to be constructed on the site of the Empire Theatre and on former areas of housing and railway land. Office blocks and cultural and entertainment facilities were planned near Wood Green underground. Alternative sites for displaced light industry were to be made available west of the shopping centre. Secondly, new housing was to be incorporated in the re-modelled central area. Thirdly, a new road system would be built to allow through traffic (80 % of the total) to by-pass the main shopping street. Special access routes would cater for service vehicles and shoppers arriving by car.

In the eight years since redevelopment was first announced Wood Green has undergone the planned chaos of demolition and reconstruction. In place of the Empire Theatre a layered scheme includes shops at ground and first floor levels, car parking at second and third levels, capped by an elevated deck of ninety-two housing units known as Page High. A further 225 dwellings have been built on the former goods yard and 400 more are under way at three other sites which include the partially constructed 'Shopping City' that will contain 46 530 m^2 of retail outlets, offices, a seventy-unit market hall and parking facilities for 1600 cars. Two major office blocks have been completed near Wood Green underground where a central library and the students' residence are also being built. Not surprisingly, the national financial crisis has bitten hard into schemes such as that at Wood Green. Residents' reactions comprise a blend of complaint about costs and rate increases, measured civic pride in the new shops and houses, and a sense of questioning as to how much of the original scheme will be completed and when.

An Entirely New Shopping Centre

For all its recent transformation, Wood Green is still a modernized version of the British High Street. By contrast, North London's other major scheme at Brent Cross is completely new and derived its inspiration from North America and Continental Europe. As far back as 1957 developers started looking for land alongside major roads in North London where a large shopping centre might be built for car using customers. Eventually blocks of land in Barnet LB to the north of the river Brent and the North Circular Road and between the Edgware Road and Hendon Way became available and were consolidated into a single area of 21·5 ha (Fig. 8·6). The accessibility of the site was enhanced by the southward extension of

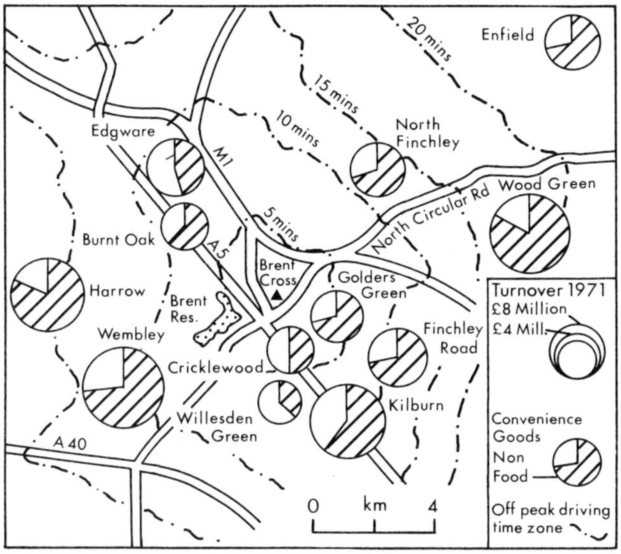

8·6 Brent Cross and Surrounding Shopping Centres.

the M1 to the North Circular Road in 1976. The developers' request for planning permission in 1965 was not granted because of objection to the proposed access roads. A revised application was made in 1968 and in the public inquiry that followed the likely advantages and disadvantages of the shopping centre were examined. Chief opponents were neighbouring local authorities (Brent, Enfield, Harrow and Haringey) and local chambers of trade who claimed that Brent Cross would remove custom from High Street shops. After almost two years planning permission was granted and development began. Brent Cross would concentrate on selling 'durable' goods rather than food and 'convenience' goods. It was planned to compete with the West End rather than with local shops. In fact only three food shops were permitted on the new site.

Brent Cross was opened in March 1976 and proved to be very different from what the developers had proposed in the 1960s, when a boating lake, swimming pool, restaurants, bowling centre and service station had been mentioned. Ultimately only shops were built, in a fully enclosed air-conditioned building. It involves 92 905 m^2 (with 73 393 m^2 devoted to retail activity) and is serviced from roof level. A double-decker shopping mall runs for 185 m between two department stores, located at either end of the centre and accounting for half of the total sales space. There are branches of four major stores, with sales floors on both levels and about eighty other shops, including an 1800 m^2 supermarket. Escalators link the two carpeted sales areas, where approximately 3000 staff are employed. Long opening hours make Brent Cross available to after-work as well as daytime shoppers. Free parking spaces are available at ground level for 3500 customers' cars and there is the possibility of building multi-storey car parks. Nine bus routes serve the site and the re-named Brent Cross underground station is nearby.

Undoubtedly Brent Cross is well placed to act as a major shopping focus for north-west London, which lacked a major strategic 'centre' between Ealing and Wood Green, and has proved to be a financial success. Official shopping surveys are being undertaken to monitor the impact of Brent Cross and the changing fortunes of North London's High Streets. Already it is well known that one major company changed its decision to locate a new suburban department store in Wood Green and chose Brent Cross instead.

Prospect

Redevelopment and rehabilitation will continue to be vital themes in the urban geography of London's northern suburbs during the final quarter of this century. It is not possible to anticipate how widely or rapidly these changes may take place. Expenditure cuts imposed on local authorities will slow down redevelopment but in the mid-1970s central government agencies have shown increasing concern for the problems of inner urban areas. That concern may be matched by finance and if so London's inner suburbs could hardly fail to qualify for support.

New kinds of management scheme will have to be devised for landscape elements that have outlived their initial function but which are considered worthy of conservation. In this respect the challenge of providing space and facilities for leisure time use offers important opportunities. London as a whole is well endowed with public open spaces, ranging from the ancient Royal parks to much more recent recreation areas, but the fact that there are strong variations in provision between districts cannot be denied. The GLDP recognized six parts of inner London that not only contained high residential densities and poor housing but also lacked sufficient public open space (Fig. 8·7). The worst of these areas is in the LB of Islington, which has only 0·1 ha of open space per 1000 residents, with parts of Camden, Hackney and

8·7 Areas of Greatest Need of Public Open Space. (After GLDP).

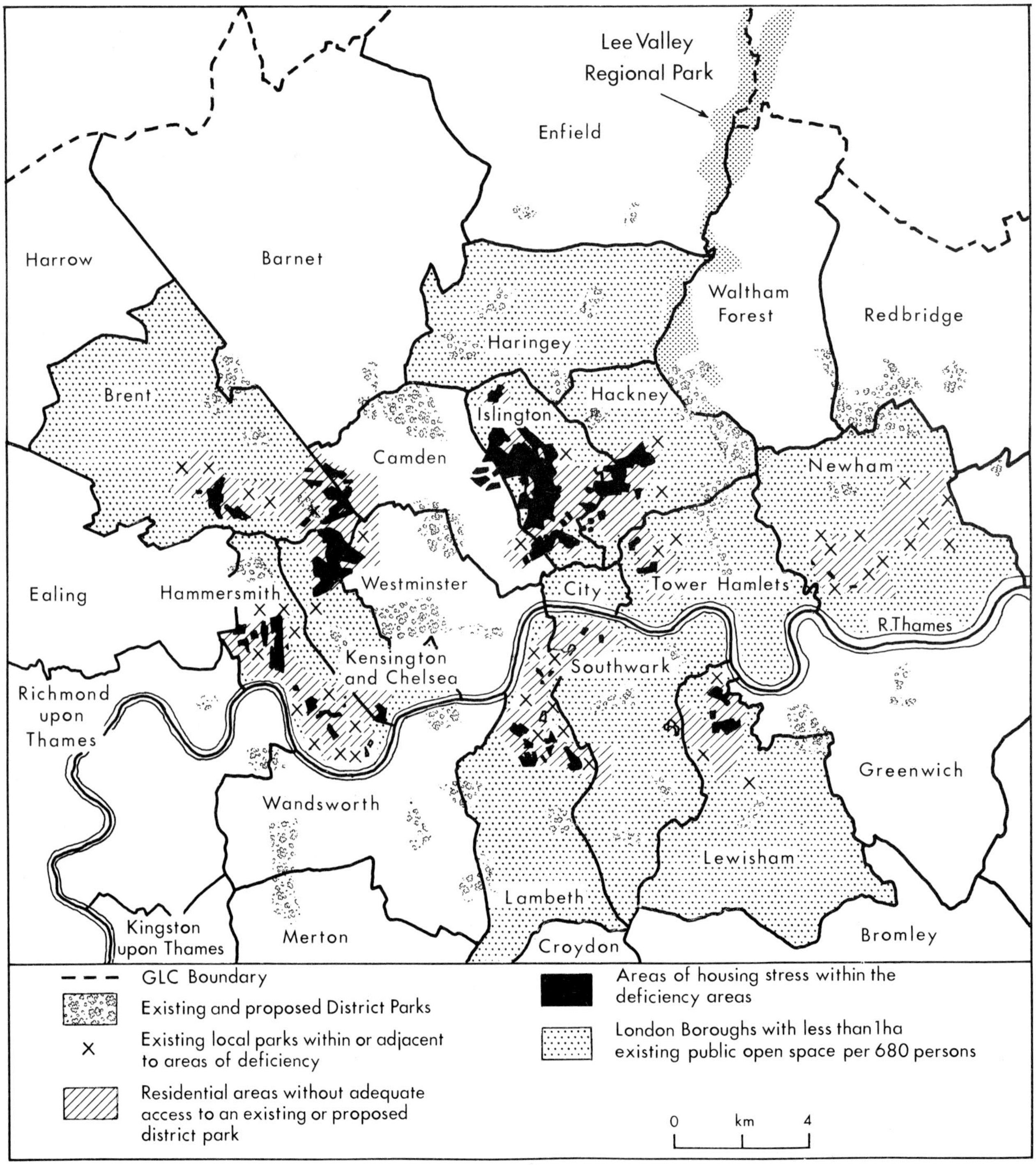

Tower Hamlets following closely. As elsewhere, the demand for recreation facilities in the inner suburbs is a complicated matter. Day or half-day outings by the whole family, whether or not they own a car, normally involve travelling to the urban fringe or beyond (see Chapter 11). However, large open areas like Hampstead Heath manage to accommodate part of that demand within the built-up area. Teenagers and young adults display a second kind of demand, wanting special facilities where active sports may be played. An important start has been made to meet their needs by installing floodlit 'astroturf' football pitches on vacant land, making some schools' facilities available after hours, and building special sports centres, such as the Sobell Sports Centre in Holloway. All the remaining types of demand may be considered together. Young children, with or without their mothers, need play space; middle aged and retired people, workers with spare time in the lunch hour, and indeed, virtually all residents need local areas in which they can sit or stroll for short periods. Small or irregularly shaped patches of redundant land can be adapted successfully to cater for these needs.

The 13·5 km Regents Canal from Paddington to Limehouse is no longer in commercial use and provides a good illustration of this kind of possibility. To the east of the well-known section in Regents Park the canal has suffered from years of neglect, pollution and public indifference. Old workshops and warehouses treated it as their backyard and piles of refuse and scrap were stacked beside it. Some of the canal basins were in particularly bad condition and there were long stretches of dilapidated fencing and buildings. But the canal and its towpaths offer tremendous amenity potential as a linear walkway in the heart of North London. Already Camden and Islington have taken important action in opening towpaths to public access and promoting an environmental facelift, but great scope remains for imaginative and sensitive management.

The same may be said of Alexandra Park and Palace (Haringey), a few kilometres to the north. Some 80 ha of the 180 ha Rhodes estate were set aside as public open space in the 1860s and a 'people's palace' was opened in 1873 on a site giving excellent views over inner London. After a disastrous fire, a new building was opened in 1875. But as the years passed, its concert hall, theatre, terrace, gardens and race-course failed to attract the crowds. Costs of maintenance and repairs soared and as early as 1925 the Palace was being described as a 'white elephant'. That judgement has been echoed many times since. High costs put extensive restoration of the Palace out of the question but there is ample scope for moderate cost schemes. A GLC survey of public opinion showed that most North Londoners wanted the building to be retained and 'utilized to its maximum potential as a people's palace' with appropriate attractions for the final quarter of the twentieth—rather than the nineteenth—century. Indeed it may be that growing public opposition to large redevelopment schemes will combine with the constraints of the financial climate to put much more emphasis on rehabilitation and conservation in North London than has been the case in the past two decades.

Further Reading

Collins, M. F. and Pharoah, T. M., *Transport Organization in a Great City: the case of London* (George Allen and Unwin, London, 1974)

Jackson, A. A., *Semi-detached London* (George Allen and Unwin, London, 1973)

Rowland, J., *Community Decay* (Penguin, Harmondsworth, 1973)

Taylor, N., *The Village in the City* (Temple Smith, London, 1973)

Wates, N., *The Battle for Tolmers Square* (Routledge and Kegan Paul, London, 1976)

9 Changing South London

Richard Dennis

Introduction

This chapter, on the changing social geography of south London, is concerned primarily with the geography of housing. In a city developed by private enterprise, like the North American cities on which Burgess and Hoyt based their famous concentric and sectoral models of urban structure, the oldest housing is located close to the centre, with newer housing on the urban fringe. In Britain most houses built before 1914 were intended for renting from private landlords, whereas most private housing built since then has been for occupation by its owners. Not surprisingly, therefore, private tenants are concentrated in inner London boroughs and owner-occupiers in outer suburbs. But the situation is complicated by the construction of council housing, especially since 1919 (either slum clearance and redevelopment schemes in inner areas or new estates on greenfield sites on the urban fringe). In London the situation is confused even more by the existence of multiple nuclei: villages which were once independent, but are now absorbed into the continuous built-up area of Greater London. So within London each borough has its share of each type of housing tenure although, in aggregate, owner-occupation increases with distance from the centre, private renting decreases, and council housing both decreases in importance and changes its character from modern flats to cottage estates.

Variations in housing tenure are important because different groups in the population—people of different ages, marital status, race or social class—do not share equal access to all types of housing. Only people with sufficient income or status can afford to buy their own home; only people who are homeless, or whose existing home has been compulsorily purchased by the council, or who have lived in the locality long enough to reach the top of the waiting list, can get a council house. Most single people, temporary residents and new arrivals, including overseas immigrants, are forced into privately rented accommodation. So the location of different housing tenures influences the spatial distribution of social and ethnic groups.

The relationship between housing tenure and social groups is not constant because periodically the government alters the rules of 'the housing game'. At present, council housing and owner-occupancy are favoured tenures. New council housing is subsidized, rent rebates are granted to needy council tenants. Local authorities can grant mortgages so that lower-income families can become owner-occupiers. Tax relief is granted on mortgage interest repayments, reducing the real cost of buying a house with a mortgage. All these actions mean that families prefer to own their home or be council tenants if they cannot afford to buy. Other government activity, like the passing of successive Rent Acts, which control rents or grant security of tenure to sitting tenants, may make private renting more attractive for tenants but less attractive as a source of income to private landlords. The apparent result has been the withdrawal of

TABLE 7 POPULATION CHANGES IN SELECTED BOROUGHS

	Population (000's)			
	1951	1961	1971	1975
Lambeth	347	342	308	297
Southwark	338	313	262	236
Wandsworth	331	335	302	288
Croydon	310	324	334	325
Merton	200	189	177	173
Sutton	176	169	169	166
Greater London	8197	7992	7379	7111

	Private Households	
	1961	1971
Lambeth	117 120	111 940
Southwark	104 750	93 270
Wandsworth	112 657	109 835
Croydon	103 805	112 900
Merton	63 322	64 420
Sutton	54 684	59 275
Greater London	2 658 166	2 651 815

privately rented accommodation from the housing market, although the demand for such housing has not contracted to the same extent. This chapter will explore some of the changing relationships between central and local government activity, supply and demand for housing, and the distribution of social groups in the context of south London.

South London, like London as a whole, is losing population. For example, three inner boroughs (Wandsworth, Lambeth and Southwark) lost 195 000 inhabitants between 1951 and 1975; three outer boroughs (Merton, Sutton and Croydon) lost 23 000 (Table 7). But population decrease has not reduced the demand for housing. The number of separate households continued to increase until the early 1960s and is still increasing in outer London. Average household size in Greater London fell from 3·1 in 1951 to 2·9 by 1966: completed family size has decreased, young people marry earlier or move from their parents' home into their own flat, old people live longer and remain independent. The result is a substantial increase in the number of one- and two-person households. Housing demand is as great as ever, but the demand is for smaller dwellings than previously.

In 1971 there were 59 275 households in Sutton living in 59 015 separate dwellings. In Lambeth, despite a decline in the number of households since 1961 the shortage of dwellings is much worse: 111 940 households in 97 280 dwellings. In fact the problem is more severe than these figures imply. More accurate indications of a deteriorating situation are the lengthening of council house waiting lists and the growing numbers registered as 'homeless' (Table 8). Furthermore, not all dwellings are in a satisfactory condition. In 1974 it was estimated that 3 % of London's housing stock required demolition and 14 % was in need of repair. Most unfit housing is concentrated in inner London: 3510 houses were demolished in Southwark between 1971 and 1974. Another index of unsatisfactory housing is the proportion of dwellings without either hot water, a fixed bath or an indoor toilet. In 1971 only two-thirds of inner London households had exclusive use of all three amenities. The remainder had to share with another household or, in about one-tenth of cases, went without one of the amenities altogether. In outer London nine out of ten households had exclusive access to all three amenities.

Housing and Class in Inner London

The greatest problems of insufficient and unsatisfactory housing occur in areas of privately rented housing developed in the nineteenth century and now incorporated into inner boroughs like Lambeth. But the supply of privately rented accommodation is diminishing while other forms of tenure increase in importance (Fig. 9·1).

Owner-Occupation Between 1961 and 1971 the proportion of households in Lambeth who owned their home increased slightly from 18 to 20 %. This compares with an increase in Greater London as a whole from 36 to 40%. There are wide variations within the borough. In 1966 the most northerly ward (Bishop's) contained only 2% owner-occupiers, the most southerly (Streatham South) 56%. In the south owner-occupiers are middle-class residents in inter-war terraced and semi-detached houses, bought with mortgages from building societies. In the central wards of the borough (Ferndale, Town Hall and Tulse Hill) are large Victorian terraced houses, structurally sound but lacking in amenities and in poor decorative order. Building societies are not prepared to lend money for the purchase of such properties, whose buyers must resort to private finance companies, which lend money at high rates of interest to be repaid within 5–10 years, compared to a building society repayment period of 20–30 years. The only way a borrower can afford such high repayments is to let spare rooms in his house, often at very high rents for sub-standard accommodation. In Brixton many West Indians, denied access to other sectors of the housing market, have been forced to become owner-occupiers with the aid of expensive 'back-street mortgages', letting rooms to other immigrant families to help repay the loan.

A minority of owner-occupiers in inner London live in select enclaves of upper-middle-class status, like Dulwich Village. These areas may be explained in terms of the sentiment and symbolism with which they are associated, which strengthen middle-class resistance to invasion by lower status groups moving out from the centre. In Dulwich the park, art gallery, public school, common and Georgian and Victorian houses are strong middle-class symbols. But the resis-

TABLE 8 Council Housing Supply and Demand

	Size of waiting list			*Number of households rehoused from waiting list*			
	1972	*1973*	*1974*	*1966–71*	*1972*	*1973*	*1974*
Lambeth	12378	14390	15574	3495	783	375	111
Southwark	7976	8752	9013	5405	1534	742	557
Wandsworth	7860	8994	8878	4837	1087	452	286
Croydon	5651	5638	6489	4898	261	129	486
Merton	4089	4455	5358	2027	676	429	238
Sutton	2128	2609	2505	2396	218	196	278
Greater London	208 205	229 554	233 677	114 711	21 150	n.a.	14 928

	Homeless families Number of Applications		*Homeless families Number rehoused*		
	1972–3	*1973–4*	*1972*	*1973*	*1974*
Lambeth	827	1025	570	740	751
Southwark	595	479	285	436	358
Wandsworth	1032	1259	383	568	756
Croydon	562	389	236	286	595
Merton	195	183	83	86	170
Sutton	84	113	10	26	53
Greater London	11 926	16 066	4586	n.a.	9356

Notes: The 'waiting list' overestimates need to the extent that many families fail to deregister when they no longer require assistance, but underestimates need to the extent that many families in need do not apply.

Some applications from homeless families are subsequently withdrawn without official action being necessary.

Some data not available for 1973.

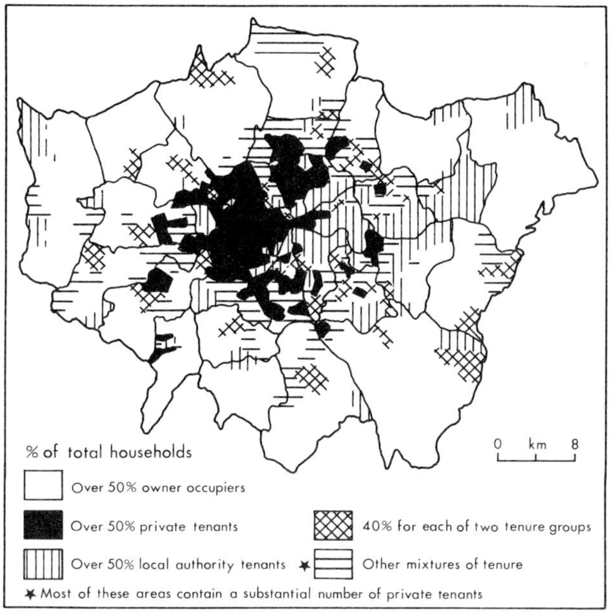

9·1 Types of Tenure in the GLC, 1971 (by ward).

tance is successful primarily because of the careful management policy of the College Estate. Unlike new housing elsewhere which is usually sold freehold, properties on the estate are sold leasehold, so that restrictions can be imposed on housing density and cost. Non-residential land uses can be excluded. College Road, the geographically central north–south axis, is privately maintained as a toll road, thereby diverting most through traffic to parallel roads east and west of the estate.

Dulwich is one area in which building societies will lend money to prospective homeowners because there is little danger of the area losing status, or of property values declining. In general, building societies prefer to grant mortgages to applicants with guaranteed incomes who are buying modern houses in pleasant areas. But most private housing in inner London is neither modern nor in areas that are environmentally very attractive. Lambeth Council has encouraged national building societies to lend on cheaper, older houses to 'marginal owner-occupiers'—people who can afford to buy only cheap dwellings and would otherwise be on the waiting list for council housing. Their efforts have been unsuccessful, however, even in General Improvement Areas, where improvement grants for both housing and the surrounding environment are available and there is a guarantee that property will not subsequently be compulsorily purchased by the council.

In 1969 Lambeth Council instigated a housing policy aimed at providing 2000 new dwellings annually: 1500 built by the council, 500 erected by private builders. In fact only 5454 new dwellings were completed in the following five years, barely half the objective. Private completions slumped from 153 in 1971 to 39 in 1974. The problem is that land in inner London is too expensive. In Lambeth, in the early 1970s developers were willing to pay £85 000 per ha but available sites were valued at £150 000 per ha. There was little likelihood of attracting private builders, even if the local authority offered subsidies towards the purchase of land (Fig. 9·2).

However, there are other factors working in favour of owner-occupation in inner London. During the late nineteenth and twentieth centuries many large houses designed for the middle classes filtered down to multiple occupancy by low status groups. Now they are being reoccupied by high status people favouring a more cosmopolitan lifestyle than the suburbs can provide. This is the process of 'gentrification'. Property companies purchase multi-occupied houses often very cheaply if sitting tenants are still in residence, then offer the tenants alternative accommodation or money to leave. Next, the houses are modernized, usually by converting them to self-contained flats with the aid of government improvement grants. The converted flats are sold on long leases to young professional people. Although the major building societies rarely grant mortgages on converted property, many property developers are associated with finance companies or local building societies, so that they not only sell flats, but also lend the buyers the money they need to pay for them! Gentrification is particularly important in parts of Clapham, Kennington and Stockwell, partly as a result of the extension of the Victoria line underground through Stockwell.

The local authority (both the GLC and individual

boroughs) can also grant mortgages to prospective owner-occupiers who fulfil certain qualifications, for example, families who already live or work locally and who have been refused a building society mortgage. But the local authority's principal role is in the provision of council housing to rent (Table 8).

Council Housing The proportion of council tenants in Lambeth increased from 22 to 31 % between 1961 and 1971, varying from more than half of households in Stockwell and Bishop's wards to less than one-tenth in Streatham South. In North Lambeth, as in Southwark, council housing has increased at the expense of unfurnished privately rented accommodation. Much of the latter comprised small Victorian houses rented by skilled and semi-skilled workers from small-scale private landlords. The houses were not overcrowded, but lacked indoor toilets and baths. Where they were beyond improvement they were compulsorily purchased by the council, demolished and replaced by blocks of multi-storey flats. More recently, policy has moved against redevelopment, in favour of rehabilitation in areas designated as General Improvement Areas. After rehabilitation dwellings are let to families on the council waiting list, or to families from compulsorily purchased housing whom the council are obliged to rehouse. One example of rehabilitation is in Vassall Road and Foxley Road, Lambeth, where the GLC has renovated several villas and terraces of mid-nineteenth century origin.

Another reason for the increasing importance of council housing is 'municipalization'. This occurs where the council purchases private housing, usually to maintain working-class rented accommodation which a private landlord might otherwise sell to a middle-class owner-occupier. The effect is to reduce the degree of segregation between public and private housing. The opposite process, the sale of council houses to sitting tenants, was operated by the GLC between 1967 and 1973 and by Lambeth Council from 1970 to 1972. It has the same effect as municipalization: to increase mixing of public and private housing.

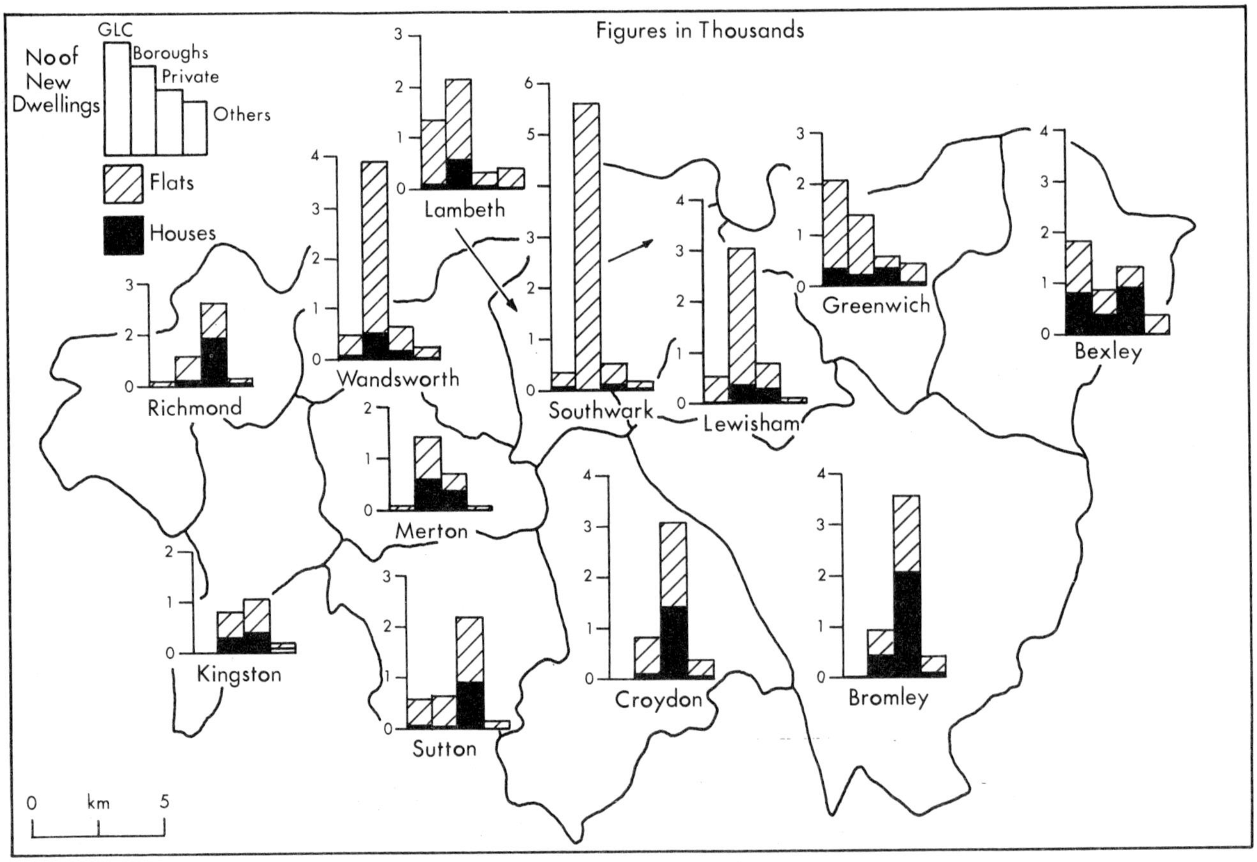

9·2 New Housing in South London, 1971–4.

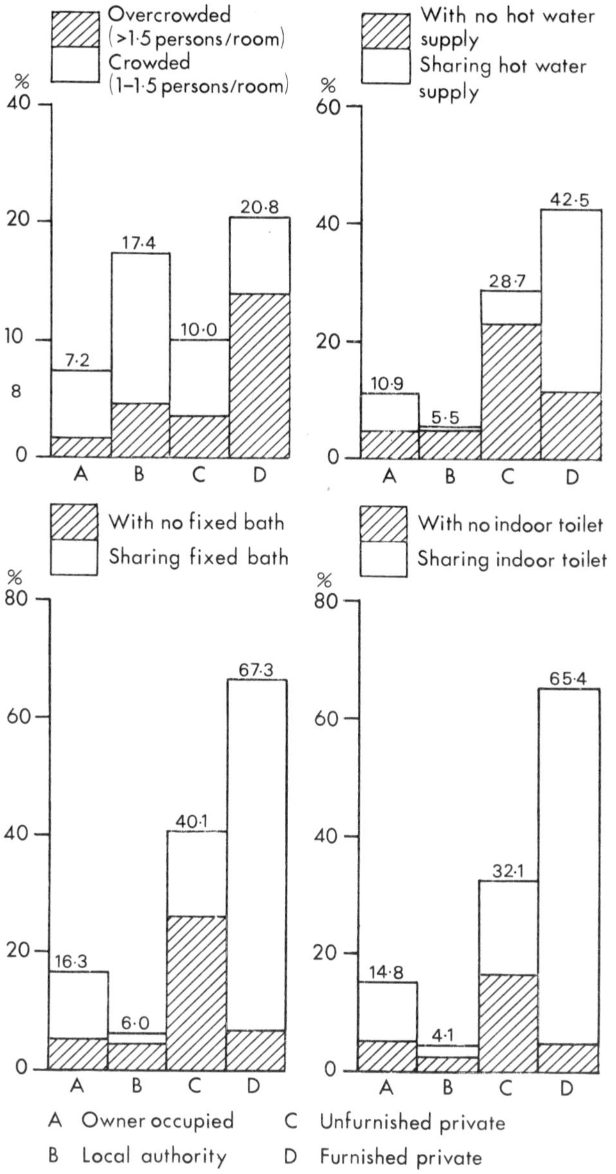

9·3 Overcrowding and Provision of Amenities in Lambeth, 1971.

Private Renting Between 1961 and 1971 unfurnished private tenancies declined from 45 to 33 % of households in Lambeth. Furnished tenancies increased from 13 to 15 %, but since 1971 both types of private renting have declined. Unfurnished tenants have the worst sanitation, often without hot water or a fixed bath, whereas furnished tenants usually have access to basic amenities but frequently have to share and live in overcrowded conditions (Fig. 9·3). Only 8 % of council tenants were denied exclusive use of all three amenities (hot water, bath, indoor toilet). Twenty-one per cent of owner-occupiers—owners of old dwellings or resident landlords who shared a bathroom or toilet with their tenants—lacked exclusive access. There was little sharing among unfurnished tenants and of the 48 % without exclusive use of all facilities, most lacked *any* access to at least one facility. By contrast, among the 73 % of furnished tenants without their own facilities, most shared, either with other tenants or with resident landlords.

Housing density figures provide further evidence of overcrowding in the furnished sector. Overcrowding is normally defined as a density of more than 1·5 persons per room; 5·2 % of Lambeth households, and 9·5 % of inhabitants, lived in overcrowded conditions in 1971, but in the private furnished sector the figures were 14 and 24 %.

One reason for the decline in unfurnished tenancies lies in their inclusion in slum clearance or council rehabilitation schemes. Another reason has been the decreasing financial return to be obtained as a private landlord, as commercial interest rates have risen far above the rate of return that a landlord could achieve by letting property, and as successive Rent Acts have made it more difficult for landlords to increase rents or evict undesirable tenants.

In 1964 32 % of privately rented dwellings in London were owned by landlords with more than one hundred properties. Many were 'mansion flats' owned by property companies and built between the wars. There are large numbers of these blocks in the south of Lambeth, especially between Brixton and Streatham. Some companies continued to let unfurnished flats until the early 1970s, but as residents have grown aware of their rights through the formation of tenants' associations and as profits have decreased, many companies are now selling their flats on long leases, either to sitting tenants or by advertising to the general public when the tenants leave. The result is a change in tenure from unfurnished private renting to owner-occupation, but there is no change in the social status of the residents. The tenants of mansion flats were from higher income groups. The new owner-occupiers, if not the same people, are the same type.

The response of small landlords to early Rent Acts was often to convert to furnished tenancies, from which the tenants could be evicted more easily prior to the 1974 Rent Act. Hence, the slight increase in furnished tenancies between 1961 and 1971. In this case there was a change in the status of occupiers. Unfurnished tenants were often working-class families who had been resident locally for a long time. Furnished tenants are more frequently young, single, temporary residents, immigrants or problem families, *eg* unmarried mothers and their children. A survey of furnished tenants in housing stress areas showed that half had children, of whom one-third were fatherless, more than half were coloured and two-thirds had semi-skilled or unskilled occupations. Many would have preferred unfurnished accommodation, but although there are more unfurnished than furnished tenancies in inner London, unfurnished tenants rarely move and when they do, the tenancy is relet, if at all, without being advertised. So it is difficult to get an unfurnished tenancy unless you have the right personal contacts.

Relatively few furnished tenancies have been subject to compulsory purchase, partly because they are not in poor structural condition but also because their replacement by council housing is unlikely to yield a major 'housing gain'. This occurs where the number of people rehoused on a site exceeds the number living there before redevelopment. It is easier to achieve a 'housing gain' where each house is occupied by only one family than where properties are multi-occupied. So it has been left to 'gentrification' to reduce the stock of furnished tenancies by converting them to owner-occupation, thus replacing poor families with rich single people and young childless couples. Since the 1974 Rent Act, which extended security to furnished tenants, many private landlords have sold their properties or kept them vacant in the hope of more favourable future legislation.

The recognition that private tenancies have a continuing role to play in housing students, single people, immigrants and temporary residents—all denied easy access to council housing—led Lambeth Council to aim at the improvement of 1000 existing dwellings every year and the conversion of large houses into flats to provide an additional 1000 dwellings annually. Half of these conversions were to be undertaken by housing associations, which are registered as charities, receive financial support from either the borough council or the GLC, and often cater for particularly disadvantaged groups such as unmarried mothers or discharged prisoners.

Between 1971 and 1974, 1771 improvement grants and 2886 conversion grants were made for housing improvement in Lambeth. These figures fall far short of the target but exclude grants on GLC-owned property. The role of housing associations has been disappointing: only 470 conversions in four years. Because associations are small organizations with limited budgets they cannot afford to risk too many tenants who may default with their rent payments. Nor can they charge sufficiently low rents to attract many low-income tenants, although the special groups for whom they were intended are usually also very poor. A final problem of the improvement grant system is that the properties most in need of improvement rarely benefit. Their owners, often burdened by expensive mortgages, cannot afford their share of the costs of improvement. Their tenants cannot afford to pay the increased rents which would follow improvement.

Environment and Employment

Although housing is a major problem in inner South London, it cannot be isolated from associated problems of environment and employment. There is little sense of community in areas of North Southwark and Lambeth where slums have been replaced by monolithic, multi-storey blocks of flats which are poorly maintained and for which the tenants do not feel personally responsible. More attention should be paid to landscaping, the provision of play areas and open space, if problems of vandalism, delinquency and a general feeling of anonymity are to be overcome. It may be desirable to demolish some dwellings on the grounds that it is better to house some of the people in an attractive environment than all of the people in a 'concrete jungle'. Lambeth Council planned to demolish two rows of mid-Victorian houses in St. Agnes Place, Kennington in order to enlarge Kennington Park. Critics of the scheme claimed that it was more important to preserve the housing, which could be repaired to serve as short-life accommodation for homeless families, who are often housed in local boarding houses at great expense to the ratepayers. They also argued that people would prefer several small parks to one large open space.

Changes in the composition of the housing stock are benefiting professional people who can move into gentrified property or buy their own house. Skilled manual workers benefit from council mortgages and the increasing proportion of housing that is council-owned. Yet skilled workers also benefit from decentralization policies, moving with their employers to new and expanded towns outside London, or gaining GLC nominations to council houses in outer boroughs. But the unskilled have suffered from the reduction of privately rented accommodation, are ignored by the outer boroughs and are also finding it more difficult to get jobs even in the inner city. The *Inner Area Studies Report* (1977) noted that in Stockwell there was a slight increase in the higher socio-economic groups, a decrease in skilled manual workers and an unchanging number of unskilled workers, despite their decreasing national significance.

Until the early 1960s the south bank of the Thames around London Bridge was the site of numerous warehouses, wharves and small industries associated with printing, engineering and food processing and distribution. Their workforce came from throughout south-east London, but especially from adjacent areas of North Southwark where the population had already fallen from over 40 000 in 1961 to 26 000 by 1974. In 1967, 77 000 workers were employed in North Southwark but in the following five years, as industries and services closed and were replaced by offices, 17 000 industrial jobs were lost and more than 8000 redundancies were officially registered. A survey of the fifty largest firms remaining in North Southwark in 1974 concluded that of 6085 jobs, 1657 (27 %) were likely to disappear by 1977. New office jobs are intended for middle-class commuters from outer London; local skilled workers may move out with their employers; the less skilled are abandoned in inadequate housing with little prospect of employment. The Inner Area Studies Report advocated industrial retraining and job creation in inner city districts, but also recognized the necessity of continued dispersal from inner London.

Population Dispersal

Public housing in London began with LCC schemes at Bethnal Green and Millbank in the 1890s, but the LCC soon realized that cheaper and more attractive locations for council housing existed on the edge of the then County of London, for example on the Totterdown Estate, Tooting, begun in 1903. The first 'out-county' estate, in which the LCC purchased land outside the county, was in Norbury, at the northern extremity of the borough of Croydon, where 498 small houses were built between 1906 and 1910. Land cost £21 per house compared with £454 for each three-bedroom flat erected by the LCC in central London at the same time. Tenants could still work in inner London, travelling by train or at workmen's rates on electric trams operated by the LCC from central London to the county boundary at Norbury.

Between the wars each local authority built council housing for its own population. In addition, the LCC built council flats and houses both within and beyond its county boundaries to meet those needs which local authorities were unable to satisfy. This role passed to the GLC in 1965. Part of the GLC's work involves rehabilitation, slum clearance and redevelopment in inner London: between 1971 and 1974, while Lambeth Council completed 2241 houses and flats, the GLC built 1332 dwellings in Lambeth. But the estates built by the LCC and GLC to rehouse inner Londoners in outer London are more distinctive.

Overlapping the boundaries of Sutton and Merton, the St. Helier estate dates from between 1928 and 1936. It originally comprised 9068 dwellings, housing nearly 40 000 inhabitants. Most residents continued working in inner London, their journeys to work eased by the underground extension to Morden (1926) and the construction of a new surface railway between Wimbledon and Sutton (1930). So popular is the estate that many inter-war residents still live there, producing problems of 'under-occupation'. Two- and three-bedroom terraced houses originally accommodated young married couples and their small children. Now the children have grown up and moved out, leaving their elderly parents occupying houses which could comfortably accommodate twice as many people. Not surprisingly, the elderly decline offers of smaller accommodation on post-war estates where they would be separated from their friends and the community with which they identify. Sutton Council, which took over part of the estate in 1971, is converting large four-bedroom houses into pairs of one-bedroom flats, so that residents can remain locally but in appropriately sized dwellings.

Another problem of St. Helier concerns its rudimentary facilities. When the estate was built few council tenants owned cars, so there were no garages. Today the narrow roads are choked with parked vehicles. Many houses had baths in the kitchen, necessitating a modernization programme in which bathroom extensions were added to the backs of houses, some swung over the roof by crane!

Between 1968 and 1971, 86 % of families rehoused in St. Helier came from inner London. By comparison with inner London families rehoused in inner London, St. Helier nominees came from larger families and had higher incomes. The very low rate of residential mobility at St. Helier—only about 2 % of tenancies fall vacant each year—also means that in absolute terms the estate now contributes little to the solution of inner London's housing shortage. Its future contribution has also been reduced by the policy of selling council houses to tenants, often at discounts that vary with the time that tenants have been in residence. In seven years, the GLC sold about 16 000 houses throughout London, including 5–10 % of its dwellings at St. Helier. Since 1973 Sutton Council has operated a similar policy although by early 1977 only about 150 houses had been sold.

A more recent example of an estate intended to rehouse inner Londoners in outer London is the Roundshaw estate, built between 1967 and 1971 on the site of Croydon Aerodrome. The estate comprises 1637 dwellings, mostly one- and two-bedroom flats and maisonettes. The importance of the car is recognized by the provision of as many garages and parking spaces as there are dwellings, and by complete segregation of cars and pedestrians. The initial allocation of tenants included families from Sutton's own waiting list, nominees from four neighbouring outer London boroughs (Richmond, Kingston, Merton, Croydon) and GLC nominees, many from older estates in Brixton, Streatham and Mitcham.

Roundshaw's obvious architectural contrast with conventional private housing in neighbouring parts of Sutton and Croydon reinforces its physical and social isolation. By outer London standards, Roundshaw has disproportionately high numbers of juvenile delinquents, single-parent families and families in receipt of supplementary benefits.

The argument continues over the outer boroughs' responsibility for solving inner London's problems. Several boroughs stipulated that the GLC could nominate tenants to vacancies on their estates only after agreeing not to build its own estates in their areas. Since most agreements referred to the GLC's right to nominate tenants to a fixed percentage of vacancies and new dwellings, the GLC was powerless when many boroughs reduced their building programmes towards the end of the 1960s. Smaller building programmes meant fewer GLC nominations. For example, Sutton Council has limited public housing to the north of the borough, apart from Roundshaw, and provides new housing principally for the old and the physically handicapped. In the four years, 1971–4, Sutton completed 265, 164, 0 and 90 new dwellings. In Merton completions fell from 699 in 1972 to 15 in 1974.

Proposals for a London-wide housing pool for families on borough waiting lists have met with considerable opposition. The London *Evening Standard* (2 December 1976) reported a Croydon housing spokesman as saying: 'The sort of people the inner boroughs want to spill out are those they don't want, the unemployed and the problem families who are a big drain on the social services.' In return, the GLC accused outer boroughs of offering only low standard houses to families from inner London stress areas, and reserving their better properties for their own families. In the first eight months of 1976, Merton housed only three families nominated by the GLC, Sutton six and Croydon nineteen. However, the answer to inner London's problems cannot lie entirely in outer London. One reason why the unskilled do not move to Sutton is that there are few unskilled jobs there and they cannot afford to commute to central London. St. Helier and Roundshaw are close to the Wandle Valley industrial zone and the industrial estates along Purley Way, but these factories provide jobs primarily for skilled and female labour. This is also true in dispersal schemes where housing and employment are linked, as in the case of London's new towns.

Crawley: An Old New Town

London's eight new towns were created under the New Towns Act, 1946, as a means of dispersing industry and making up the backlog of housing that had accumulated during World War II. Each new town was built by a development corporation appointed by central government and faced with co-ordinating development with local authorities and county councils in its designated area. These regional authorities provided services such as schools and council houses sufficient for local residents, while the development corporation built housing for the incoming population. In Crawley, the borough council has built over 3000 houses for rent. The development corporation and its successor, the Commission for the New Towns, built over 13 000 houses but about a quarter have since been sold to sitting tenants on similar lines to council house sales in Greater London. To ensure some degree of social mixing in new towns, sites are also reserved for houses for private sale. In Crawley this sector comprises over 4000 dwellings. Nevertheless, public housing constitutes a much bigger share of housing than in ordinary towns, because there is little privately rented accommodation apart from property owned by housing associations. One of the newest neighbourhoods in Crawley—Broadfield—includes developments administered by the Guinness Trust and the Quadrant Housing Association.

Crawley is built as a series of neighbourhood units, each focused on a community centre, church, primary school, pub and low-order shops, and separated from adjacent neighbourhoods by open space and main roads. The earliest neighbourhoods were designed for populations of 6–9000. The more recent 'Broadfield' was planned for 14 000 inhabitants, and includes a larger shopping mall with its own Sainsbury's, shared with the final neighbourhood, 'Bewbush', constructed by the borough council for a further 10 000 people. The increased population and higher-order shopping facilities of these two neighbourhoods reflect not only their remoteness from the town centre but also the age of the town. It is no longer necessary to build compact, identifiable neighbourhoods to engender a sense of community. Neighbourhoods were planned to be 'socially balanced' containing people from each social class in the same proportion as they are found in Crawley as a whole. In practice many better-off families have abandoned Crawley for surrounding villages in the Sussex countryside, and migration between the town's neighbourhoods has produced social segregation within Crawley.

Initially, housing and jobs were planned together. Many firms moved to Crawley from South London, their workforce guaranteed accommodation in the town. Now, the process of job creation is complete, the town's population exceeds 75 000 and any future growth will result from natural increase within Crawley. The housing stock of the Commission has been pooled with that of the borough council, to be allocated to satisfy local need as in other local authorities.

How successful is Crawley? The town provides homes and jobs for thousands of Londoners who might otherwise still be living in inner city areas. But from the perspective of the inner city the problems are as bad as ever, possibly worse because of the selective nature of new town migration, whereby the unskilled and the uneducated have been left behind.

Middle – Class Suburbia

This chapter has concentrated on changes in

working-class housing. But middle-class suburbia is also changing as small town-houses and blocks of flats replace Victorian and Edwardian villas built when the area first became commuter country. The 'housing gain' achieved by such redevelopment often exceeds that associated with slum clearance, where the number of new dwellings may be little more than the number of slums demolished. Between the wars new private housing took the form of low-density estates added to the edge of built-up areas. But the imposition of the Green Belt has curtailed this type of development. Large scale, low-density estates must now be located beyond the Green Belt in Kent and Sussex. Furthermore, rising costs of land and construction have attracted private developers to sites where all services—water, gas, electricity, sewerage—are already provided. Given the scarcity of completely open sites, the favourite strategy is to replace one or two large old houses with blocks of flats. Councils are unlikely to refuse planning permission if a site is already in residential use. The only restrictions may relate to height, density and the provision of parking facilities. For example, the height of flats may be limited to three or four storeys to preserve the character of an area. Particularly favoured locations are within walking distance of commuter railway stations, as at Sutton, Wallington and Beckenham. Of private dwellings completed in Sutton between 1971 and 1974, 932 were houses, 1301 were flats. In Croydon the figures were 1445 and 1664. In Sutton 582 private houses and 1561 flats were started in 1973 and 1974.

The concentration on small sites usually means development by small companies. Large companies prefer extensive greenfield developments beyond the Green Belt. Small companies tend to build relatively expensive flats and houses, whereas large companies favour the mass market. The result is a reversal of Burgess's concentric-zone model on the urban fringe. Instead of a regular increase in status with increasing distance from London, we find high-status families on the edge of the built-up area and within the Green Belt, and less wealthy, middle-income families as 'reluctant commuters' in cheaper housing farther out.

Private redevelopment has the effect of intensifying existing patterns of residential segregation. Selected sites invariably lie in the middle of existing high-status, owner-occupied areas. The new residents are high-status owner-occupiers. Neglected sites are areas of poorer old housing which are redeveloped, if at all, by the council as housing for relatively low-status tenants. Sites requiring considerable expenditure before they can accept buildings—abandoned railway yards and industrial sites, poorly drained or polluted land—are also left to the council to develop. Piecemeal private redevelopment also leaves street layouts unchanged. On maps of land use or social class nothing has changed, but the fabric has been renewed, thus making subsequent change—invasion and succession of Burgess's theory—even less likely.

Conclusions

It has been customary to interpret the social geography of British cities in terms of the zonal and sectoral models of North American social scientists. We contrast high-density, low-class inner areas—like Bermondsey and Battersea—with low-density, middle-class suburbs—like Chislehurst and Cheam; or we contrast high-status sectors following the upper Thames through Richmond and Kingston, or commuter railways through Beckenham and Bromley, with low-status sectors following the lower Thames from Deptford to Erith, or the Wandle Valley from Wandsworth to Mitcham. But the processes envisaged by researchers like Burgess and Hoyt have few parallels in London today. This chapter has emphasized instead the roles of government, both local and central, and institutions like building societies, property companies and developers, in influencing where people live. It has also demonstrated that behind a façade of relatively minor changes in land use, complex processes are in operation which affect the extent to which more radical changes will be possible in the future.

Further Reading

Ambrose, P. and Colenutt, B., *The Property Machine* (Penguin, Harmondsworth, 1975)

Harloe, M., Issacharoff, R. and Minns, R., *The Organization of Housing* (Heinemann, London, 1974)

10 London's Green Belt

Richard Munton

Introduction

The growth of suburbia has been the dominating feature of urban development in the twentieth century. In Western societies its expansion has been more a consequence of car ownership than either increasing numbers of city dwellers or improved public transport, although these have also played their part. Populations have been consistently redistributed from inner-city areas to the urban fringe, creating planning problems that local and central government have found difficult to resolve.

In the urban fringe there are two interrelated land-use planning problems. The first concerns the spatial *pattern* of urban growth. Uncontrolled urban development can lead to excessive urban sprawl along lines of communication. This was evident in parts of south-east England in the 1930s, particularly southern Essex, and is still apparent today around cities in North America. Not only can an irregularly distributed and widely scattered urban population create difficulties for farming but it can also lead to high costs in the provision of public services. Urban areas may also coalesce leaving minimal open space easily accessible to the public. The second problem stems in part from the first and concerns the *composition* and *nature* of urban fringe land uses. There is the danger that the urban fringe can become dominated by unwanted but necessary, land uses such as sewage works, refuse dumps and sand and gravel extraction. Informal recreational space may be underprovided, as no great profit can be derived from supplying it, and agricultural land may fall idle because of various forms of urban nuisance or because the prospect of urban development removes the incentive to invest in its improvement. Aesthetically unpleasing landscapes and inappropriate mixes of land uses are the result.

These land-use problems have long been recognized and are not particular to London. Various forms of planning and financial legislation have been passed to try to create an acceptable land-use pattern and to attempt to develop orderly means of transferring land from rural to urban uses. Green belts have been a favoured planning device. They exist, although only provisionally in some cases, around a number of British cities and conurbations, including Belfast, Clydeside, Merseyside, the West Midlands, Oxford and the Bath/Bristol area. The Metropolitan Green Belt around London is probably the best known because it is the largest and has been a planning reality since 1947, longer than any other in the UK. It is the purpose of this chapter to describe its evolution and land-use composition, and to assess its present role. Recreational open space in London's urban fringe is discussed in Chapter 11 and so particular attention will be paid here to the present pattern of agricultural activity although green belt policy has had little to say about agriculture directly. This is unfortunate as in areal terms farming is still the major land use in the urban fringe. Its economic viability and enterprise structure significantly affect the appearance of the Metropolitan Green Belt and the achievement of landscape planning goals.

London's Green Belt: Its Establishment and Early Development

Calls for the establishment of a green belt around London, often with different objectives in mind, have been made repeatedly since the end of the nineteenth century. Not until the 1930s was much progress made. Then in 1935 the LCC launched its Green Belt Scheme under which the Council, in conjunction with county councils on the edge of London, proposed to buy land with public money. The land purchased was to be retained in its existing rural use. The Scheme received statutory backing in 1938 (The Green Belt [London and Home Counties] Act) and was enthusiastically taken up by the county councils of Middlesex, Essex, Buckinghamshire and Surrey in particular. By 1944, 100 km² of land had been purchased.

A more comprehensive approach was proposed by Patrick Abercrombie in the Greater London Plan of 1944. He argued for the maintenance of a belt of countryside in agricultural and recreational use up to 16 km in depth around the edge of London. It would contain with it those towns and villages already in

10·1 Extent of London's Green Belt.

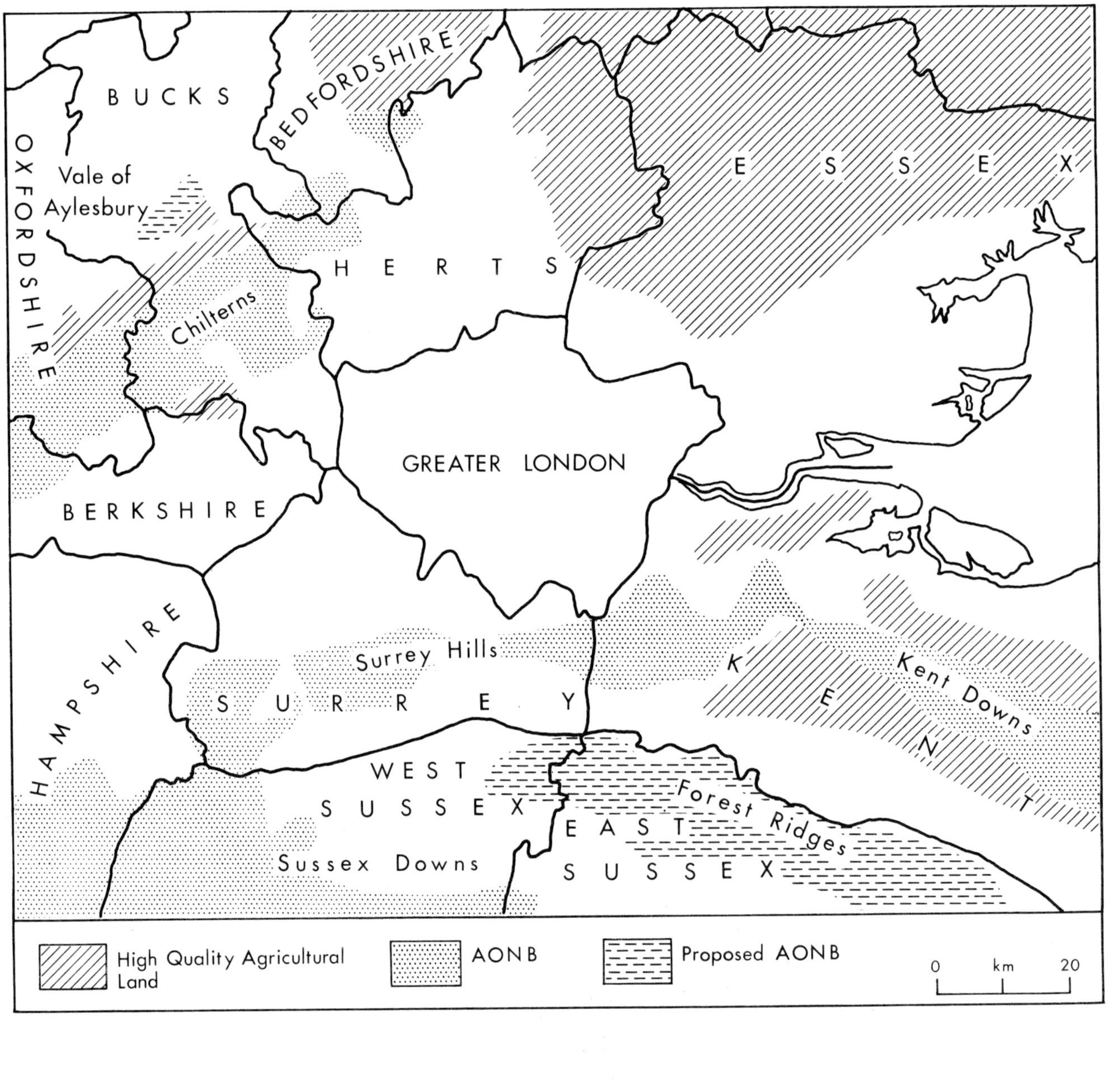

existence, but was nevertheless to act as a barrier to the further outward expansion of London. Abercrombie's proposals were largely accepted by central government, the proposed area, in excess of 250 000 ha was too large and too costly for public authorities to contemplate purchasing. Instead, it was to be maintained in rural use through the strict implementation of the development control procedures contained in the land-use planning system set up under the 1947 Town and Country Planning Act. This Act required all landowners to obtain permission from their local planning authorities for most proposed changes in land use. Proposed changes that were unacceptable were to be refused. But the definition of 'acceptable uses' of green belt land and, indeed, the very existence of a green belt at all, have been matters of debate.

TABLE 9 Land Use in London's Green Belt and 'green belt zone' in 1960

Land Use	*Green Belt (%)*	*'green belt zone' (%)*
Residential and Commercial	6·2	14·3
Manufacturing Industry	0·2	0·7
Extractive (*eg* sand and gravel)	1·8	1·6
Transport	1·5	2·1
Public Services	0·9	1·2
Institutions in Extensive Grounds	1·1	1·4
Woodland	11·8	10·3
Water	0·6	0·5
Recreational Land	6·2	5·4
Agricultural Land	69·5	62·3
Unused	0·2	0·2
	100·0	100·0

Percentages rounded to one decimal place

Arguments in favour of green belts have emphasized their value as a means of creating a desired spatial pattern of urban land use as well as preserving and promoting certain rural land uses in the urban fringe. The position of central government was made clear in 1955 when the Minister of Housing and Local Government issued a circular providing guidance to those authorities that wished to follow London in establishing green belts. Three general principles were enunciated. Green belts were to be seen as appropriate planning measures if they checked the growth of large built-up areas, or prevented the merging of towns, or preserved the special character of a town. As such they paid little attention to the appearance of land in the urban fringe, or how some rural land uses might be encouraged at the expense of others.

This is not to suggest that views were not expressed in the circular as to which land uses were acceptable or unacceptable. In the case of London's Green Belt (capital letters are used for statutorily approved areas) it was clear that no new residential development was to be permitted, except in such special cases as housing for farm workers. Towns and villages within the Green Belt were not to be allowed to grow, except for infilling on undeveloped land within the settlement. This 'infill' land became highly valued as a result and housing on such land dating from the 1950s and 1960s is in evidence in many villages and towns in the Green Belt.

The first detailed analysis of land use within and around London's Green Belt was carried out by David Thomas and is described in his book *London's Green Belt* (1970). Thomas recognized three general categories of land use. First, undesirable uses whose presence extend from their existence before the Green Belt was established, and include housing, roads and manufacturing industry. Second, undesirable uses that are to some extent inevitable in the urban fringe, such as refuse dumps. Third, approved uses such as agriculture, forestry, sports grounds and informal recreational space. Thomas produced land-use statistics for both the statutorily designated Green Belt (land under green belt notation) and for a 'green belt zone', a belt of land 16 km wide beyond the outer edge of London's built-up area. The latter zone contained some land beyond the Green Belt and included towns within it but not recorded as being under green belt notation. The results are shown in Table 9.

Land uses were allocated to one of eleven categories, the first five being regarded as unacceptable or 'non-conforming'. It can be seen that in the Green Belt only 10·6% of the land area fell into these categories, although the percentage varied from 8·1% in the north-east quadrant of the Green Belt to 14·0% in the south-west. The great majority of the land was in agricultural, woodland or recreational use and, as Thomas also pointed out, land-use changes between 1955 and 1960 had only increased the area covered by residential and commercial uses by approximately 0·3%. This apparently satisfactory situation was less obvious in the urban fringe 'green belt zone'. Here almost 20% of the land was in non-conforming uses, this higher proportion being the result of including a number of large free-standing towns on the edge of London around which the boundary of the Green Belt had been drawn. Even more significant, Thomas's analyses also indicated that the rate of urban development between 1955 and 1960 was considerable on land unprotected by green belt notation. Green belt policy seemed to be working by keeping non-conforming uses out of the approved Green Belt, but partly at the expense of shifting use changes to land just beyond its boundary. Indeed, this was a period in which infilling continued apace and it may be that the relatively loose drawing of green belt boundaries around many towns permitted a rate of urban development in the urban fringe not much less than might have occurred without a green belt at all.

Green Belt Policy in the 1960s and 1970s

Despite some success in influencing the pattern of urban growth in South-East England, criticisms of green belt policy began to be made in the 1960s. In particular, the policy operating in the 1950s was regarded as having been negative and inflexible. It was considered negative because of the lack of encouragement given to those uses regarded as acceptable. Inadequate attention, it was argued, had been given to the following kinds of question. What objectives should be set for agriculture? How much land should be allocated to recreational use? How should public access to the countryside be ensured? Green belt policy was considered inflexible because it was based on the economic premises employed by Abercrombie in the 1940s. For example, should there not be some relaxation in the restrictions on urban and industrial development in some parts of the Green Belt so as to meet the rising demand for housing land?

These questions also reflect changing attitudes on the part of planners to the planning process as a whole during the 1960s. There was a general move away from the inflexible land-use plan approach implicit in the 1947 Town and Country Planning Act. In as much as London's Green Belt dates from the same period then it is not surprising that a more flexible policy-orientated approach to it has been sought since the mid-1960s. This is reflected in the kinds of statement contained in the GLDP (1976) and the structure plans now under preparation or seeking government approval. Detailed green belt proposals will undoubtedly be contained in the local plans to be produced by local district authorities outside the GLC area and boroughs within.

Inflexibility in green belt policy arose from an awareness in the early 1960s that the rate of growth in the regional economy and population had been much greater in the 1950s than had been anticipated. At the same time, people were moving from central London to towns within and beyond the Green Belt at a faster rate than had been expected. One major outcome of these trends was that more housing and industrial land had to be found in South-East England outside the GLC area than had been planned. A series of government circulars and regional studies all made different proposals on where the new urban growth should be located, but they all agreed that authorities close to London would have to make some contribution to solving the land shortage problem. The sacrosanct nature of the Green Belt was questioned and in 1963 and 1973 central government initiated enquiries as to whether some green belt land could not be released for housing. Some was released for housing and commercial development between 1964 and 1974, partly in response to these initiatives and partly as a result of planning applications permitted by central government on appeal (see Table 10, category 1), but the seriousness of the land shortage problem has receded during the 1970s as the rate of economic growth and population increase have declined. Moreover, the greatest rates of population increase are now in areas beyond the Green Belt but this in turn has raised a potential difficulty.

This difficulty stems from attempts by various county authorities on the edge of London to extend the Green Belt. At present, most of the extensions are still interim, that is to say they do not yet have final government approval (see Fig. 10·1), but planning decisions in them are made on the basis of 'green belt principles' by the local authorities concerned. These proposed extensions, if approved, would more than double the size of the original Green Belt so as to cover the whole of Hertfordshire and Surrey, as well as large parts of Kent and Essex. An inflexible regional planning situation could recur if a blanket restriction was imposed on urban development over the whole of this area. This situation, however, is unlikely to occur for practical reasons. In the first instance the pressures exerted on different authorities to permit development vary. Marked differences exist in the planning context of green belt land between say Hillingdon and Bromley LBs in the outer suburbs of Greater London and the more rural district authorities of Waverley (Surrey), Rochford (Essex) and North Hertfordshire (Fig. 10·1). But not only do demands for urban development vary spatially but so also does the environmental character of green belt land. Even within the original Green Belt there were, for example, parts of the Surrey Hills and Chilterns Areas of Outstanding Natural Beauty. The proposed extensions will also lead to the inclusion of large areas of high-quality farmland in Kent, Essex and east Hertfordshire (Fig. 10·2). Finally, with the division of

TABLE 10 Major Land Uses in the Green Belt, 1964 and 1974*

	hectares 1964	*hectares* 1974	*% of total area* 1974	*% change in area* 1964—74
1. Villages, groups of houses and land where other surface development predominates	6880	7972	3·5	+15·9
2. Airfields, War Department land reservoirs and waterworks, mineral workings, tips and other land uses of a predominantly open character	11 331	11 089	4·8	−2·1
3. Institutions in extensive grounds, cemeteries, playing fields and other uses appropriate to the Green Belt	16 188	16 957	7·4	+4·8
4. Public open space	16 188	17 280	7·5	+6·8
5. Remainder, mainly agricultural land and woodland	178 875	176 244	76·7	−1·5
TOTAL	229 462	229 542	100·0	
6. Areas which have been acquired, or for which financial contributions, covenants dedication agreements or preservation orders have been made to preserve the land in its present state (included in figures above)	27 115	30 352	13·2	+11·9

* Percentages rounded to one decimal place. Based on information contained in Report 620 of the Standing Conference on London and South-East Regional Planning (1976).

planning powers between both County and District authorities in 1974, over fifty planning departments are now concerned with the implementation of green belt policy. Differing interpretations of what is acceptable development, based on local circumstances, seem bound to be made.

Thus the present justification of flexibility rests more on the enormous variety of local circumstances in the extended green belt than on an ever rising demand for housing land. These practical reasons, among others, led a recent study of London's Green Belt to suggest that the definition of what constitutes an acceptable use should be reviewed, not only to acquire a clear redefinition of acceptability, but also with the possibility of applying different definitions to different parts of the Green Belt. Up to the present all proposed changes in use on land in the Green Belt have been treated in basically the same way using the same criteria; but this suggested change in policy would imply zoning *within* the Green Belt, a view that has yet to receive public acceptance or government recognition. As yet no criteria by which zones could be delimited have been put forward.

Land-Use Changes 1964–74

It has been argued that it is not enough merely to indicate that some land uses are unacceptable whilst at the same time not encouraging, or at least having a policy for, those that are deemed acceptable. In short, a positive approach to achieving prescribed land-use

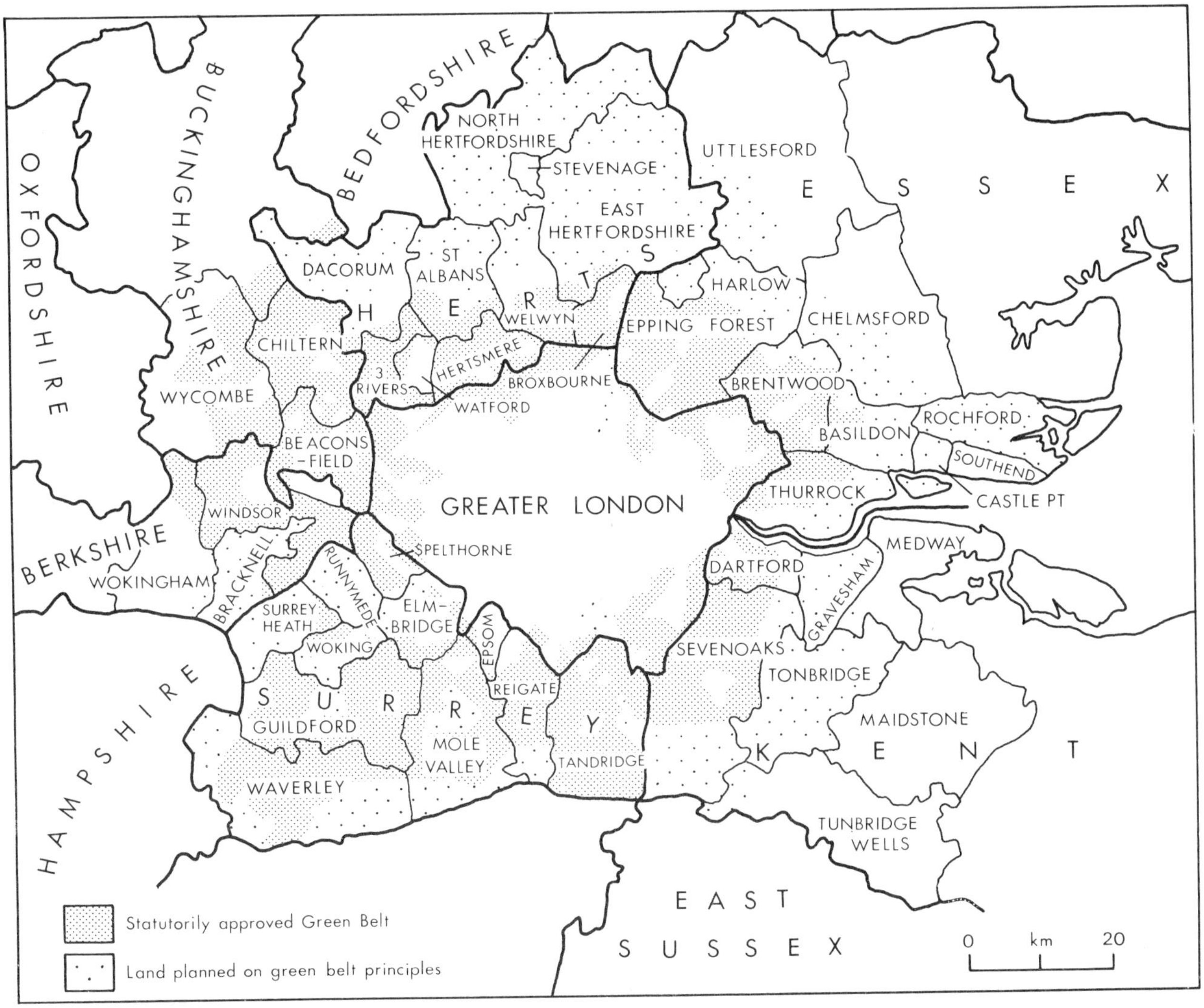

10·2 Areas of Outstanding Natural Beauty and High Quality Agricultural Land.

and landscape objectives is required. Discussion has centred on three issues, namely, extending the provision of public recreation facilities, defining a role for agriculture and maintaining, enhancing and even rehabilitating the landscape. But before considering the questions of landscape and farming it is necessary to bring land-use changes in the Green Belt up to date.

A recent report entitled *The Improvement of London's Green Belt* contains estimates of land use for the Green Belt for 1964 and 1974 (Table 10). These figures should not be compared with those of Thomas for 1960 (Table 9) as they have been compiled on a different basis. A relatively slow-moving situation in terms of total land use is revealed, but one in which agriculture and woodland are declining in area, and residential development (despite controls) and public open space have been expanding their areas. These trends are most evident when the proportional change for each use over the period is calculated. Even then, the full impact of the changes cannot be inferred from Table 10. In the first place the figures underestimate the extent of urban uses by excluding areas of less than 2 ha. Secondly, the spatial pattern of urban development has not been uniform, development being most rapid in some of the most vulnerable areas of the Green Belt, such as southern Hillingdon. Finally, even small developments can have an intrusive effect on the landscape and can interfere with farming activities. It is to agriculture and its problems that the chapter now turns.

Agriculture in the Green Belt

Surprisingly little is known about the distribution of different farming activities in the Green Belt. Some useful information can be obtained from the second edition of J. T. Coppock's *Agricultural Atlas of England and Wales* which uses data collected in 1970. At this time about 55 % of the farmed area was under tillage (arable crops) compared to the national average of 43 %. There was a marked difference in pattern with Hertfordshire and the areas in Essex shown on Fig. 10·3 recording 70 % tilled land. The remaining districts to the south and west of London averaged only 42 %. In every area barley was the most important single crop in terms of land coverage, followed by wheat, except in south-east Essex where the order was reversed. Over 80 % of the tilled area of Hertfordshire was in one of these two crops, but this particular measure (area) significantly underestimates the importance of field vegetable production and horticulture to the regional agricultural economy. In national terms beef cattle were under-represented over the whole area, and sheep markedly so. Dairy cattle were the dominant form of livestock in all but four of the districts, dairying being especially important in Buckinghamshire, Berkshire and Surrey. Pigs and poultry were evenly distributed throughout the Green Belt, except for an area of concentration in south-west Hertfordshire, east Buckinghamshire and east Berkshire. If the data are analysed by major enterprise groups (Fig. 10·3), and their measurement standardized in terms of their labour requirements, their order of importance in 1970, taking the Green Belt as a whole, was as follows—horticulture (32 % of all labour requirements), cropping (24 %), dairying (20 %), poultry (9 %), pigs (7 %), beef cattle (7 %) and sheep (1 %). Horticulture was especially important in east Hertfordshire and west Essex (Lee Valley), west Kent, south-west London and north-west Surrey.

The information is insufficiently disaggregated into small areal units for the impact of urban proximity to be measured effectively. But a comparison of those districts that bound London with those that do not, reveals one important difference. Horticulture is significantly more important in the inner areas. It accounts for 42 % of all labour requirements (compared with 21 % in the outer districts) gaining primarily at the expense of general cropping. It is also worth noting that labour inputs in agriculture are very high over much of the Green Belt and that in 1970 the district covering north-west Surrey and south-west London employed fifty-two workers for every 400 ha of crops and grass, the highest number for any district in the country.

Farms in the Green Belt tend to be smaller in terms of their area than the national average. There are few very big holdings and most of those greater than

120 ha are in the general cropping area to the north of London. The small size of farm reflects the large number of highly intensive vegetable and horticultural holdings, the importance of dairying, pig and poultry enterprises and the numerous part-time and hobby farms. From her survey in the mid-1960s Ruth Gasson estimated that perhaps 60 % of holdings were farmed part-time in the Green Belt to the south-east of London. The proportion was increasing, mainly the result of a continuing expansion in hobby farming. Hobby farming, a term used to describe a situation in which the farm provides only a nominal source of income, often financially non-essential, to supplement that earned in urban employment, inevitably introduces professional people with an urban background to farming. Many of them enter farming with mixed motives including the desire for a preferred residential location and the purchase of land as an investment. The latter has an unwelcome effect on land prices, raising them for those landowners genuinely seeking an economic return from full-time farming. Gasson's study was able to conclude, however, that hobby farming is neither less efficient economically than full-time farming nor does it lead

10·3 Structure of Agricultural Enterprises, 1971.

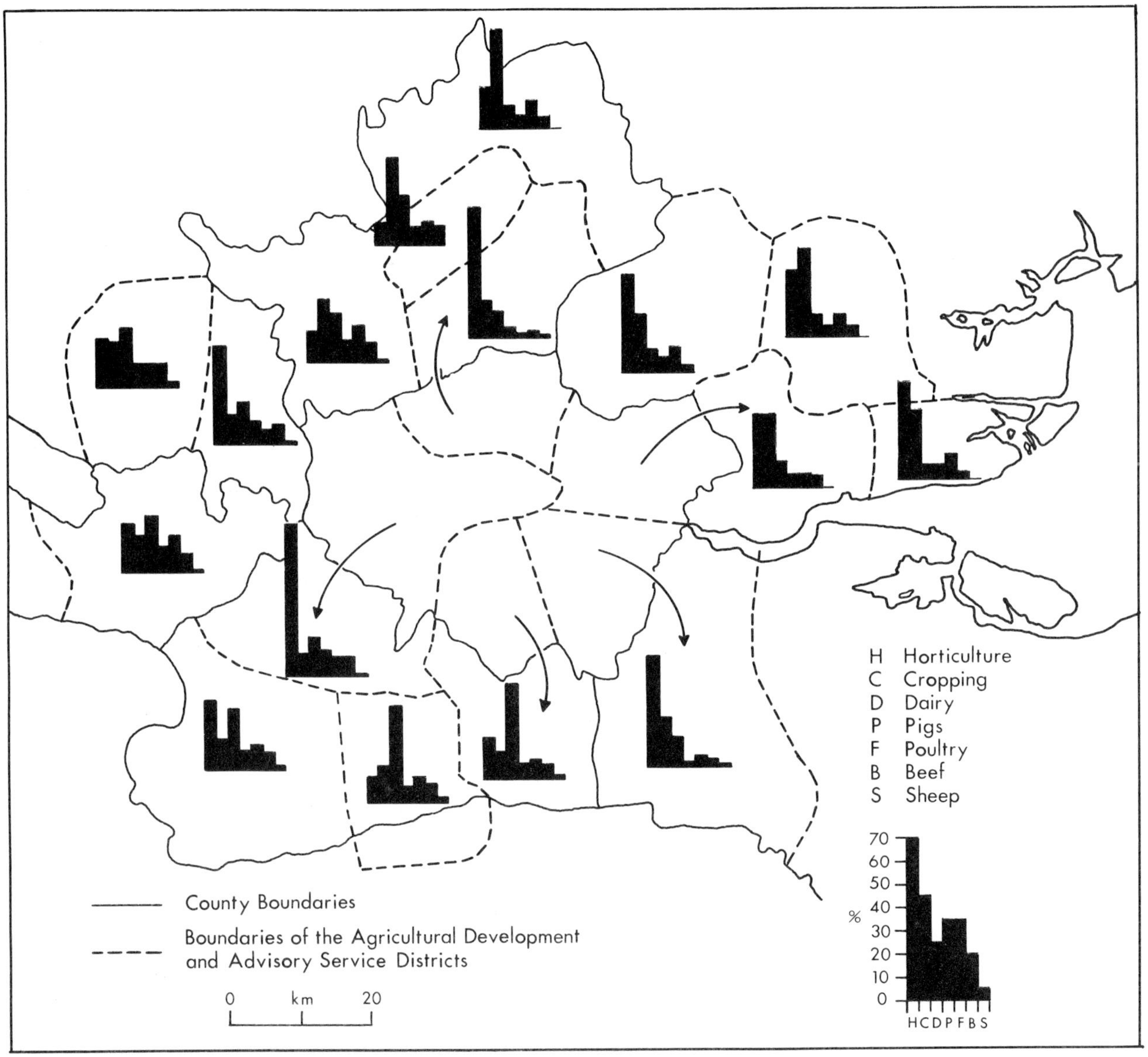

to markedly different systems of production, although hobby farmers tend to prefer simpler and less time-consuming enterprises.

Farmers in the Green Belt can experience additional problems but acquire extra financial benefits from their urban fringe location. Locally, urban interference can be a serious problem, particularly to those farmers whose land is adjacent to residential areas. The most widespread forms of interference are trespass, dumping and theft. The limited presence of sheep and beef enterprises could be put down to this latter difficulty, but it is also a consequence of the higher levels of profit normally made from more intensive arable enterprises. The evidence on urban interference suggests that it imposes a significant cost on a few farmers and an additional worry on many. Farmers also complain generally about planning uncertainty in the urban fringe, and the inadequate consultation between planners and farmers in particular. Why invest, they ask, in farm improvements when their land may be developed for an urban use in the near future—sometimes, however, at a handsome profit to themselves. In principle, this should not be an issue in question in the Green Belt if planning restrictions are being strictly imposed, but because planning permission has been given in some cases for urban development (Table 10, category 1) landowners continue to entertain the possibility of selling their land or having it acquired compulsorily. The latter situation has occurred quite frequently with motorway and trunk road development which takes place outside the normal development control procedure.

Some farmers benefit from their location. Some develop farm gate sales and the selling of produce direct to the public. Although profit margins can be substantial the amount of business is usually small and variable unless retail outlets are systematically developed. Few farmers are prepared to restructure their businesses to accommodate this kind of selling and so those growing fruit and vegetables and other produce that can be readily sold at the farm gate tend merely to capitalize on their existing farming systems. Other farmers gain financially from recreation demands through the establishment of stables and farm trails, the selling of shooting licences and, where planning permission is granted, the construction of golf courses. At a general level, both advantages and disadvantages exist for farmers in the green belt, but what has yet to be established is whether those farmers that suffer financially from urban interference fail to gain from, say, farm gate sales.

Little attention has been paid to the question of what should be expected from farmers and landowners in the Green Belt. The urban pressures exerted upon them vary enormously and it may be unreasonable to expect agriculture to play a single role over the whole of the Green Belt. For example, close to the edge of urban areas farm-based leisure activities, such as shooting and horse riding could be encouraged leaving less vulnerable farming areas to commercial food production. In the light of the White Paper *Food from Our Own Resources* (Cmnd. 6020, 1975), which expresses a wish for an expansion in food production in the UK, then the best quality farmland in the Green Belt (Fig. 10·2) should be rigorously protected. But with the exception of the north-east quadrant of the Green Belt the area of high quality land is fairly limited. The Green Belt as a whole cannot be treated as more than an important, and certainly not a strategic, national agricultural resource. Moreover, some of the very best land is to be found near Slough, in Havering and in southern Hillingdon, all areas experiencing severe residential and industrial development pressures.

The importance of agriculture to the land-use pattern makes its contribution to the maintenance of an aesthetically pleasing landscape a matter of major concern. There are parts of the Green Belt that have been so severely affected by sand and gravel extraction and industrial pollution that they cannot be returned to agricultural use in the foreseeable future. These areas are most evident east of Slough, in Spelthorne, in the Lee Valley, in Havering and along the Darent Valley between Dartford and Sevenoaks. But other areas presently in agricultural use are threatened, and in the absence of either new forms of financial assistance or further planning restrictions over what the landowner may or may not do, persuading him to plant trees, keep hedges and invest in farm improvements, largely depends on an economically viable farming industry. It will also be necessary to assure the full-time farmer who wishes to stay in the industry that there are good long-term prospects for him in his present location. As soon as the farmer loses interest in farming, for whatever reason—planning blight, urban interference—he will stop investing in improvements and may seek ways of realizing a large capital gain by selling his property to a developer. Indeed, it is absolutely essential to indicate to landowners that by deliberately running down their properties, and some examples of this have occurred, they will not enhance their chances of acquiring planning permission for some form of urban development. Because of the difficulties of determining criteria and delimiting boundaries any attempt to zone the Green Belt will only exacerbate this particular problem.

Some attention has been given recently as to how particular land use and landscape goals could be achieved. For example, it has been suggested that 'Landscape Conservation Orders' could be introduced. These would result in landscapes of great beauty or historical significance outside Areas of Outstanding Natural Beauty being managed on the basis of practices agreed between public authorities and landowners, the latter possibly receiving financial aid to offset any loss of income. The particular attraction to the local authorities of the Orders is that they would increase the authorities' powers of enforcement, as it is their view that many green belt problems are created by the non-compliance with planning conditions rather than the intrusion of undesirable land uses. The increased public ownership of land is also an attractive possibility. Access for the public to the countryside could be ensured and recreational facilities developed, but progress would necessarily be slow because of the cost of land acquisition and because of the political objections that would inevitably be raised. An alternative approach to a large-scale increase in public land ownership is being tried in the Urban Fringe Management Experiment. This has been established jointly by the Countryside Commission and local authorities in Hertfordshire, Barnet and Havering as an example of a practical land management exercise. It is the successor to that in the Bollin Valley to the south of Greater Manchester and was set up in 1975 in the belief that landscape objectives are most readily achieved by the detailed working out on the ground of local land-use conflicts. It is an approach with considerable potential for effecting change at the local level but its success in the London Green Belt context has yet to be demonstrated.

The Present Position

The Green Belt was greeted with enthusiasm in 1947, heavily criticized in the 1960s and is coming under review again in the late 1970s. Doubts have been expressed whether the benefits it bestows offset the costs it incurs. By restricting development on the edge of London it has raised housing costs and led to longer commuting journeys. The recent decline in the region's rate of population and economic growth has temporarily reduced the demand for building land and muted these concerns. Nevertheless, without a readjustment of green belt boundaries pressures could easily build up again as infilling possibilities are few and high fuel costs now favour shorter journeys to work.

In spite of these doubts, the Green Belt remains a planning instrument with strong public support, although opinions as to what is wanted within it vary. The inhabitants of Greater London are faced by an apparent shortage of building land, high house prices and rents, and frequently inadequate provision of public open space. Many local authorities are constantly seeking means of acquiring additional land resources to meet these needs, if necessary at the expense of the Green Belt. Small pieces of low quality agricultural land surrounded by urban development become prime targets. On the other hand authorities outside Greater London, and even more the public they represent, take a protectionist, amenity-orientated view of the Green Belt, whilst those living within it hold the most conservative outlook of all, resenting even the best intentioned decisions that lead to changes in use.

With such differences in attitude it is extremely difficult for the large number of authorities responsible for implementing green belt policies, often themselves being pressured by local action and amenity groups, to produce consistent and fair decisions over changes in use. In principle, the Department of the Environment can provide consistency as it acts as the final arbiter on all planning decisions on appeal and on matters requiring a public enquiry. But many decisions are taken at a local level and the sheer variety of green belt planning situations militate against conformity and comparability. Moreover central government has to take into account regional and even national considerations and these will not only vary over time and space but also may be at odds with local wishes. Indeed central government has taken many decisions that have met with local disapproval.

It would seem that the Green Belt is here to stay, even if the realities of the situation—a precisely defined zone but with vaguely defined land-use policies—suggest that 'local flexibility' will be invoked to achieve most of the specific objectives of central and local government where particular land-use decisions are concerned. Yet this pragmatic approach could contain the seeds of its own destruction, especially when the aggregate effects on the landscape of such decisions are observed. For example, if this approach is not seen to be implemented with fairness, or concern for the needs of farmers, how can they be persuaded to keep the landscape aesthetically attractive, and largely for free?

Further Reading

Johnson, J. H., (ed.), *Suburban Growth: geographical processes at the edge of the Western city* (Wiley, London, 1974)

Thomas, D., *London's Green Belt* (Faber, London, 1970)

11 Recreation and Ecology in London's Urban Fringe

Carolyn Harrison

Introduction

Land adjacent to most large cities in Britain is subject to recreational pressure of many different kinds and intensities throughout the year. Often urban fringe land has to serve as the local playground for schoolchildren, the golf course for businessmen, the open country for equestrians and dog walkers, the laboratory for naturalists and students, the 'wilderness' for ramblers and the picnic area for the whole family. Recreational pressure is greatest on fine summer weekends but the suburban nature of large tracts of urban fringe land means that some activity goes on throughout the year. London's Green Belt therefore can be seen as an area to which hundreds of thousands of people regularly turn for their leisure pursuits and it is not surprising to find that land set aside for public access and enjoyment is regarded as one of the most acceptable and 'conforming' uses of green belt land.

A closer inspection of the pattern of land available for undertaking informal recreation activities such as walking, sightseeing, riding and picnicking in London's Green Belt reveals three important points. First, the fragmented nature of the pattern of provision, in which some areas are well served and others only poorly provided for. This means that some people have to go farther, and spend more money than others in order to enjoy themselves. Second, much of the publicly owned recreational land, as well as private estates, can be reached only by car-owners and hence those people dependent upon public transport are unable to participate in a full range of recreational pursuits. Such a pattern of accessibility suggests that even those public bodies and agencies which could be expected to serve the interests of *all* potential recreational users (not just car-owners) do not do so in respect of recreational land. Third, the uneven pattern of supply can mean that certain well-known beauty spots and open spaces are subjected to very heavy visitor use, which takes its toll of the physical and natural features of the environment that the public come to enjoy. To some this environmental deterioration may seem insignificant but to others, such as the committed naturalist, teacher or student, the disappearance of particular plants and animals presents serious problems. Such losses become even more significant in those areas acknowledged to be of particular scientific interest. These three themes form the basis of this chapter, namely:

(1) the provision of a range of facilities to meet a large demand;
(2) the provision of a pattern of facilities which is accessible to large numbers of people; and
(3) the management of sites in such a way that the most scientifically interesting sites are not irreparably damaged.

The Provision of Informal Recreational Facilities

The physical setting of London, at the centre of a

basin fringed by the girdle of chalk hills of the Chilterns in the north and the Downs in the south, provides varied landscapes in which several semi-natural communities (such as woodlands, heathland and downland) play their part. To the west of London the Bagshot Sands support some of the last remaining tracts of heathlands in south-east England, to the east the mixed oak and hornbeam woods of Epping Forest surmount the sandy ridge overlooking the valley of the Lee, and between them the Thames valley sands and gravels have been worked to provide an interrupted chain of abandoned and partially landscaped water-filled basins that are fringed by willows and reeds. To the south, the open chalk downland of the Hog's Back commands magnificent views, north across the London Basin and south across the Weald. Many of the semi-natural communities are green islands in a sea of buildings and intensively cultivated land and they owe their presence in the landscape to the protection afforded by particular legislative measures taken at various times in the past. It is to these areas that most Londoners look for countryside recreation.

Some of the most ancient open spaces in the urban fringe areas around London are commons preserved for their use as areas for public exercise and enjoyment during early Elizabethan times, *eg* Wimbledon Common. They are now normally managed by county and local district authorities and by groups of conservators as areas for formal and informal recreation. In addition, the GLC has entered into several agreements with outer-fringe local authorities to ensure the joint provision and management of recreational land, following the traditions of the Corporation of the City of London which purchased land within 40 km of the City's boundaries from 1878 onwards for the provision of public parks and open spaces, *eg* at Chislehurst, Kenley, Hayes, Burnham Beeches and Epping Forest. The twentieth century has seen a more concerted effort on behalf of public authorities to acquire land with preservation and recreational use in mind, culminating in the Green Belt (London and Home Counties) Act 1938. Under this Act the GLC continues to purchase additional land for purposes of preservation and makes financial contributions to other authorities in the furtherance of Green Belt policies. The 1938 Act accepted that recreational land had both an amenity and public health function and subsequent legislative measures (*eg* Town and Country Planning Act 1947 and Countryside Act 1968) have reinforced the powers of local authorities to withhold planning permission or to purchase land in areas set aside for recreational purposes. For example in Surrey alone, the public has access to approximately 56 000 ha of which the greater part is common land, the remainder being land owned or managed by agreement by the county and district authorities. There is also additional land (*c.* 17 500 ha) owned by the National Trust. Many of these areas are 'open' land, in the sense that little or no agricultural activity takes place over them other than a limited amount of commercial forestry, and are dominated by semi-natural vegetation. The peculiar status of common land may render such areas subject to the intermittent exercise of traditional common rights (such as grazing, turf-cutting, firewood collection and fishing) and a few commons in London's urban fringe continue to experience such uses.

The role of the National Trust as a public agency concerned with the preservation of landscape and promoting public access to the countryside is an important one in the Green Belt area of London. Established towards the end of the nineteenth century, the Trust owns and manages substantial tracts of open country and parkland in many urban fringe areas. Sites of particular importance for recreational purposes are the beauty spots of Leith Hill and Box Hill in Surrey and Ivinghoe Beacon in the Chilterns. In conjunction with local authorities, the Trust has also entered into agreements with the Countryside Commission for the establishment of Country Parks on some of their properties. Under the terms of the Countryside Act 1968, the Countryside Commission can make financial contributions towards the costs of setting up and improving a country park, which is defined as an area of land with or without water, within the countryside, normally more than 10 ha in extent, with the basic facilities for the public to enjoy informal open-air recreation (Fig. 11·1). At Frensham Common in Surrey, for example, the National

Trust has leased part of their holding to Waverley District Council which manages it as a Country Park catering for the needs of thousands of visitors each year.

Other Country Parks are owned and managed by county or district authorities offering visitors a variety of facilities ranging from the beauty of the formal gardens and parkland at Trent Park on the northern outskirts of London through the golf course and football pitches available at the Hainault Forest Park on the Havering Ridge east of London, to the wooded walks of Northaw Great Wood in Hertfordshire. The purpose of all these parks is to provide outdoor enjoyment for the public but, in some cases, it is not clear whether this enjoyment is to be gained by providing a minimum of facilities or whether people expect a wide range of facilities to be available in a countryside setting. The latter approach suggests an 'urban' park functioning in the countryside.

Other public agencies that have come to take an interest in providing land for informal recreation include the Forestry Commission and the Nature Conservancy Council. In these cases the primary function of the land is not recreational but in highly suburbanized areas of the Green Belt many of their properties are subject to considerable use by the

11·1 Publicly owned Land in the Green Belt.

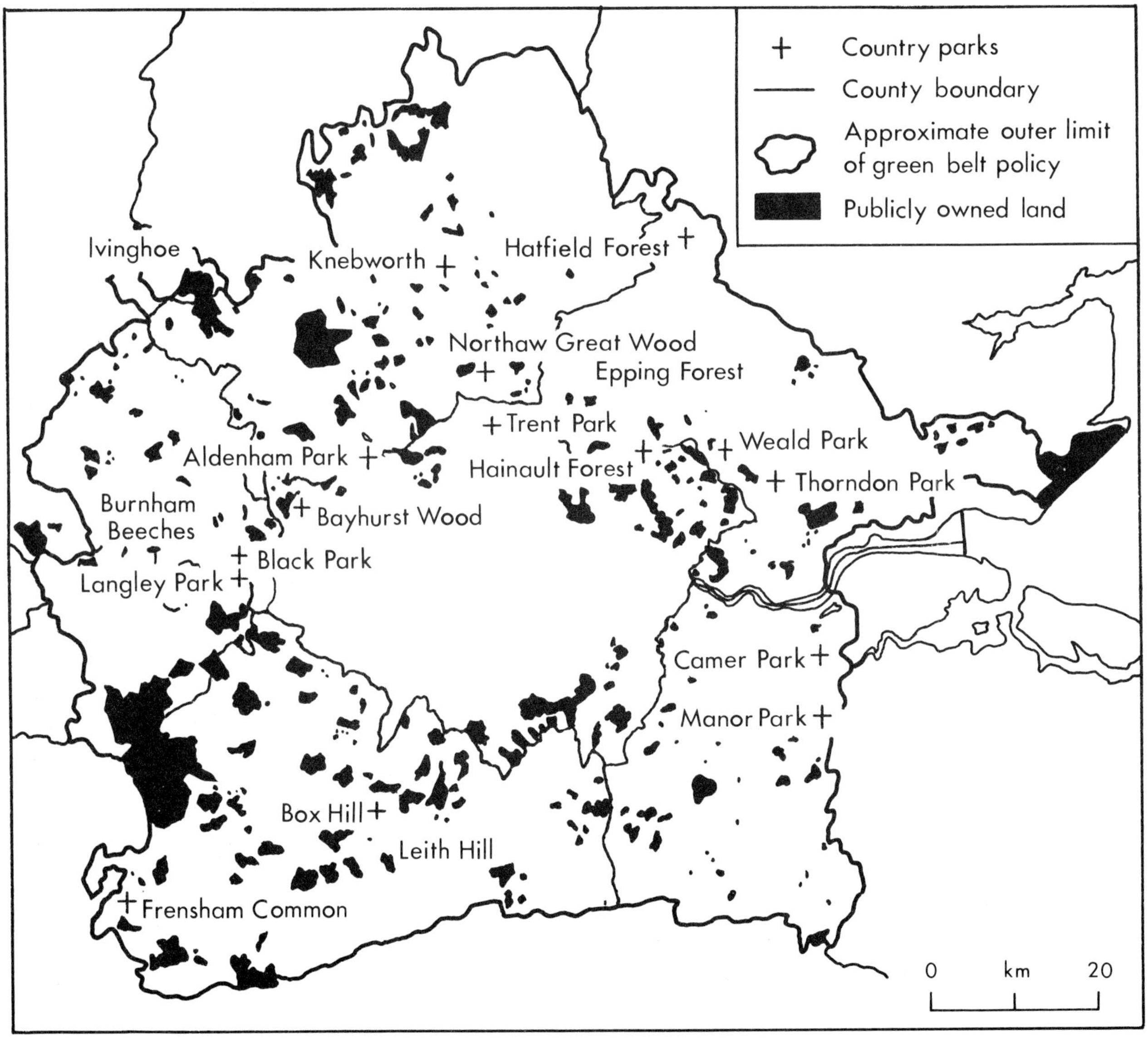

public. As far as the Nature Conservancy Council is concerned access can be gained to most National Nature Reserves, but few are in the immediate vicinity of London. On the other hand, a very large number of sites used for informal recreation are scheduled as Sites of Special Scientific Interest under the National Parks and Access to the Countryside Act 1949. In Surrey, for example, a recent survey of seventeen public open spaces reveals that eight sites were already SSSIs, four were proposed SSSIs and an additional site was pending review. Clearly, recreational use of these sites is not always compatible with their declaration as sites of scientific interest and the sympathetic management of such areas requires co-operation between landowners, the Nature Conservancy Council and the management agency. The Forestry Commission encounters similar management conflicts where public access is not always compatible with growing commercial timber. In the Chilterns, for example, a management programme has been worked out which allows for selected felling and planting in a manner consistent with maintaining the biological richness and essential character of the woodlands.

Various water authorities also own land holdings over which the public enjoy access. Certainly the bank sides of rivers, canals and reservoirs form foci of attraction for weekend walkers, ramblers and picknickers, and several authorities are now entering into more formal agreements with local county authorities to provide a wide range of water and bank-side facilities. Perhaps the most ambitious of these is the Lee Valley Regional Park in north-east London, where the GLC, neighbouring authorities and the water authority have together financed a linear park containing provision for a variety of water-based activities. The Colne Valley Regional Park to the west of London is a similar venture, comprising four authorities (including the GLC) and involving the rehabilitation of gravel workings along some 22 km of valley.

Other areas of land open to the public include those owned by the Crown Estate and the Ministry of Defence. In Surrey, for example, substantial tracts of the heathlands associated with the Bagshot Sands and the sandy outcrops of the Folkestone and Hythe Beds are owned and used by the Army. In some cases access is prohibited, as at West End Common, whereas in others, as at Hankley to the west of Guildford, the public enjoy access on foot and on horseback.

The pattern that emerges as a product of these land holdings is complex. Figure 11·1 depicts land which is publicly owned and, although not all of this is open to the public, the recent report *The Improvement of London's Green Belt* (1976) records that 17 080 ha are designated as Public Open Space in the Green Belt over which access is available. This area represents 8 % of the London Green Belt. The irregular broken chain of sites around London provides a variety of landscapes for public enjoyment but the spatial pattern clearly shows that those residents, in south-west Surrey are better served than either those in Kent or north Essex. There are also important implications of this pattern for the residents of inner London. What is less clear, is the reduced flexibility of management options in those areas that offer only a few scattered and frequently small sites. Nor is it clear that certain sites experience very heavy levels of use which can result in severe environmental deterioration.

Accessibility

A recent GLC study (1975) of how Londoners spend, and would like to spend, their leisure in recreational activities away from home reveals that Saturdays and Sundays form the peak period of demand, with Sunday trips of an informal recreational nature being twice as numerous as Saturday trips. The major locations for visits include the coast, the countryside, parks and zoos, where the major attraction is the range of informal activities of particular importance for family outings. For stops made in the countryside 83 % of the journeys were by car and 13 % on foot. These figures emphasize the negligible proportion of trips being made by public transport and the overwhelming importance of car ownership. However, more than half of inner London's population is made up of households without cars and so existing recreational use of the countryside reflects the socio-economic status of the urban population rather than total possible or latent demand.

In an earlier study researchers were able to demonstrate that recreation provision around London varied sectorally on a *per capita* basis and that car-less residents of inner London in the lower socio-economic groups had very limited opportunities for countryside recreation. For example, pressure in the southern sector (which includes parts of Surrey within 50 km of central London) is of the order of 250 persons/ha, that in the south-east sector (including the north-west of Kent) of the order of 1185 persons/ha and in the north-east approximately 570 persons/ha. When travel and distances are taken into account, particularly those associated with public transport, the potential pressure on the zone within one-and-a-quarter hours' reach of the inner London social areas rose to an average of 1895 persons/ha (Fig. 11·2). Again the southern sector was well off and the south-east poorly provided for. In these circumstances car-less people have limited opportunities for countryside recreation because leisure time is reduced by long journeys dependent on public transport and also because of the high costs involved, particularly where the whole family wishes to participate. Clearly any concerted effort to provide an egalitarian approach to recreation provision would need to take such issues of accessibility into account as well as the purchasing power of individuals who do not take part currently in countryside recreation.

There are, of course, important exceptions but very large numbers of Londoners do participate already in informal recreation out of town. On an average summer Sunday, 189 000 trips are undertaken to the coast plus countryside and some 120 000 trips to the countryside, to areas of inland water or to stately homes. Many of these trips involve whole families so that an estimated 750 000 people might be seeking recreational facilities in the urban fringe around London, with demand peaking between 14·00 and 16·00 on a Sunday. Add to this figure the substantial number of people who live in the urban fringe and also participate in countryside recreation and then the full extent of demand becomes clear. Against the background of this level of demand and the uneven

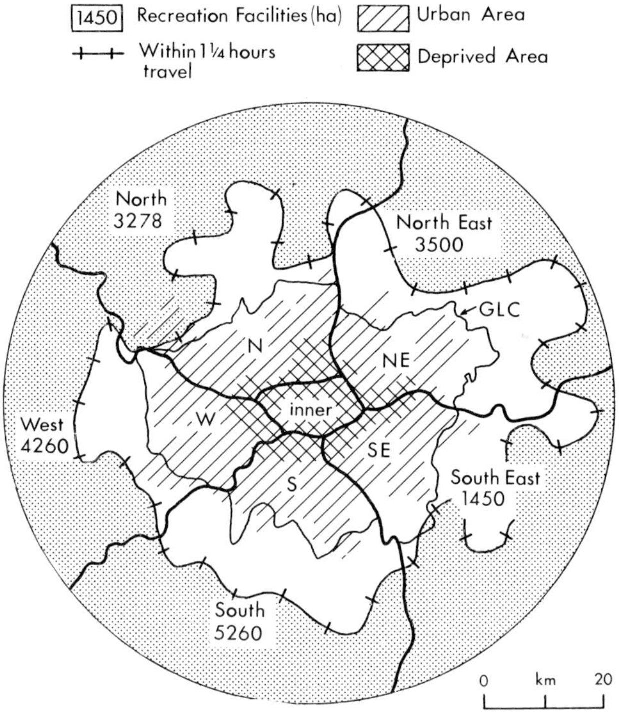

11·2 Accessibility to London's Countryside. (After Law and Perry).

pattern of supply it is not surprising to find that some sites experience very heavy public pressure with serious consequences for the well-being both of users and of the site itself.

Managing Sites for Informal Recreation

Much published work on recreational need has been unable to assess adequately what people require. But, as far as informal countryside recreation is concerned, many users appear to be able to satisfy their needs on the same site and at the same time because few people want specialist facilities. Toilets and refreshment facilities are normally provided, as are car-parks and picnic sites, but most people who use sites for the general pleasure of being out of doors seem to require little else. This does not mean to suggest that all conflicts between users can be avoided. The most noticeable type of problem arises because of the sheer number of people using a site at any one time. Car-parks fill up, access roads become blocked, litter bins spill over, quiet and solitude evaporate, plants are bruised or eroded, and animals move away or fail to breed. The accumulated effect of large numbers of people using the same site at the same time leads to a lessening of enjoyment and in some cases produces irreparable environmental damage. For those concerned with site management for purposes of informal recreation, managing people becomes a prime concern and when those sites have special scientific interest, restrictive management measures may have to be enforced to conserve them. At a more general level, an effort has to be made to manage *groups* of sites, so that the greatest recreational pressure may be diverted to areas that may tolerate it most efficiently. In this way areas that are particularly vulnerable to pressure may be protected.

Evidence of environmental deterioration on sites used for informal recreation is observed all too readily. For example, at Box Hill in Surrey, the chalk slope leading up to the Soloman Memorial at the summit shows signs of advanced damage and erosion and some of the rarer chalk species are declining in abundance. This site is owned by the National Trust, forms part of the Surrey Hills Area of Outstanding Natural Beauty and is notified as a Site of Special Scientific Interest. At Frensham Common in Surrey, which is also owned by the National Trust and is leased to Waverly District Council and managed by them as a Country Park, the shore of the Great Pond is fringed by an extensive sand-field, having been produced by vehicular and pedestrian traffic which now supports scattered patches of the sand-dune plant *Carex arenaria* where previously heathland species such as *Calluna vulgaris* and *Erica cinerea* had been present. On this latter site the only means available to revegetate the area and so contain further erosion is by preventing public access by erecting fences. However, this measure conflicts with the designation of the site as a Country Park and is inconsistent with its use by thousands of visitors each year. Such drastic measures demonstrate the need for an approach to site management that is based on sound understanding of the resilience displayed by various soils, slopes, and plant and animal communities to differing intensities and frequencies of visitor use. Visitors may be directed along particular tracks and trails specially designed to withstand the passage of thousands of feet. For example, one may quote the use of gravel tracks or duck boards on clay substrates and the use of wooden risers on steep slopes. In Epping Forest gravel has been laid on some of the horse tracks in an effort to reduce erosion and at Hindhead in Surrey artificial steps have been cut into the steep, sandy slopes of the western rim of the Devil's Punch Bowl. On other sites special seed mixtures of grass species that are resistant to trampling have been sown in an effort to reduce the impact of cars and people.

A more subtle approach to site management is achieved by providing way-marked paths and trails which direct visitors away from vulnerable habitats and concentrate them on the more resilient substrates. Similarly, a fringing vegetation of spiney gorse or hawthorn can act as a barrier along paths which pass through sensitive areas. Spatial zoning is perhaps the most important concept at the heart of site management. Public pressure may be channelled on to the more resilient substrates by siting car-parks, picnic areas and refreshment facilities on them, allowing other zones to take on a 'wilderness' role and be enjoyed by those who make the effort to do so. For example, the main car-park at Headley Heath in Surrey is sited on the summit's sandy deposit overlying the chalk and the picnic sites on adjacent flat land, leaving the steeper chalk slopes below (which support the most interesting flora and fauna) for a much lower intensity of use. In this way the requirements both of the family group, which does not wish to move more than a few hundred metres from the car, and those of the committed naturalist or seeker of solitude may be satisfied on the same site and at the same time.

However, spatial zoning requires large areas to be implemented successfully. Unfortunately one of the most characteristic features of sites that are available for informal recreation in London's urban fringe is their limited extent. For example, in Surrey the size class distribution of public open spaces (Fig. 11·3) demonstrates that there are few large sites but many small ones that are no more than a few ha apiece. In most cases, therefore, only a very limited amount of spatial zoning may be achieved at any one site. The small size of many sites has implications for the survival rate of some of the plants and animals that are valued by naturalists, students and casual observers alike. Many biogeographers have commented on the relationship both between the size of a site and its biological richness and between its biological richness and degree of isolation. In general the larger the site the more species it contains and the nearer a site is to another of comparable community composition the better the chances of recolonization by individual species. Conversely, the smaller the site the fewer species that are found and the more isolated it is the greater the risk of species becoming extinct. A rule of thumb suggests that for most open, semi-natural communities in England, excluding woodlands, an increase in site area by a factor of ten roughly doubles the number of species present. This means that approximately twice the number of species will be encountered in an area of 200 ha than in one of 20 ha. For this reason it makes good sense to try and conserve large sites if, as a general principle, we wish to retain a diversity of plants and animals in those semi-natural areas that still remain. However, if large sites are not available, a number of small sites may offer an equal variety of ecological conditions and hence habitats such as bog, wet heath, dry heath, scrub and mixed woodland are of particular importance. However, unless these sites are close one to another, areas within them that are subject to uses leading to a decline in species (for example, repeated accidental firing of heath and grassland sites or draining of wet and boggy sites to make way for car-parks or picnic sites) are unlikely to be recolonized from species outside the area concerned. It has been suggested that a distance of 5 km is sufficient to prevent some heathland animal species from recolonizing an area. As a working rule, therefore, it may be just as important to consider the joint management of a range of sites in close proximity to each other if we wish to conserve a variety of wild-life habitats.

11·3 Open Spaces in Surrey.

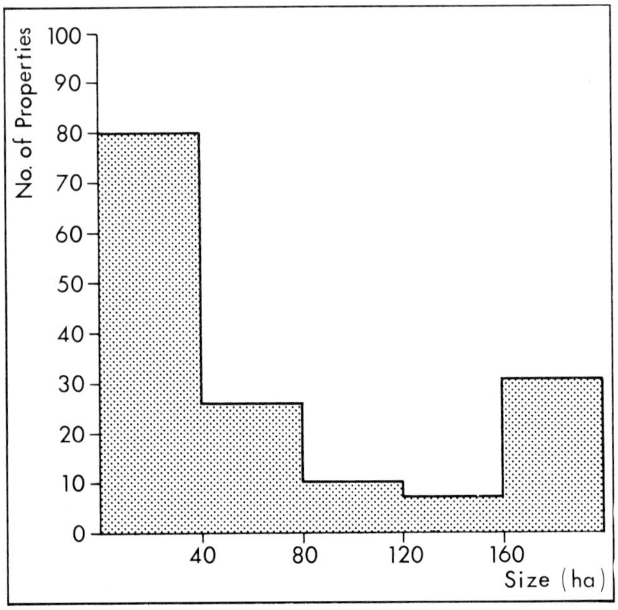

The Regional Park Formula

Where several small sites are close to each other it is possible to manage them on a joint basis and thereby achieve a segregation of uses whilst contributing to the conservation of a range of natural areas. This approach to management is perhaps most easily developed in areas where relatively few landowners are involved and where a single management body has responsibility for each site. It is on this basis that the Regional Park was founded in the Lee Valley, with a single autonomous body. The Colne Valley Park is a co-operative effort between local authorities. In each case the physical setting of the park focuses on water and the fringing plant communities. The upper reaches of the Lee Valley Park support aquatic and marsh communities which are managed as local nature reserves, while its central reaches contain reservoirs and provide yachtsmen and motor boat enthusiasts with ample scope for their pursuits. In the Colne Valley different flooded gravel pits are set aside for specific users and are called 'activity centres'. Intensive activities, such as waterskiing and power-boat racing, are restricted to a limited number of sites while rowing, bathing and organized games occur more widely in other activity centres (Fig. 11·4). Other free-ranging activities include walking, horse riding and cycling and take place throughout the park. Two major routes will run the length of the park, with one following the canal and the River Colne close to the eastern boundary and the other proposed to run close to the western edge. Wildfowl sanctuaries could be located at Stockers Lake, Harefield Moor, the Old Slade Gravel Pit complex and Staines Moor and between them would complete a chain of refuges through and

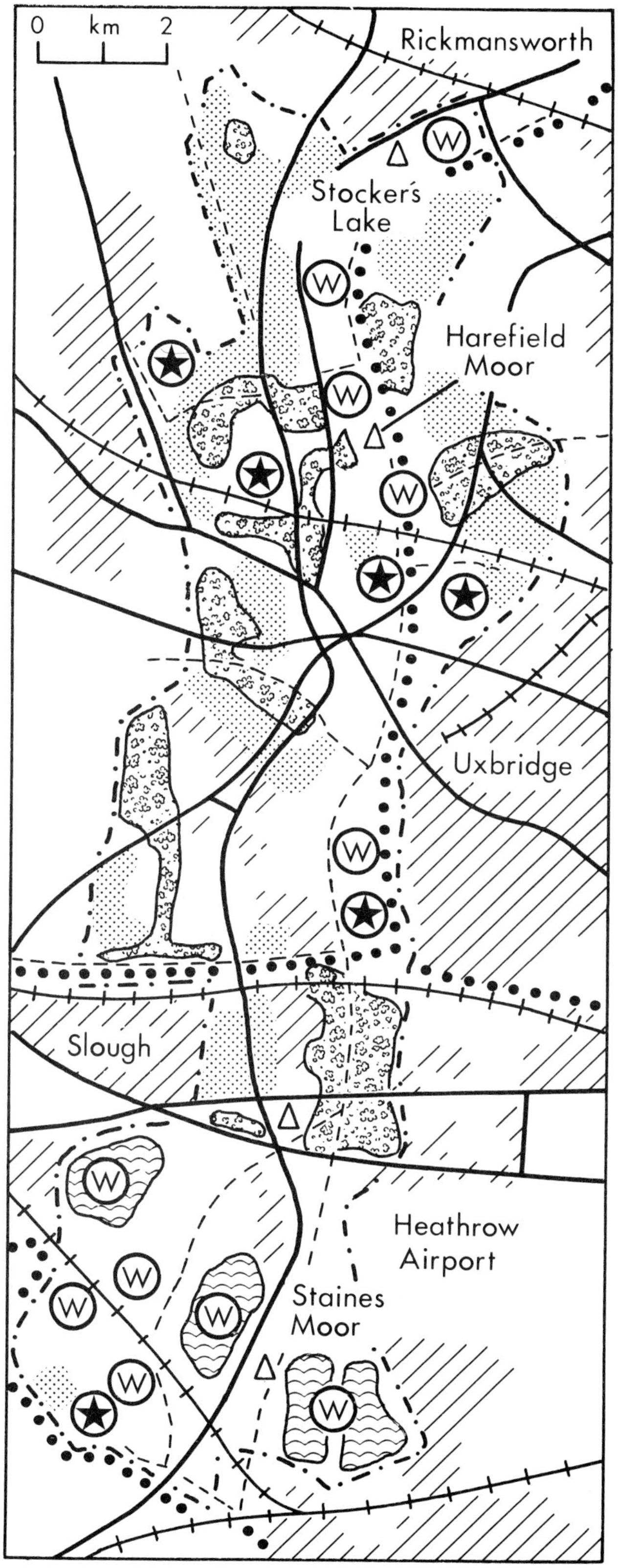

11·4 Colne Valley Regional Park.

beyond the Colne Valley and could therefore assist the migration of wildfowl not just on a regional but also on a national scale.

The concept of the Regional Park has found favour elsewhere in Europe as a means of reconciling the numerous recreational needs of a highly urbanized population. In the urban fringe, where opportunities for creating a better environment are being lost perhaps more quickly than elsewhere, regional parks can serve four valuable functions. First, they can provide a range of facilities that are easily accessible to many people. Second, they can provide opportunities to segregate different users on a controlled basis. Third, they can contribute to wildlife conservation by providing a means of managing groups of adjacent sites on an integrated basis. Finally, they can contribute to a general improvement of the urban fringe landscape. Unfortunately the regional park formula is not applied easily in areas of complex and fragmented landownership that are found in many sections of London's urban fringe. However, the management ideas associated with these parks may be implemented in a more informal sense provided that there is co-operation between landowners, local authorities and advisory bodies concerned with recreation and resource conservation.

Further Reading

Denman, D. R., Roberts, R. A. and Smith, H. J. F., *Commons and Village Greens* (Leonard Hill, London, 1967)

Law, S. and Perry, N. H., 'Countryside Recreation for Londoners', Quarterly Bulletin of the Intelligence Unit GLC, 1971, **14**, pp. 11–26

MacArthur, R. H. and Wilson, E. O., *The Theory of Island Biogeography* (Princeton University Press, 1967)

Stamp, L. D. and Hoskins, W. G., *The Commonlands of England and Wales* (Collins, London, 1963)

12 Water for London

Ted Hollis

Introduction

Cities require water for drinking, sanitation, cleansing, navigation and industrial purposes. Angling, yachting and riparian leisure activities need clean water which conflicts with the function of rivers and estuaries as self-flushing sewers for effluents. Farmers also need water for irrigation and for stock. Their demands must be added to those of city people because of the interrelated nature of the hydrological cycle. Conversely, cities may be threatened by flooding because of heavy rainfall or tidal inundation of estuarine sites.

London meets its water demands from groundwater and from the Thames and its tributaries. Figure 12·1 shows the importance for the Thames of groundwater flow in summer and the significance of winter rainfall for water resources. London's main aquifer is the Chalk and lower Tertiary sands of the London Basin syncline which is recharged by rain falling over the Chilterns and the North Downs. The overlying impermeable London Clay causes the metropolitan watercourses of London to have a flashy regime with low flows between falls of rain. Permeable sands and gravels, which cap London's hills and form the terraces of the Thames and the Lee, store small volumes of groundwater and feed springs. The freshwater flow of the Thames, incorporating treated effluents from upstream towns and from London, discharges to the estuary and thence to the sea. Tides remove these water-borne wastes and are important for navigation but also threaten London with serious inundation.

This chapter examines three themes. First, the water demands of London which have been met by progressively developing its regional water resources. The legacy of capital equipment is proving to be both a valuable legacy and a major liability. Second, the growth of London's demand for water, the sheer size of the urban region and the complexities of the water cycle have required a management framework that is suitable for handling the hydrological cycle and its users. Third, problems are now being encountered because of the continuance of past trends or the

12·1 Monthly Rainfall, Surface Run-Off and Ground-Water Flow averaged over eighty-five years (1883–1967).

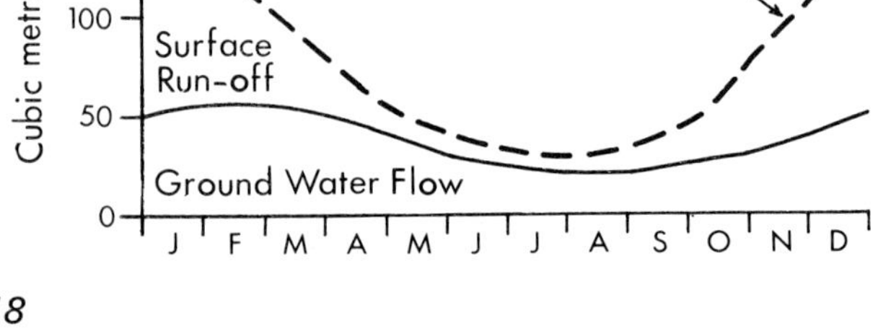

impact of recent changes. A concluding case study of the Lee Valley juxtaposes these themes in a spatial context.

The Inheritance

The nineteenth-century era of poor, polluted water supplies and discharge of untreated sewage to rivers gave way to a drainage system designed by Joseph Bazalgette, safe supplies of water drawn from the Chalk and an ethos requiring public health to be safeguarded before all else. In Bazalgette's scheme (Fig. 12·2) the culverted 'lost rivers' of London were prevented from discharging their rainwater and sewage directly to the Thames by a series of intercepting sewers which took the flow eastwards to Beckton and Crossness. They were designed to flow into storm relief sewers at times of heavy rainfall, with stormwater overflowing into the Thames only during severe storms. Well digging started when steam engines became available for pumping, but the peak rate of well construction was around World War I when about fifty-five wells were bored each year. The Water Act of 1945 introduced a licensing system for wells and precluded further speculative exploitation. The desire to protect public health was pursued through constructing treatment works both for water supplies and for sewage. Two other important hydrological legacies from the nineteenth century are formed by the docks and by London's canal system.

Suburban expansion in this century has greatly enlarged the inheritance. Beyond the LCC area separate sewer systems were normally adopted so that foul water flowed to sewage works and rainwater

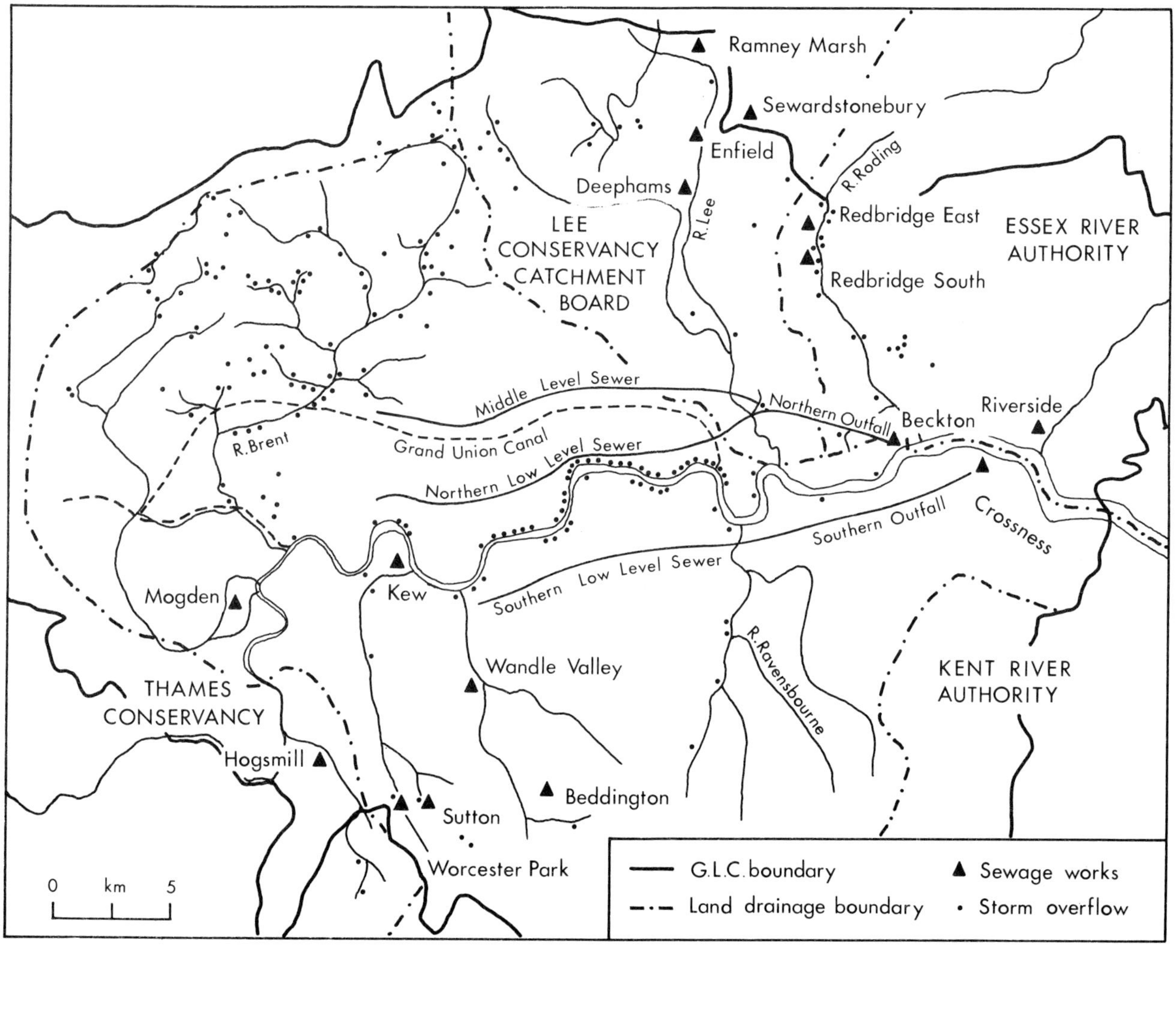

12.2 Land Drainage in Greater London.

discharged to open rivers via a surface water sewer network. Water services were provided for the suburban ring by a few works. The water supply reservoirs, which hold about eighty-eight days' supply, are filled mainly from the Thames (71 % of the total supply), and the Lee (14 % of the total supply). They safeguard supplies during periods of inadequate riverflow and also have an important secondary function in the first stage of water purification. The remaining 15 % of London's water is derived from the Chalk via wells mainly situated south of the Thames. This modest contribution results from excessive pumping prior to 1945 which left the aquifer seriously overdrawn. The well at the National Gallery (Trafalgar Square), for instance, fell by about 48·8 m between 1850 and 1950 but since then its level has been stabilized

The daily average volume of water supplied to the 5 830 000 consumers of the Metropolitan Water Division is around 1 818 400 m^3. This is equivalent to 309*l* (about 0·33 t) per head and approximates an average natural August discharge of the Thames (Fig. 12·1) at Teddington of 2654 tcmd, since 773 tcmd must be allowed to pass over the weir to refresh the estuary. The potable water is distributed via 16 266 km of water mains, of which 16 % is over 61 cm in diameter, and by two major tunnels which convey water from the Thames to augment supplies in the Lee Valley and in south-east London. The sixteen sewage works of greater London serve 8 000 000 people, with the four largest works (Fig. 12·2) alone serving 6 630 000. By comparison, the other 4 000 000 people in the Thames Basin are served by 470 works.

Organization of Water Management

The water management structure for London has evolved to cope with a number of problems which are common to most British cities but are at their greatest in the capital. Such problems include a dependence for water supply upon rivers which are used by towns upstream, a threat of estuarine flooding with major national implications and the need to treat a massive volume of sewage each day. The 1974 reorganization of the water industry in England and Wales, which continued a long-established trend towards fewer and larger authorities, left four organizations and seven water companies in charge of London's water.

The Thames Water Authority has responsibility for all aspects of the water cycle upstream of Teddington Weir and in the river Lee catchment. It has charge of London's water supply through its Metropolitan Water Division and the water companies which act semi-autonomously as its agents. It runs London's sewage works and is responsible for water quality in the Thames estuary. The creation of ten regional water authorities in 1974 was very important for water management in England and Wales because, for the first time, responsibility for all aspects of the water cycle for any one region were vested in a single authority. In the case of London, a unitary view may be taken of the Thames Basin which allows the quality and quantity of water arriving at Teddington to be managed for the benefit both of London and of water users upstream. An optimal regional pattern of resource use, including perhaps local water grids such as the Thames–Lee Tunnel, can be established instead of smaller authorities each pursuing local schemes as happened in the past. Moreover it facilitates sensible water planning so that all water use is accommodated efficiently with a minimum of conflict. Finally, the personal and financial resources of such a large organization make it more able to tackle the problems arising from the great scale of water operations in the Basin.

The GLC is responsible for flood prevention along the tidal Thames and the watercourses of London. The Thames Water Authority is soon to give it responsibility for water based recreation and amenity throughout the GLC area. This arrangement recognizes the comprehensive powers of the GLC and leaves the beneficiaries of flood alleviation works to fund the projects with assistance from government grants. The British Waterways Board owns and operates the Lee Navigation, the Grand Union Canal, the Regents Park Canal and the Brent reservoir. The final organization concerned with water in London is the Port of London Authority, which is responsible for the management of shipping in the estuary and the docks.

Probable and Possible Changes

Six inter-related areas of change will be considered in turn. Some elements in this changing scene continue past trends but others are very recent in origin.

The Ageing of London's Sewers and Water Mains The water mains and sewers of central London are now over one hundred years old and are reaching the end of their useful life. Burst water mains are progressively more frequent, costs of repairs escalate and, perhaps most important of all, huge volumes of treated water can leak away into superficial gravels without being detected for a long time. The condition of the sewers is even more problematical and illustrates a forthcoming national problem as the infrastructures of all our major cities wear out. The sewers of central London are in a doubtful structural condition with more and more being discovered to be in a state of structural decay even nearing collapse. Often they are inadequate in capacity and this produces flooding and the operation of storm overflows which cause pollution by taking dilute sewage direct into the Thames and other rivers. Furthermore, low gradients and frequent roof falls result in considerable deposition of grit which requires regular and expensive removal. It is not easy to give the cost to London of this aged infrastructure. For the whole of the Thames Water Authority area in 1974–5 water mains, waste prevention and inspection made up 19·7% (£9 630 000) of all expenditure on water supply, whilst pumping and sewer maintenance involved a further 19·8% (£9 900 000) of the budget. The replacement or major renovation of mains and sewers will be very costly, even with the new tunnelling techniques already proven in the capital and Thames Water's new responsibility for both systems. Moreover, it will need very careful planning since the urban region has been built on top of the network and water and sewage services will have to be maintained during reconstruction.

Population Changes The population of the London region grew steadily until after World War II. However, intra-regional movements have moved population from inner areas out to the suburbs and particularly to towns and villages beyond the Green Belt. The Metropolitan Water Division area, for instance, served 7 000 000 consumers in 1931–2 but thereafter the number fell to 5 600 000 by 1974–5. Corresponding rises in population in the suburban ring are exemplified by the 10% growth in the number of consumers in the Lee Valley Water Company's area of east Hertfordshire and north-west Essex between 1966 and 1972. This population movement increases the pressure upon resources in the recipient areas which has to be met by schemes such as the Three Valleys Direct Abstraction Scheme which was designed to take up to 227 tcmd from the Thames at Sunnymeads for treatment at a new works at Iver, Buckinghamshire prior to distribution to the Colne and Lee Valley areas. The other major shift in population results from large developments, such as the Grahame Park estate on the site of the old Hendon Aerodrome, and schemes for comprehensive redevelopment such as that proposed for Dockland. A major extension of water and sewage services was required in the former example and a substantial redevelopment of these facilities will be needed in Dockland.

The Increase in the Demand for Water There has been a steady rise in the *per capita* consumption of water nationally and in the London area ever since records began. Within London *per capita* daily consumption has risen steadily from 168*l* in 1912 to 309*l* in 1975. Historically the adoption of bathrooms and indoor toilets increased demand; nowadays the spread of central heating and the use of washing machines and dishwashers continues the long-established trend. The water-supply industry has kept pace with this growth in demand because it reflects improved public health and welfare which form part of the inherited ethos of the industry. This expansion of water supplies requires more waterworks and more sewage works since the volume of sewage that needs treatment rises directly with the water supply. Existing waterworks will accommodate the increased demand from London's declining population but by 1985 the Thames area as a whole will be deficient in water resources by between 140–240 tcmd. There is, however, little land for further reservoirs and the Lee Valley, in particular, has no further sites for reservoirs. This difficult situation led the predecessors of the Thames Water Authority to experiment with two entirely new ideas in British water resources planning. The first scheme increases flows during the critical summer months in the river Kennet near Newbury by pumping water from the Chalk of the Berkshire Downs. The augmented riverflow is then available for use and re-use as it passes down the Thames until it is abstracted for Londoners who are thereby assured of a slightly higher Thames flow in the vital summer months. The scheme uses the underground Chalk of the Berkshire Downs as a river-regulating reservoir which does away with the need to store water artificially and demonstrates how integrated planning of water resources on a catchment basis can provide huge benefits with minimal environmental disruption. The second new scheme involves the storage of up to 205 000 000 m³ of water in the Lee Valley by means of artificial recharge. The dewatered Chalk and Tertiary sands beneath the London Clay in the lower Lee Valley are part of the inheritance, but at the same time they now provide a storage capacity equal to all the existing reservoirs of London. The project involves pumping potable water down a north to south line of wells in the winter and drawing the same water out of the wells in the summer. The scheme is designed to yield 65·9 tcmd at a cost of 6·6p/m³, which is very similar to the cost of water from new surface reservoirs and is obtained without using large areas of valuable land. In addition, because of the new management structure introduced in 1974, more efficient use can be made of existing resources through their linkage or redeployment. A new link is proposed between the west London reservoirs and the Three Valleys Scheme, whilst a rudimentary regional grid system already exists in the form of the Thames–Lee Tunnel.

The growth in population and in the *per capita* quantity of sewage to be treated was more rapid than the improvements undertaken at sewage works. The condition of the Thames steadily deteriorated in consequence and Fig. 12·3 shows that the river was at its worst during the 1950s. Since then there have been major investments at Beckton and a completely new works at Crossness which have cut the polluting effects of 4 600 000 Londoners to less than 25 % of the 1950 value. The quality of the effluent should continue to improve without further major investments because of the declining population and the tidal Thames should also become cleaner. A more direct indication of the improved water quality is the fish life of the Thames. In 1957 there were only eels in the river. Eleven years later a one-day fishing competition was begun with catches during successive years of 0, 169, 40, 52 and 352 fish. A 1974 survey found eighty-two species of fish living in the river, including the first salmon since 1833.

The pressure upon the sewage works in the outer

12·3 Third Quarter Oxygen Sag Curves for Periods 1895–1971.

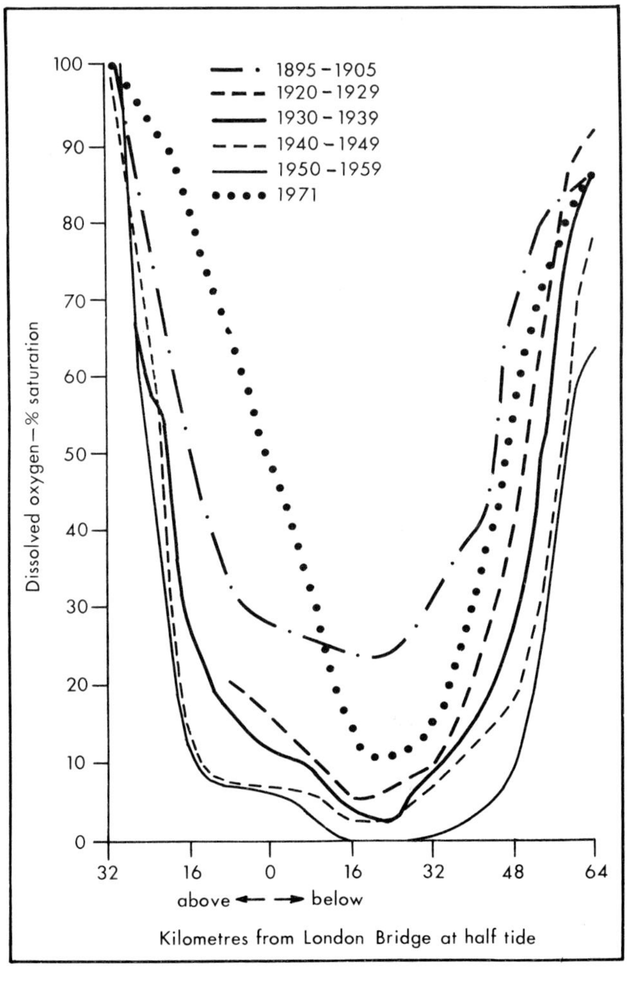

suburban ring is continuing to increase. Their effluent must be of good quality because most of it reappears as someone else's water supply. The lessons of the past have been applied carefully in this area and very large works have been constructed as part of regional schemes rather than under the auspices of single local authorities. The Rye Meads works, for instance, serves Harlow, Stevenage, Welwyn Garden City and surrounding areas. Its effluent is discharged into the river Lee where it is normally of as good quality as that of the river itself. Even though the mixing ratio is often as low as 1:1, with the one part of river water being mostly Luton sewage effluent, the river Lee is tapped 15 km downstream to provide drinking water for London.

The Growing Demand for Water-based Recreation and Amenity The recent escalation of the demand for the amenity use of water led the government to make water-based recreation one of the duties of the Regional Water Authorities. This integration is important because conflicts can very easily occur between recreation and other water uses. For example, anglers and yachtsmen require high water quality, but its maintenance adds significantly to the costs of effluent dischargers. The range of recreation activity fostered by the Thames Water Authority in the London area is shown in Fig. 12·2. The recreational use of storage reservoirs, other than for angling and bird watching, was resisted until very recently because of the fear of pollution of domestic supplies. Modern purification techniques, reservoir water management methods and the growing public demand for access have eased this total prohibition although power boats are still not permitted. Angling has not been downgraded by this extension of recreation, in fact the Authority established trout fisheries at Walthamstow and Kempton Park during the 1970s. Outside London by far the largest recreational use of the Thames is for cruising and sailing. Thirty thousand craft were registered on the freshwater Thames in 1974 and this represented a 43% increase over 1965.

The Grand Union Canal, the Regents Park Canal and the Lee Navigation have some 1600 moorings and are extensively used by cruisers. In 1974 a one-day mid-week count found 301 pleasure boats on the Regents Canal, 161 on the Paddington Branch Canal around Little Venice and 704 on the Grand Union Canal between Brentford and Berkhamsted. The Brent Reservoir also serves some 400 yachts and its banks have a nature reserve, parkland and a schools' project area. In the past the tidal Thames through London has been little used for active recreation because of the tidal range, the poor quality of the water and the dearth of moorings. Nowadays it is sharing in the growth of recreation because of its improved water quality and the development of major new marinas, such as that at St. Katharine Dock. This scheme increased the number of berths between Teddington and Barking Creek by nearly 38% and until the opening of the Royal Albert Dock basin was the only major enclosed area of wet berths. The tidal Thames has seen power-boat racing and perhaps most important of all in terms of participation an extension of leisure activities on moored craft. The World War II heavy cruiser HMS *Belfast* is now moored in the Pool of London; the *Tattershall Castle*, once a paddle-wheel ferry on the Humber, is at the Embankment as an art gallery; and *Gypsy Moth IV* has been set alongside the *Cutty Sark* at Greenwich. The final type of water related recreational development involves the regional parks set up in the Colne and Lee Valleys where linear strips of open land penetrate into densely populated areas. In both of these parks there are large areas of open water as a result of gravel extraction. Both areas now have authorities that are developing a wide range of pursuits, from indoor athletics in large sports centres, to sailing, angling and informal recreation.

Hazards

London is threatened by three hazards associated with water. Tidal inundation is becoming more probable, flooding as a result of excessive rainfall has become a serious problem since the suburban expansion of London in the 1930s and the 1970s have seen insidious rises in the nitrate content of river water which threaten drinking water supplies.

The low-lying land of London has always been subject to flooding by high tides which can be raised by up to 2 m by a North Sea surge caused by strong north-easterly winds. The increasing threat of tidal flooding shown by Fig. 12·4 results from two things. First, south-east England is sinking at a rate of about 30 cm every hundred years. This is largely the result of isostatic readjustment following the disappearance of the Pleistocene ice sheet but the settling of the London Clay and Chalk as a result of the lowered watertable has also contributed to a small extent. Second, the progressive banking, walling, and reclamation that has taken place in the Thames estuary has, paradoxically, exacerbated some flood problems whilst also alleviating others. The East Coast floods of 1953 had little effect on London largely because the breaching of the defences in Essex allowed large volumes of water to spill on to the land instead of moving up the estuary. Since then there have been major improvements to the coastal defences in the outer estuary and reclamation work has continued, often using garbage, brought by barge from London itself. The Ford works at Dagenham, Barking power station and the GLC housing development at Thamesmead are all built at least partly on reclaimed land. This progressive raising of banks and reclamation of marshland prevents flooding but it keeps all of the water in the river which causes it to rise to a higher level than would have been the case without defences. As an interim measure the Thames barrier project will protect the threatened areas outlined on Fig. 12·2. Because the threat was considered so immediate, all the banks and walls were raised by 45 cm between April 1971 and December 1972 and a mov-

12·4 Thames Flood Prevention (showing defence levels 1791–1953 and the structure of the Thames Barrier).

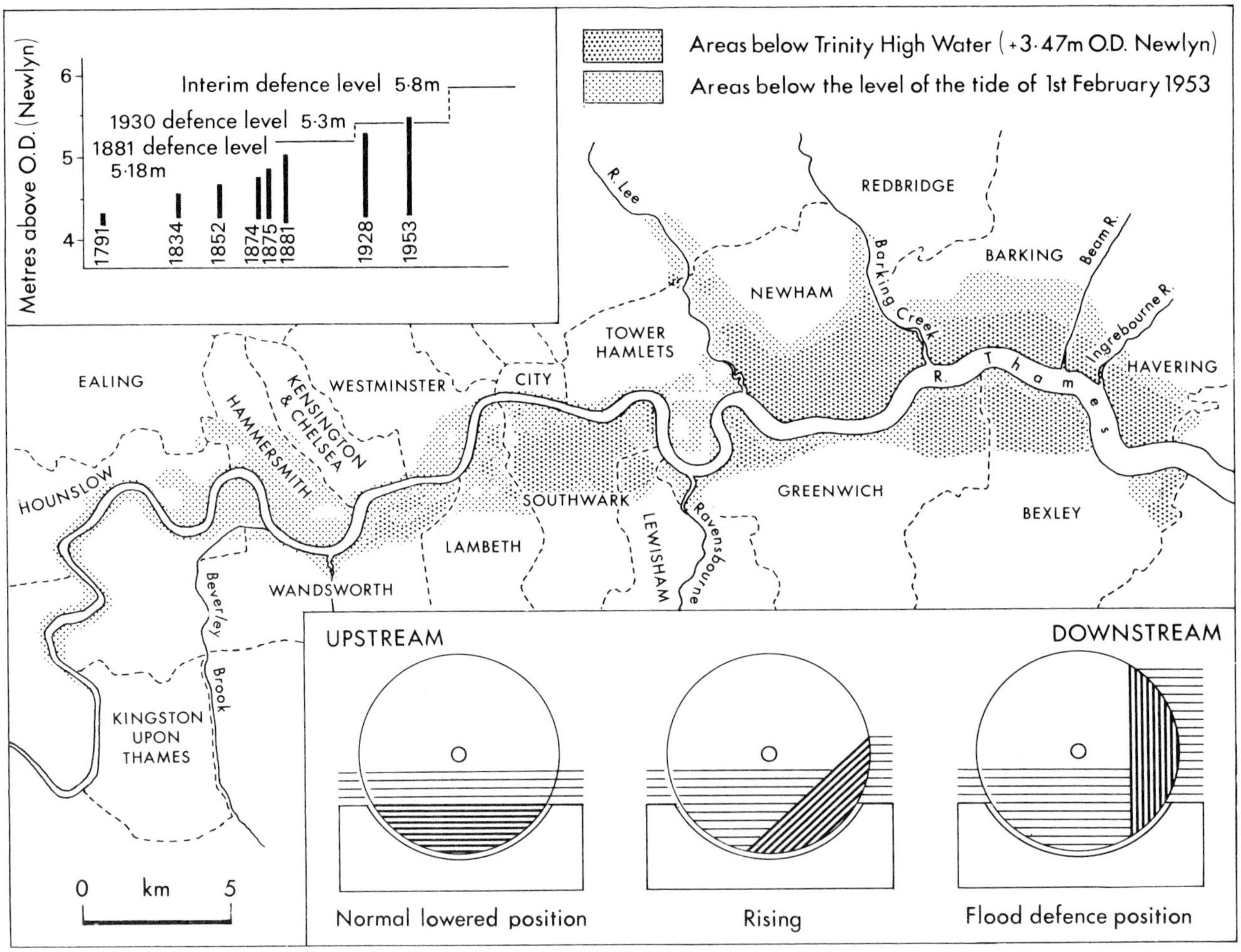

able barrier was built in Bow Creek to avoid the need to raise the banks in the highly industrialized Lee Valley. The barrier project is in two parts. A rising sector gate flood barrier is being constructed in the Silvertown reach of the Thames at Woolwich and 130 km of banks are to be raised along the estuary as far as Southend and the Isle of Grain. The barrier (Fig. 12·4) will prevent flood surges moving up the Thames and the high banks will retain the tide and accommodate the wave that will be reflected from the barrier itself. The cost of the barrier is of the order of £200 000 000 and the banks and walls will involve a further £150 000 000, some of which will be spent at the rate of £2000 per m of wall in areas where it fronts industrial development. The barrier is likely to be closed against floodwater twice a year initially but this may increase to ten times per annum by AD 2030.

A quite separate flooding hazard is that posed by excessive rainfall. There were twenty-five direct flooding incidents between 1965 and 1976 as a result of the overflow of the non-tidal rivers of the London area. This hazard is increasing for four reasons. First, there is some evidence to suggest that intense convectional rainstorms are especially frequent over London. The mechanisms suggested are that London heats the air itself, creates turbulence in the airflow by the roughness of the buildings, and helps rain formation through the release of condensation nuclei in air pollution. Second, the paving of large areas of once permeable land increases the amount and rate of runoff to rivers. This paving is continuing in areas where, for example, Victorian houses are being redeveloped as maisonettes and in new developments such as at Brent Cross, which has the M1 extension, the widened North Circular Road and the new regional shopping centre. Third, the outer London boroughs are steadily improving their surface water sewers. This relieves local flooding caused by the inadequate capacity of sewers but adds significantly to the flow in the rivers. Finally, in spite of planning control, there are still incursions of new development into flood-risk areas and so the potential damage in flood plains is on the increase. The net result of these increases in the Brent catchment is that the once in fifty-year flood will increase in frequency and become the once in ten-year flood later in this century.

Flood relief schemes normally involve a series of elements which may be fitted to local circumstances. Wherever possible open spaces are retained as washlands over which flood water can be stored on sports fields, allotments or parks with a minimum of disruption. Channels are often enlarged where space permits and their efficiency can be improved by aligning concrete or steel piles. Finally, flood water may be stored in flood-regulating reservoirs which may or may not contain a permanent water body. Examples of such schemes may be seen in the Lee Valley, where a new flood relief channel, the widening of the river and extensive improvements to Pymmes Brook, Salmon Brook and Moselle Brook were completed in the 1960s. In the Brent catchment the parks and sports grounds between Hanwell and Perivale are used as washlands. A channel improvement scheme has been undertaken between Brent Cross and Staples Corner; a flood regulating reservoir has been constructed as an integral part of the Grahame Park housing development; and the Brent reservoir is kept 1 m below the spillway by the British Waterways Board in order to store flood water from the upper part of the basin. Once the GLC's planned programme of flood alleviation works is completed the potential flood damage from tidal and non-tidal hazards will be cut to about 5 % of its 1970 value.

The final hazard involves the nitrate content of the Lee and Thames. This has been increasing for many years and after a sharp rise in the early 1970s it equalled or slightly exceeded the maximum level for drinking water recommended by the WHO. The nitrate originates from the solution of agricultural fertilizer, from natural processes in the soil and from effluent where it is a by-product of sewage treatment. The relative importance of the three sources is under investigation but the latter is clearly of considerable importance in the valleys of the Thames and the Lee with their substantial re-use of water. The problem was exacerbated by the dry, mild winters of the early 1970s which increased nitrate production in the soil and reduced riverflows which dilute sewage effluents. The problem was tackled in the short term by taking relatively old and nitrate-free water from the reservoirs and by Thames–Lee transfers of water abstracted when nitrate levels were acceptable in the

Thames. For the longer term, studies have shown that 50% removal of nitrate from sewage effluent is possible at minimal cost, whilst 90% removal is possible before water is put into supply. The nitrate problem therefore appears to be under control but it provides an interesting example of how the intensive use of water and unusual weather conditions can conspire to produce new problems.

Future Management Changes

In spite of the enormous reorganization in 1974, the government has initiated discussion about a National Water Authority to supervize the regional authorities, to undertake national planning of water resources and to equalize charges for water supply and sewage disposal. The implications of this additional management tier are two-fold. First, national planning of water will be the norm, as it was with the Water Resources Board until 1974, and so future supplies of water for the Thames Basin and London may come from the Wye, the Severn, Grafham Water on the Great Ouse and perhaps eventually from the Wash. Second, equalization of water charges will penalize London. Historically, London has invested in an efficient system for water supply and sewage disposal which provides relatively low-cost services so any equalization will involve Londoners paying more in order to subsidize rural areas where there is a much poorer inheritance.

The Case of the Lee Valley

Some of the issues discussed in this chapter are not visible in London. Some are underground, like the 'lost rivers' and the water mains, others are invisible, like the nitrate in river water, the management structure is intangible, and floods are too infrequent for most observers. Conversely, other things are open to view, and a brief survey of the Lee Valley will illustrate many of the points raised and will demonstrate the interrelationship of the parts of the hydrological cycle. The river Lee discharges into the Thames estuary through Bow Creek in the heart of Dockland. As part of the interim bank raising in 1971–2 a falling gate flood barrier was constructed in Bow Creek. This saved the expense and inconvenience of raising flood defences throughout the lower Lee Valley where virtually all of the flood plain is occupied by factories and warehouses. Industry throughout the valley mostly discharges its effluents to the Lee or the Lee Navigation under the surveillance of the Thames Water Authority or the British Waterways Board. Industrial water supplies, abstracted at many points along the Lee Valley, are derived from the river or canal when low-quality water is required for cooling, whilst wells in the Chalk furnish high-quality supplies. The Lee Navigation, which continues to be successful commercially as well as a recreational waterway, has links to the Thames and to the Grand Union Canal.

At Hackney factories give way to the vast open spaces of the Hackney Marshes recreation ground. These are not, however, washland marshes for flood storage because the level of the flood plain was raised by filling it with the rubble left after bombing during World War II. With floodplain storage reduced, flood water merely moves elsewhere and so this reclamation has exacerbated the difficulties of the land drainage engineer. Across the river are the Coppermills waterworks of the Metropolitan Water Division of the Thames Water Authority, where much of the research on nitrate removal has been undertaken. The works can supply 491 tcmd of potable water to east and north-east London. The water is supplied to the works from the Lee Valley reservoirs, notably the Lockwood, Banbury, William Girling and King George reservoirs. These are filled with water from the Lee, which has a very large sewage effluent component, and by Thames water, brought via the tunnel to the pump house at Lockwood reservoir. Much of the water supplied from Coppermills returns as sewage to the nearby Deephams treatment works. The Deephams effluent is discharged to the Pymmes Brook, Salmon Brook and the Lee Navigation, so it reaches the river downstream of the reservoir intakes. The sludge from the works is pumped via sludge mains to Beckton or the Rammey Marsh sludgeworks, just to the north of the King George reservoir. An indication of the degree of development in the floodplain and consequent land drainage problems in this area is given in Fig. 12·5. A major sports and recreation centre for the Lee Valley Regional

Park is located at Picketts' Lock, beside the William Girling reservoir. Beneath the valley, between Coppermills and Waltham Abbey, the Chalk and Tertiaries provide the source of about 4 % of London's water and is the site of the proposed artificial recharge scheme. To the north of Waltham Abbey and comprising the northern part of the Lee Valley Regional Park, there are extensive water-filled gravel workings through which pass the Lee Navigation and the greatly improved channel of the Lee itself. At Broxbourne, the open aqueduct of the New River comes close to the Lee and parallels it to the springs at Amwell, from which water has been carried to London for 460 years. At the confluence of the Stort and the Lee is Rye Meads sewage works that was described earlier as one of the main sources of water for the Lee Valley reservoirs. It was also the site of Thames Water's successful experiments involving the removal of nitrate from sewage. North and eastwards from this point in the valley is the dip slope of the Chilterns. Here, rainfall feeds the rivers and aquifers and the countryside attracts even more people from the metropolis who bring with them their steadily growing demand for water and water services.

Further Reading

Barton, N. L., *The Lost Rivers of London* (Phoenix House and University of Leicester Press, 1962)

12·5 Development in the Middle Section of the Lee Flood Plain.

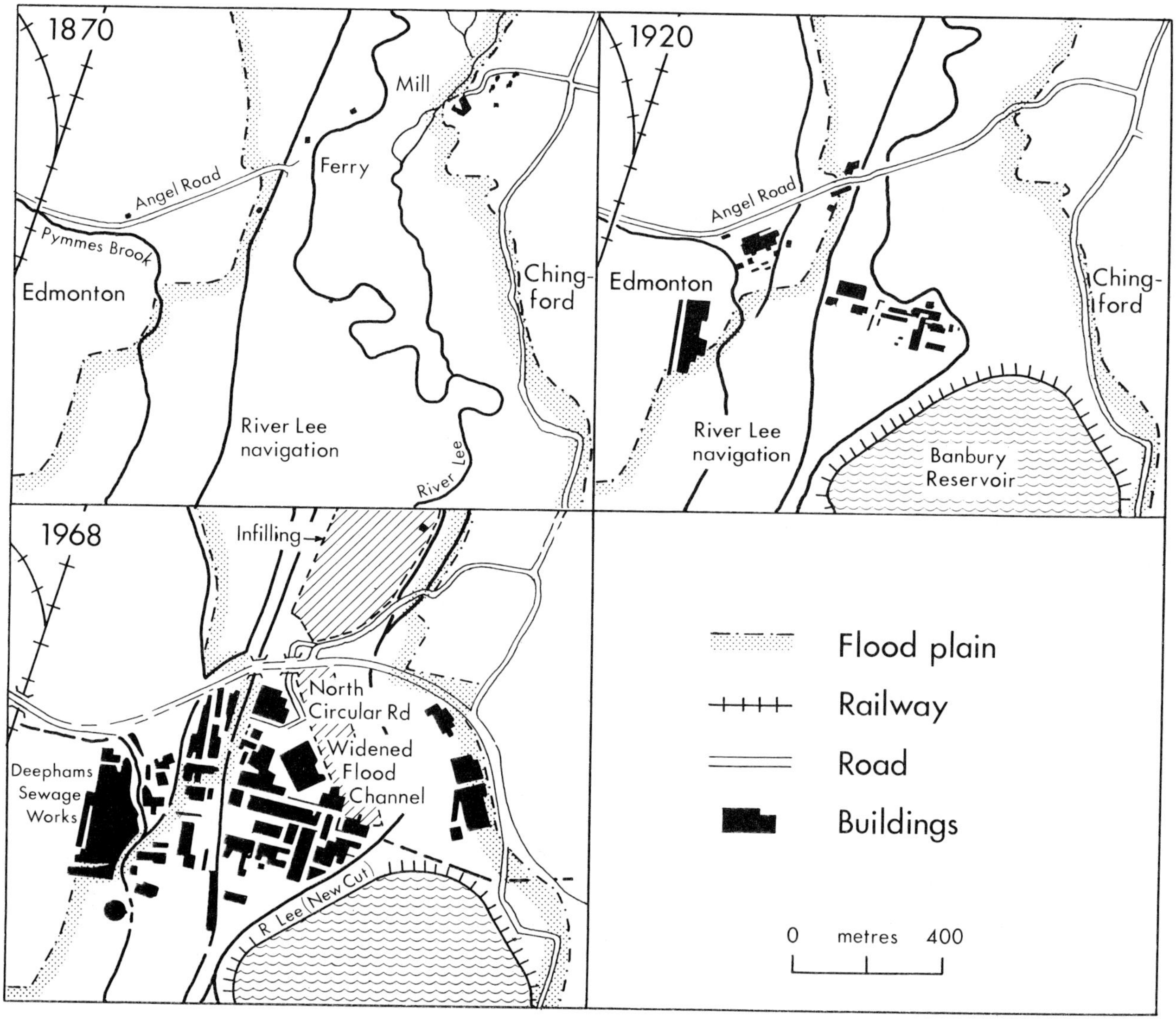

13 London's Changing Meteorology

John Thornes

Introduction

London's meteorological character may be said to be composed of four elements: atmosphere, weather, climate and landscape meteorology. All four are intimately linked but it is the changes within its atmosphere and, in particular, its air chemistry that have produced the most dramatic changes within the other three. London's meteorological atmosphere has been almost as rich a source of inspiration for writers, artists and poets as its social atmosphere. London's 'smog' or 'pea souper' forms an integral part of an 'outsider's' mental image of the place. The term 'smog', a combination of the two words smoke and fog, was first coined with reference to London's air in 1905. However it had been a notorious feature of London's winter weather since probably as early as the thirteenth century, when coal was first used in any quantity in the city. Charles Dickens' characters, in an attempt to drive out the smog, sat snug in front of roaring fires unwittingly adding to the human volcano of smoke. For Shelley, London was a parody of Hell complete with smoky atmosphere. Sherlock Holmes endured the frightening smog enveloping Victorian crime. Victorian London bursting with industrial revolution became known affectionately as 'The Smoke'.

In this century, however, London's air quality has changed dramatically. In the 1970s smoke is no longer a problem in the city but other pollutants, less obvious than smoke, have come to the fore. Central London has one of the highest sulphur dioxide levels in Europe (Fig. 13·1) and displays summer ozone levels comparable with those in other European cities. Vehicular pollutants, such as carbon monoxide (CO), oxides of nitrogen (mainly NO and NO_2) hydrocarbons, photochemically produced ozone (O_3) and aldehydes, have gradually increased in parallel to the growth of London's traffic. The weather and climate of any area is intimately linked to the chemical composition of the air above it. In London and other cities, the vast outpourings of air pollution alter the chemical composition, and hence the weather and climate, to recognizable urban climates. As the chemical composition of London's air has changed so has its urban climate.

In general, the climate of London is a tamed version of the climate of south-east England, although far enough from sea influences to maintain a measure of continentality. London's urban climate has been well documents, however it must be recognized that its influence has changed and expanded with the growth of the city. For example, the landscape artist John Constable, with a studio in Charlotte Street, wrote in his diary for 31 March 1837 of a 'premature ebullition of winter', adding that 'the snow lies very deep and all since four this morning'. At that time Charlotte Street was on the edge of London, near to Marylebone fields and the countryside of Middlesex. Today it is in a closely built-up area just west of Tottenham Court Road where deep snow in winter would be regarded as truly surprising. In fact, snow ploughs have not been used in central London since the notorious winter of 1962–3.

The weather over south-east England manifests a struggle between the influences of land and sea, which give rise to a good deal of undecided, indifferent weather, interspersed with short spells of sunshine and pouring rain. The wet summer of 1974 and the long hot summer of 1976 illustrate the unpredictability of English weather and climate on both daily and annual time scales. Such conditions of change give rise to spectacular skies over London which are rarely appreciated by urban commuters. But, of course, London's landscape meteorology is typically 'urban'. The sky is masked by towering buildings, the wind channels down the streets, and people look anywhere rather than at the sky. However, London is blessed with numerous parks, heaths and bridges which make fine observation points. As Bonacina (1951) remarks 'On many a day of variegated sky in the London region you may see most of the common types of cloud . . . at a high level will be an exquisite web of cross-fibred cirrus, in another direction poised in the blue a band of delicate altocumulus . . . set off in another quarter by a cumulus across whose mountain-like crest shreds of scud may be drifting rapidly—all in endless transmutation throughout the day'.

The view southwards from Hampstead Heath looks into an ideal atmospheric laboratory—exploited to the full by John Constable who was a Hampstead resident. 'Our little drawing room commands a view unsurpassed in Europe.' He painted many such views and usually gave them a sparkling clear atmosphere. By contrast, J. M. W. Turner, his contemporary, observed and painted a smoky London through more realistic eyes for instance in his view of 'London from Greenwich' (1809).

Today a view over London from either Greenwich or Hampstead will surprise the visitor. Very few sources of air pollution are in evidence and visibility over the city is scarcely different from that over the surrounding countryside. This represents a definite change from the traditional image of 'The Smoke'. Why has this change taken place? How noxious is London's present air in comparison to the past? How

13·1 Sulphur Dioxide Pollution in Major European Cities.

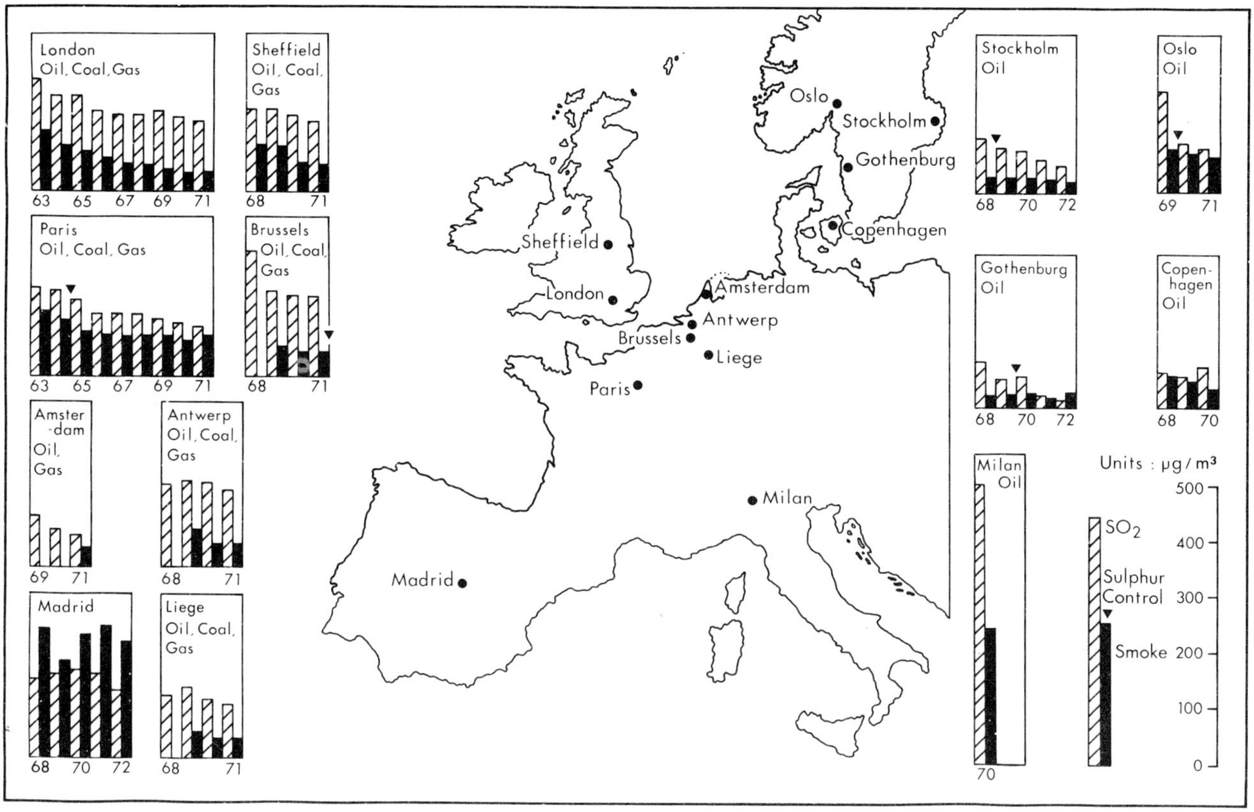

have the weather and climate changed? In order to attempt an answer to these questions we shall look at how the air quality has changed with time and then discover how these changes have modified London's weather, climate and landscape meteorology.

Changes in Air Quality

Particulate Matter Smoke, grit, dust and ash are the four common terms used to describe the particulate matter that is released into the atmosphere. 'Smoke' is often used as a more embracing term to cover smoke, grit and ash that are either produced naturally, as in a forest fire, or by man through the combustion of fossil fuels. 'Air pollution' is usually defined such that only man induced pollutants are considered. Strictly speaking smoke only refers to very small particles (radius $\sim$ 0·035 mm), usually tarry hydrocarbons and resins, which are the product of incomplete combustion. Combustion is a chemical process in which oxygen combines with the fuel being burned to form a new chemical product and the liberation of heat. Much larger particles left as the final product of complete combustion are called ash, grit or dust (typical radius approximately 1 mm − 200 mm +). The very small sizes of smoke particles allows them to penetrate buildings just as a gas, and also to enter the lungs easily.

Coal is the chief source of particulates and the history of smoke as an air pollutant mirrors the history of coal as a fuel. Coal was first brought to London in appreciable quantities from Newcastle in the early thirteenth century being used as ballast for boats returning from Tyneside to London. By 1620 the annual import was approximately 100 000 t, but its acceptance as a replacement fuel for wood was slow, chiefly due to the obnoxious smoke it produced in comparison to wood. However supplies of wood dwindled and became more expensive, and gradually the sales of 'sea-coal' increased.

The first serious indictment against the deleterious effects of smoke from the running of sea-coal came in 1661 from John Evelyn in *Fumifugium*.

'That this Glorious and Ancient City . . . should wrap her stately head in clouds of smoke and sulphur, so full of stink and darkness, I deplore with just Indignation.'

'. . . the City of London resembles the face rather of Mount Etna, the Court of Vulcan, Stromboli or the suburbs of Hell, than an Assembly of Rational Creatures.'

The adverse effect of smoke mixed with accompanying sulphur dioxide was also recognized by Evelyn.

'For is there under Heaven such coughing and sniffing to be heard, as in the London churches and Assemblies of People, where the barking and the spitting is incessant and most importunate.'

'. . . but the chance for life in infants, who are confined in the present Foul Air of London, is so small, that it is highly prudent and commendable to remove them from it as early as possible.'

John Evelyn was an environmentalist centuries ahead of his time. He suggested moving industries downwind of the city and planting gardens along the Thames. However, as with other attempts to limit the use of coal, the relentless economic power of industry and capital triumphed. Coal fired the industrial revolution in London and became the domestic heating fuel for all classes of society. Not that London was covered in a perpetual blanket of smoke. On 3 September 1802 Wordsworth wrote his poem 'Composed upon Westminster Bridge' in which he noted:

'Ships, towers, domes, theatres and temples lie
Open unto the fields, and to the sky;
All bright and glittering in the smokeless air.'

In the nineteenth century came recognition of the fact that smoke affected London's climate, especially in winter, reducing visibility and decreasing the amount of sunshine. Natural fogs are darkened when condensation takes place on smoke particles rather than on natural condensation nuclei to produce smog. As London's suburban housing spread beyond the area defined by the Victorian railway termini so did the frequency of dense fogs. Domestic smoke mingled with factory smoke, railway-engine smoke, and smoke from steamers on the Thames. Victorian winter time saw more than 1 000 000 chimneys belching forth a blanket of smoke. Not that Victorian London was oblivious to all this. In 1819 a committee was appointed by Parliament to enquire 'how far persons using steam engines and furnaces could erect them in a manner less prejudicial to public health'. In 1853–6 the Smoke Abatement Acts came into force relating to metropolitan areas. In 1866 the Sanitation Acts authorized sanitary authorities to take action against smoke nuisance. Further acts followed in 1891, 1926, 1936, 1956, 1968 and 1974. Certainly smoke has been despised and legislated against almost since it first appeared in London. The smoke problem was probably at its worst at the turn of the century. In 1901 the LCC decided to spend £250 to set up a fog survey. The report states that 'the contamination of the air by smoke was forcibly brought to Captain Carpenter's (appointed by the LCC) attention by ten ascents of Victoria Tower (85·4 m at Houses of Parliament) and St. Paul's (dome 91·5 m) between 20 December 1901 and 17 January 1902—none of which were during fogs, and several of which were made on days of great visibility in the country, the visibility ranged from 0·8 km to 2·0 km only. St. Paul's has not yet been seen from Westminster nor Westminster from St. Paul's, although their distance apart is but 2·4 km'.

The study revealed that the fogs were produced in London and that light fogs were permanent in some areas in winter. Interestingly no severe fogs were recorded when the air temperature was above 5 °C. The twentieth century has seen a great reduction in smoke levels in London. It has been shown that smoke levels at Kew have declined steadily since World War I, due in part to the following factors (Fig. 13·2). Industry and commerce have, in general, switched from coal to oil and gas. The railways are now powered by diesel oil or electricity, which have completely replaced steam. Domestic central heating using oil, gas and electricity have become popular due to their convenience. Slum clearance and urban renewal has removed a large number of low-level sources, to be replaced by centrally heated flats and tower blocks. As a fuel coal has become expensive and unfashionable. The Clean Air Acts played their part in accelerating the reduction in smoke levels, however they are by no means the only factor as some would suggest. The 1956 and 1968 Clean Air Acts are most remarkable in that they are aimed exclusively at particulates and ignored other important pollutants. In 1974 the average smoke level for seven sites in central London was 34 mg/m^3 which compares well with the GLC-adopted World Health Organization recommended maximum level of 40 mg/m^3. It appears that most of this smoke in fact comes from vehicle exhausts. This is a very different situation from the turn of the century and has far-reaching effects on London's climate.

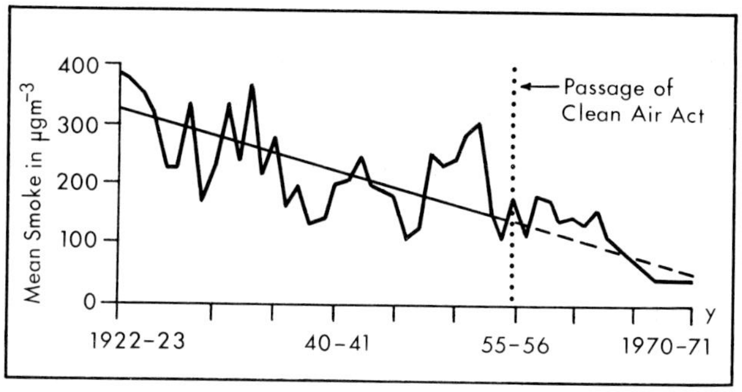

13·2 Average Smoke Levels at Kew during October–March 1922–3 to 1970–1.

Sulphur Dioxide SO_2 has been around for much the same time period as smoke. In 1587 Queen Elizabeth I found the taste of sea-coal smoke annoying. This was probably due to the fact that SO_2 can be detected by taste in the air at lower concentrations than it can by sense of smell. All fossil fuels contain an amount of sulphur which is mostly driven off in the form of SO_2 during combustion. SO_2 is a colourless and generally odourless gas in the concentrations usually found in the atmosphere. The general switch from coal to gas and especially to oil has led to an increase in SO_2 emissions in this century, although the trend towards higher chimneys has led to lower ground levels in the immediate vicinity. All government legislation has ignored SO_2 principally because it is invisible. The Control of Pollution Act 1974 was the first legislation containing regulations about the sulphur content of oil fuel for furnaces and engines. Unfortunately only part of this Act has gone through Parliament.

Central London now has the highest concentrations of SO_2 in the country. Values of more than 2000 mg/m^3 were recorded in 1974 at Crossness sewage works and the average concentration for seven sites in central London in 1974 was 103 mg/m^3 despite the oil crisis. The WHO recommended average level is 60 mg/m^3.

The London SO_2 levels exceed those of most other European cities (Fig. 13·1). It has only recently been established that SO_2 can affect London's climate. The formation of sulphuric acid aerosols in the atmosphere via photo-oxidation affects not only London's radiation balance but also its visibility. The decrease in smoke amounts has led to an increase in the amount of solar radiation reaching the ground in London. Although SO_2 levels are at a maximum in winter when space heating is most needed, nevertheless the amount of photo-oxidation has increased in summer. SO_2 is also damaging to certain plants, building materials, paper, leather, metals and works of art, although there is no evidence to suggest that it is harmful to man in the absence of particulate smoke. SO_2 remains a serious problem in London especially when it joins in the photochemical broth that is generated over London in summer.

Today, central London looks remarkably clean. However appearances can be deceptive. For instance, two notable sources of pollution in central London are Battersea and Bankside power stations. The white plume from Bankside is much more noticeable than the grey plume at Battersea, giving one the impression that the Bankside plume is more harmful, especially as it usually appears to drift horizontally when it leaves the rather short stack. However, in 1975/6 Battersea power station, which burns mostly coal but some oil, released approximately 4000 t of invisible SO_2, 300 t of particulates and 1000 t of nitrogen oxides into the atmosphere. Bankside, on the other hand, emitted only 100 t of SO_2, 60 t of particulates and 700 t of nitrogen oxides, despite burning exclusively oil which has a high sulphur content. The forty-fold difference in SO_2 emission is due to the fact that the Bankside plume is 'washed' to remove the SO_2. This reduces the temperature of the plume and makes it less buoyant when it enters the atmosphere. The visible part of the plume is water vapour. In fact, the pollution is not dispersed as efficiently as with a non-washed plume such as that at Battersea. Experiments to wash the plume at Battersea showed that the extra expense would not compensate the influence of its reduced buoyancy on residential areas nearby. This example serves to emphasize the point that visual appearance is a poor guide to the nature of a pollutant.

Vehicular Pollutants For the most part so far we have considered SO_2 and smoke to be emitted from stationary sources and to be seasonal. Vehicular pollutants, however, are emitted from moving sources in similar concentrations throughout the year. The growth of traffic in central London reached saturation point in the late 1960s and early 1970s. Since 1973 there has been a reduction in total traffic flow due to the removal of parking places and the introduction of bus lanes. Yet the summers of 1975 and 1976 saw the introduction of photochemical smog to London for long periods. The reduction in winter and summer smoke levels has meant an increase in sunshine levels, and hence the production of photochemical reactions.

Carbon Monoxide CO is an odourless, tasteless, colourless poisonous gas that appears as another product of incomplete combustion of fossil fuels containing carbon, and is now produced principally as an exhaust gas from petrol vehicles. It has been estimated that man produces 250 000 000 t annually via inadequate combustion of fuel, which makes it the commonest man-made air pollutant. In the UK in 1974 petrol engines produced $\simeq$ 7 800 000 t of CO (diesel engines produced 12 000 t) as opposed to a total UK SO_2 production of $\simeq$ 5 400 000 t and 500 000 t of smoke (Table 11).

Rush hour concentrations of 20–30 ppm CO are common in London, although values up to 300 ppm have been recorded. However in comparison to cigarette smoke, which contains $\simeq$ 500 ppm CO, the non-smoker is in less danger in a London street than a smoker in the countryside. CO has a greater affinity for haemoglobin (200x) in the blood than oxygen, and hence CO is taken up by the blood in preference to O_2. In extreme cases death can result and, even at low concentrations, athletic efficiency is reduced due to oxygen starvation. CO also takes part in photochemical reactions. Records of CO concentrations have not been kept consistently in London and therefore it is impossible to tell how levels have changed during this century. As much as 13% of a petrol engine exhaust is CO. Levels must have paralleled the growth in vehicular traffic in London. The 1974 Control of Pollution Act, if eventually passed in its entirety, will allow some control on the emissions of CO and other vehicular pollutants, however until that time recommended maximum levels for London are pointless, and actual levels will depend upon meteorological conditions.

Nitrogen Oxides and Photochemical Smog As the amount of vehicular pollution produced in London has increased so we would expect that chemical reactions within the atmosphere are more likely. Table 11 lists the other major pollutants from vehicles as hydrocarbons, aldehydes, nitrogen oxides and sulphurous oxides. Just as London was world famous for its 'pea souper' smog, so Los Angeles is equally famous for its photochemical smog. However, although the pea souper has disappeared (one hopes for good) photochemical smog in summer in London is now a reality. The intensity of vehicle exhausts in London is now at such a level, that coupled with slightly increased direct solar radiation due to a decrease in summer smoke levels, ozone is being produced in sufficient quantities to be harmful to Londoners.

TABLE 11 Estimates of Pollutants from Road Vehicles in the UK in 1974 Million Tonnes. (Consumption of Motor Spirit: 16 480 000 t; Consumption of Derv Fuel: 5 520 000 t)

Pollutant	*Petrol Engines*	*Diesel Engines*
Carbon monoxide	7·8	0·12
Hydrocarbons	0·38	0·023
Aldehydes	0·01	0·003
Oxides of nitrogen	0·24	0·07
Oxides of Sulphur	0·013	0·04

Records of O_3 concentrations have only been kept in London since 1972 but it is clear that the hot summers of 1975 and 1976 produced ozone levels much higher than the GLC/WHO recommended maximum level of 8 pphm. On 13 July 1972 a peak value of 11 pphm was recorded and on 26 June 1975 15 pphm was noted. At these levels eye irritation and aggravation of respiratory diseases may be expected. In the summer of 1976 the guideline figure was exceeded for up to forty hours per week and a peak value of 21 pphm was recorded. This is still below the peak values recorded elsewhere, *eg* 28 pphm Sydney, 30 pphm Tokyo and 99 pphm in Los Angeles, but it is an alarming trend none the less.

Ozone production is complicated but is basically a function of air temperature and solar radiation if the correct mixture of vehicular pollutants is available. The summers of 1975 and 1976 were extremely hot and dry with very high sunshine levels. This undoubtedly led to the peak levels recorded in London but there is no reason why even higher levels should not be recorded in the height of any summer. Ozone is present in the lower atmosphere at background levels of 2–4 pphm. The high levels are generated in two ways. First, some ozone is imported from the Continent during anticyclonic conditions with easterly winds (in London's case), coming perhaps from the Ruhr, Rotterdam or Paris. Ozone can travel 100–1000 km in the lower atmosphere. The second component is that which is produced *in situ* in London. The exact balance is hard to assess and varies with each anticyclone.

Ozone Production 'In Situ' Figure 13·3 shows a typical daily concentration of the constituents of a photochemical smog. Four stages can be identified:

(i) The injection of hydrocarbons and NO from vehicle exhausts during the morning rush hour.
(ii) Increasing solar radiation—decrease in NO and increase in NO_2 and aldehydes.
(iii) Decrease in NO_2, O_3 increases to a maximum around midday with a corresponding aldehyde peak.

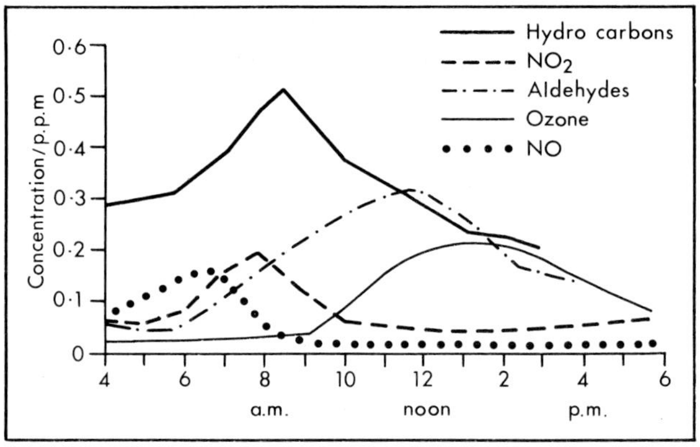

13·3 Average Concentrations of Some Atmospheric Constituents during Days of Eye Irritation in Los Angeles.

(iv) Ozone and aldehyde levels fall but note that there is no increase in NO or hydrocarbons during the evening rush hour.

How can this sequence of events be explained? In simple terms the NO is oxidized by the hydrocarbons to NO_2 which is dissociated by sunlight into NO and atomic oxygen O. The atomic oxygen then combines with an oxygen molecule to give O_3. The aldehydes are the remains of the hydrocarbon oxidation of NO. During the afternoon the O_3 reacts with any remaining NO_2 to create a nitric acid aerosol, and also the O_3 reacts with the aldehydes. The injected NO and hydrocarbons in the evening rush hour are completely removed by the O_3. Until recently it was thought that CO was inert to these reactions. However it appears that CO can help oxidize NO–NO_2, and hence ultimately increase O_3 levels.

Similarly, recent work has shown that SO_2 reacts with O_3 in the presence of hydrocarbons to form SO_3 which readily creates a sulphuric acid mist. This mist and the absorption of visible light by NO_2 and the nitric acid aerosol reduces daytime visibility via a brownish photochemical smog. Thus in summer London's climate is undoubtedly affected by the formation of photochemical smog. Legislation is needed to restrict vehicle exhaust emissions. California has already imposed very strict emission laws and, despite objections from vehicle manufacturers that the levels would be impossible to achieve, emissions have been cut to the required standard. The 1977 California standard is a maximum emission of 0·26 gm/km hydrocarbons, 5·6 gm/km CO and 0·94 gm/km NOx. The Volvo car corporation has already produced a model that produces only 0·13 gm/km HC, 1·75 gm/km CO and 0·11 gm/km NOx at an additional cost of less than £25 per car. In Britain we have no standard at all. Is it fair on the Londoner who has to breathe the smog?

Lead in Suspension Lead is the most important of the heavy metal pollutants and is principally produced into the atmosphere by motor vehicles. Levels of up to 4·1 mg/m^3 have been recorded in central London which exceeds the GLC guideline level of 3 mg/m^3. In the whole of the UK it was estimated that 7780 t of lead were discharged into the atmosphere in 1974 by motor vehicles. This could be entirely avoided if lead free petrol was used. However only in North America is lead free petrol available, and there is no sign of it being introduced in the UK. Lead levels have only been monitored very recently but it is reasonable to assume that present levels are as high as at any time in the past.

Thus it can be seen that the chemical composition of the air that Londoners breathe has changed dramatically this century, with a reduction in particulates but an increase in vehicular pollutants and to some extent in SO_2. Air pollution must affect the climate of any region and the intimate relationship between air pollution and urban climate is the subject of much research. However, some comments may be made as to how London's climate has changed as a result of changes in its air chemistry.

London's Changing Weather and Climate

Luke Howard produced the first authoritative account of London's urban climate when he published *The Climate of London* in 1818. He recognized that the very presence of a large city must interact with the atmosphere to induce an urban climate, writing:

'the temperature of the *City* is not to be considered as

that of the *climate*; it partakes too much of an artificial warmth, induced by its structure, by a crowded population, and the consumption of great quantities of fuel in fires.'

He was also very much aware of the effect of smoke on the weather. His weather diary 10 January 1812 reads:

'London was this day involved, for several hours, in palpable darkness . . . The sky, where any light pervaded it, showed the aspect of bronze . . . Were it not for the extreme mobility of the atmosphere, this volcano of 100 000 mouths would, in winter be scarcely habitable!'

The weather and climate experienced by an area are a function of a set of meteorological variables—on a given day for weather, or averaged to give the climate. The urban fabric and its inhabitants, together with air pollution, have a considerable effect on the weather and climate of the Thames Basin. Were London not present the Thames Basin would experience significantly different weather and climate. As London has grown so its climate has changed, however it is very difficult to isolate cause and effect, for instance to isolate the effect of air pollution from that produced by changes in the urban fabric or 'geoclimate'. (This term describes the climate measured by standard meteorological stations on a scale of several hundred km.)

The meteorological factors that make up the matrix of weather and climate are wind velocity, net radiation, air and surface temperature, evaporation, precipitation and visibility. It is impossible to consider these meteorological variables in isolation since they are all intimately linked. A change in air pollution is likely to have an effect on all of them. Increased winter sunshine and decrease in the number of fogs are two well documented changes that have occurred this century. Changes in the net radiation balance have therefore taken place but this is more difficult to isolate. Many studies assume that the total radiation falling on a horizontal surface is 15 to 20 % less in an urban area due to air pollution. This is based chiefly on data relating to smoke concentrations that are no longer realistic. The radiation balance controls to a great extent the heat balance at a surface. Any change in the radiation balance must affect surface temperatures and hence the strength of the heat island. The heat balance also controls evaporation rates, with the more solar radiation getting through to the surface the greater being the evaporation.

Dust and smoke undoubtedly provided condensation nuclei above London which no longer occur in such quantities as in the past. This may have had a marginal influence on condensation and hence precipitation. Increased penetration of solar radiation in summer may lead to more vigorous thermal activity and urban based thunderstorms, however this is subject to the absence of photochemical smog.

Visibility Well before the Clean Air Act of 1956 meteorologists were writing of the decline in the number of London's 'pea souper' fogs. Five-yearly running means for days with visibility less than 1000 m at 09·00 GMT at the London Weather Centre in Holborn have reduced from 48·6 in the five years ending 1950 to 5·2 in the five years ending 1975. This is a dramatic reduction, although the decline has been gradual since the peak at about the turn of the century. This reduction is almost entirely due to the reduction of smoke levels in central London over the same period. Summer visibility has declined in recent years due to the occurrence of photochemical smog. This is at its worst in the afternoon when the sulphurous and nitrous aerosols have had a chance to develop.

Sunshine Levels Corresponding to the increase in visibility in central London, winter sunshine levels have risen by comparison with locations in the suburbs and beyond. Figure 13·4 shows the duration of sunshine in hours for ten-year running means at the London Weather Centre, Kew, Wisley and Rothamsted using data for 1930–77. Whilst the values at Rothamsted and Wisley have fluctuated around a steady mean, the hours at Kew have increased from an average of 1·55 to 1·8 hours/day. The increase at the London Weather Centre is even more dramatic, rising from a minimum just below 1·0 to $\simeq$ 1·75 hours/day. These figures represent sunshine hours

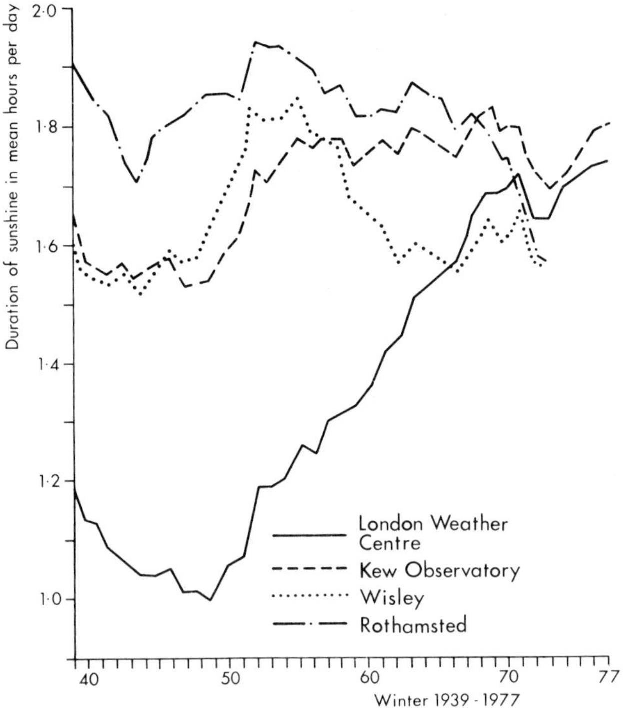

13·4 Trend of Winter Sunshine around London (by ten year running mean).

which are a function of direct solar radiation reaching the instrument. The increase is undoubtedly due again to the reduction in smoke and dust which means that less direct solar radiation is scattered into diffuse radiation. Sunshine levels have been remarkably high in the summers of 1975 and 1976, which were also the two summers of maximum ozone production in London. There is not yet sufficient information to ascertain whether or not absorption of the solar beam by ozone has led to a significant reduction in summer sunshine levels.

The Radiation Balance An oft quoted figure for the excess dust or smoke in an urban atmosphere is a factor of ten. This is said to reduce the incoming solar radiation to a horizontal surface by 15–20 %. At night that same dust absorbs terrestrial radiation and is thought to encourage the formation of an elevated inversion which forms the lid of the nocturnal pollution dome over cities on calm clear nights (Fig. 13·5). Take away that smoke and dust and replace it with ozone, nitrogen oxides, carbon monoxide and what is the resultant effect on the radiation balance? Nitrogen dioxide absorbs solar radiation which causes heating of the air layers above the surface. To a lesser extent SO_2 and O_3 also absorb solar radiation, lowering solar radiation receipt at the ground. Ozone is an effective emitter of long-wave radiation and can cause appreciable infra-red cooling rates in the air at night. The exact changes in the radiation balance have not yet been fully documented. Nevertheless it is likely that the urban heat island has been strengthened in winter due to the increased penetration of solar radiation. Perhaps a corresponding reduction might be noted in summer, but further research is needed to isolate the effects of changing pollution levels.

Conclusion

The climate of London has never been static, and any attempt to define it is likely to be out of date as soon as the report is published. One must stress that geoclimates and urban climates change on many time scales. The interrelationship between the geoclimate and the urban climate is complicated and unique for each city region. It would certainly be foolish to suggest that recent changes in London's urban cli-

13·5 The downward infrared radiation from the urban smoke layer warms the lower layers of air over the city and inhibits the formation of a night-time inversion. The night-time mixed layer is, therefore, present in the city but not in the country during periods of clear skies and light regional winds.

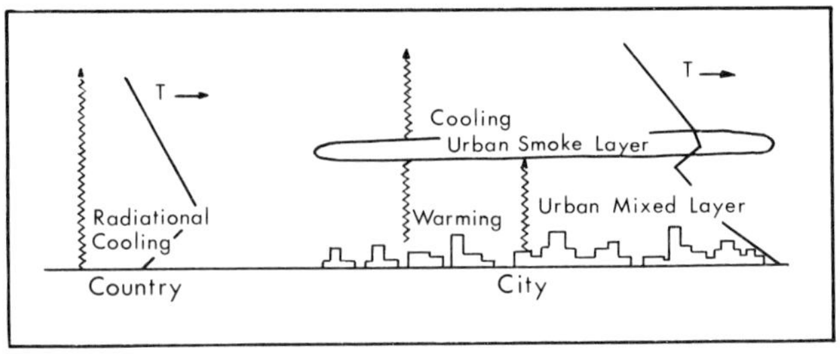

mate are due to changes in air chemistry alone. But one important question remains to be asked. Have the changes been beneficial for the Londoner? Certainly London is a much cleaner city than it was, and visually it is a pleasanter place to travel through and to live in. Its landscape meteorology has been improved by increases in visibility and in hours of sunshine. However, it must be remembered that other, less visible pollutants are present in quantities that make London's air unpleasant and even dangerous to breathe on some occasions. Legislation and other means must be sought to reduce pollution levels and to improve air quality. The full meteorological implications of such moves must also be examined. In the future, it is likely that vehicular pollution will be reduced in central London as more disincentives to exclude private cars are devised. The EEC are currently reviewing vehicle emissions and new common standards may be adopted similar to those in California. North Sea oil has a slightly lower sulphur content in general than most oil from the Middle East, so it may be envisaged that SO_2 emissions may fall marginally. However London still has a long way to go to bring pollution levels down to WHO recommendations. Purer air will certainly improve the quality of life in London. A sunnier climate, fresh air to breathe and a clearer view of the sky, clouds and urban landscape would be immense advantages.

Further Reading

Barry, R. G. and Chorley, R. J., *Atmosphere, Weather and Climate* (Methuen, London, 1976)

Chandler, T. J., *The Climate of London* (Hutchison, London, 1965)

Chandler, T. J. and Gregory, S. (eds) *The Climate of the British Isles* (Longman, London, 1976)

Scorer, R. S., *Pollution in the Air: problems, policies and priorities* (Routledge and Kegan Paul, London, 1973)

14 Land under London

Eric Brown

Introduction

The benefits and hazards inherent in the physical site and situation of London, their attendant physical resources and aesthetic values are not and never have been of an obvious kind. So muted and subtle is their influence upon the totality of the urban geography of London it is no wonder that considerations of economic social and political forces tend to dominate studies of London. Nevertheless a full understanding of the location, character and functioning of the metropolis needs not only to consider the influence of the physical environment upon London but at least as importantly, the influence of London upon its environment. For a radically new physical environment impervious in character, cellular in plan and rough in surface texture of tarmacadam, concrete, brick, stone, tile and slate has replaced the forested environment of prehistory and even the villages, farms and fields of historic times.

The Underpinnings of London

The real foundation of London is a stable platform of old hard rocks of Palaeozoic age akin to those outcropping in the Mendips to the west and in the Nuneaton area to the north but beneath London buried by some 300 m of younger Mesozoic and Tertiary sediments (Fig. 14·1). In 1870 a bore hole put down in Kentish Town by the Hampstead Water Works, in search of ground water in Lower Greensand strata, passed through the Chalk and the expected layer of Gault Clay beneath it but instead of then encountering the Lower Greensand, as the sequence of surface outcrops south of London in the Weald suggests would be the case, entered much older and harder Devonian rocks at a depth of 250 m below sea level. A similar bore at Meux's Brewery in Tottenham Court Road did the same at a depth of 299 m below sea level and in 1911 at Stonebridge Park drilling below the base of the Gault at 295 m into the basement rocks showed traces of oil, gas and salt water. A buried coalfield like that discovered in a similar situation in Kent at approximately the same time has never been detected beneath London. South of London the basement slopes steeply to depths of over 1600 m below the Weald and 4000 m below the Isle of Wight.

A 50 m or so thick layer of Gault Clay everywhere rests on the basement platform and forms a waterproof bottom to the much more permeable 4 m of Upper Greensand and 200 m of Chalk, a soft white limestone with flints. The Chalk is divisible into a relatively jointed and unfissured Lower Chalk (55–67 m) massively bedded, flintless, white and grey marly chalk, Middle Chalk (46–67 m), pure chalk with a few marl seams and flints and the Upper Chalk, very pure, frequently rough and nodular in character and containing abundant flints. In the Upper Chalk bedding planes, joints and fissures are well developed so that ground water moves more readily through it than it does through the Middle and Lower Chalk.

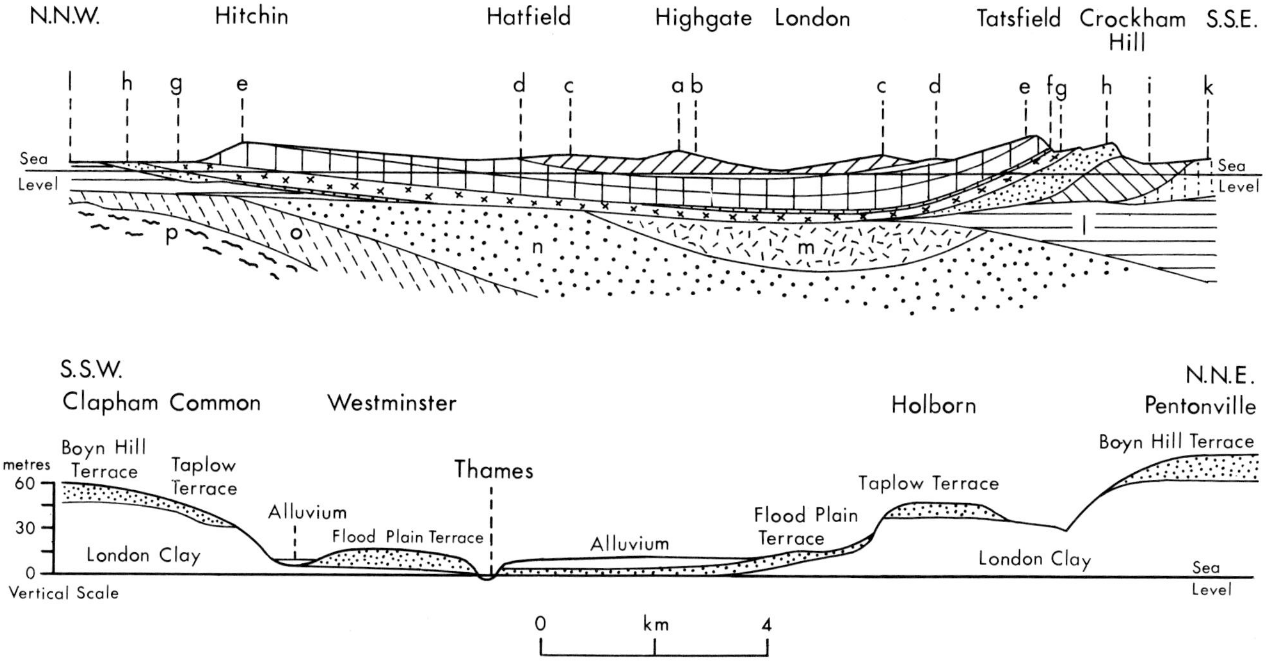

14·1 Generalized Section across the London Basin; and Section from Clapham Common to Pentonville.

This thick pile of cover rocks resting on the basement platform are folded into a synclinal downfold with a west–east axis plunging eastwards into the North Sea basin. The axis is not straight but in the vicinity of London runs north-eastwards from Wimbledon Common to Deptford. The south-eastward dip of its northern limb is less than one degree, the southern limb dips northwards at two to three degrees. As a direct consequence of this asymmetry the bounding Chalk outcrop is wider in the Chilterns than in the North Downs and, as the river Thames is on the axis of the syncline in the latitude of central London, the roughly circular urban extent of Greater London spills south to the crest of the North Downs but only just laps against the southern limits of the Chilterns.

Preserved within the heart of the syncline is a sequence of clays and sands of Tertiary age which form the surface rocks under most of London and in which the foundations of most large buildings are excavated. The oldest of them resting directly on the Chalk are collectively referred to as the Lower London Tertiaries. Their outcrop forms a distinctive type of terrain along the north margin of the North Downs and the outcrop of their contact with the Chalk is marked by a line of springs and a string of settlements from Guildford through Leatherhead and Epsom. The component Thanet and Woolwich Beds are predominantly sandy in character with subordinate clays. The sands were formerly worked as iron- and brass-moulding sands and their occurrence at Woolwich may have contributed to the location there of the Royal Arsenal. The Blackheath Beds limited to south-east London contain substantial pebble beds formerly much in demand for constructional purposes and locally cemented into conglomerates. Their edge is marked by a low escarpment between Croydon and Erith.

The outcrop of the Reading Beds, sands and clays of the same age resting on the chalk of the Chilterns is less conspicuous but numerous small hilly outliers dot the Chiltern dipslope. They are the source of the many scattered sarsen and pudding stones, silica cemented sands and pebble beds encountered in the Chilterns and even in the terrace gravels of the Thames.

The London Clay is present under practically all of Greater London. It is 132 m at its thickest but erosion has removed much of it. It is a stiff dark grey or bluish-grey clay but seen in shallow excavations it is brown in colour as a result of weathering which commonly extends to a depth of 2 or 3 m. It was the relative ease with which this clay is excavated that greatly facilitated tunnelling for the Underground. The clay holds a great deal of water and its soils are heavy and wet but it lacks permeability and wells yield water very slowly. The settlement of the London Clay plains of Middlesex, Essex and Surrey had to wait on the development of the steam pump and the iron pipe prior to which villages were limited to the outcrops of water bearing strata adjacent to and overlying the clay. In the drought conditions of 1976 shrinkage was widespread and led to cracking of foundations and walls. The sides of railway cuttings in clay, many now over 100 years old, have weathered and in wet weather have a tendency to slip. In its upper 20 m the London Clay becomes progressively more sandy in character and is mapped separately as the Claygate Beds which have in the past been dug extensively for making tiles, pipes and pottery. The clay mixed with sand makes good bricks.

The youngest in the sequence of solid rocks are fine white and buff coloured sands with thin seams of clay and locally flint pebbles called the Bagshot Beds. They outcrop extensively south-west of London and cap the tops of numerous isolated hills farther east at Harrow, Hampstead, Highgate, Epping Forest and Brentwood. Springs, emerging at the base of the Bagshot and Claygate Beds on the flanks of the hills, are the sources of minor tributaries of the Thames such as the Fleet which are dammed near their sources to form Highgate and Hampstead ponds.

Minor folds and faults within the generally synclinal London Basin are of sufficient magnitude to impress themselves upon the shape of the land. The straight north to south run of the Lee Valley between Hoddesdon and Tottenham follows the line of a monocline down which the river has shifted unclinally to the east undercutting and steepening the east side of the valley and leaving on the west a broad flight of gently sloping terraces. The broad flood plain of the Lee, the steep eastern side of the valley and the fact that ownership of Epping Forest was in the hands of the Corporation of the City of London served to hinder the north eastward spread of London and encouraged its south to north growth along the terraces on the western side of the Lee. The line of the Epping Forest ridge, Highgate and Hampstead hills and Hanger Hill marks the axis of a north-east–south-west syncline along which erosion has inverted the relief. In contrast Windsor Castle stands on an inlier of Chalk on the line of a parallel anticline which north-eastwards brings Chalk close to the surface in valley bottoms in the Pinner area. Along an east–west anticlinal axis through Cliffe, Purfleet and Grays, Chalk is brought to the surface and the outcrop continues as far west as Lewisham well within the built up area of London. In a complementary syncline to the south an extensive outcrop of the Lower London Tertiaries forms the basis of the distinctive terrains of the south-east Plateau and Lower Tertiary belt of Kent. In south London two parallel faults, orientated north-east–south-west disrupt the rocks and throw the Chalk outcrop down over 30 m to the north-east. There is no surface expression of the faults but by bringing impervious London Clay vertically against Chalk they disrupt the movement of water through the chalk and change the level of the water table. Movements along extensions of the faults into Essex may have been the origin of the East Anglian earthquake of 1883.

Superficial Deposits

An excavation almost anywhere in the London area below ground level reveals that the clays, sands and chalk of the solid rock succession are masked by a cover of superficial deposits of clay, silt, sand and gravel ranging in thickness from a scatter of a few pebbles to layers several metres thick. These have been laid down at various times during the past

2 000 000 years whilst the Thames and its tributaries have been cutting down into the solid rocks and excavating the hills and valleys which form the site of London. The deposits are therefore roughly altitudinally arranged and their varying nature reflects changes in the prevailing geomorphological and climatic environments.

Valley Floors

The Thames enters the London Basin obliquely in the north-west through a gap cut across the Chiltern Hills at Goring. Between Goring and its estuary the Thames pursues a due west to east course albeit in a markedly meandering fashion. It crosses obliquely right across the structural basin the axis of which runs more nearly south-west–north-east. Upstream of Kew the Thames performs three very large meanders about its east–west axis, the first past Reading brings it on to the Tertiary outcrop but it then somewhat perversely turns its back upon the syncline and makes a large loop northwards past Henley back into the Chilterns, in a very attractive incised valley, before returning to the west–east line at Maidenhead. Downstream to Kew it then describes an even larger loop in the opposite direction reaching its most southerly point at the confluence of the Wey. Downstream through London and into the estuary the river continues to meander but never departs very far from its latitudinal course.

Three south bank tributaries of the Thames, the Wey, Mole and Darent, have their sources in the Weald and cut across the North Downs in distinctive water gaps which, together with wind gaps at Farnham and Mersham, carry some of London's principal rail and road links with the south coast. Five other smaller tributaries, the Hogsmill, Beverley Brook, Wandle, Ravensbourne and Cray, have their origins in dip slope springs at the junction of the Chalk and Tertiaries and drain most of the built up area south of the Thames. Only one north bank tributary, the Lee, breaches the Chiltern scarp but other Chiltern valleys drained southwards at their London ends by the Gade, Bulbourne and Misbourne head back into wind gaps which together with the Lee gap at Luton, carry most but not all, of the lines of communication by road, rail and canal from London to the Midlands. Other north bank tributaries, the Colne, Brent, the lower Lee and Roding owe their characters to the fact that at one stage in their histories they carried glacial meltwater from an ice sheet which invaded the Thames Valley from the north-east.

The valley floors of the Thames and its main tributaries comprise their present floodplains together with two low gravel Flood Plain terraces a few metres above the flood plains (Fig. 14·2). In a later period of glaciation, when ice did not reach the London area, the rivers cut down the floors of their valleys to a level below present sea level in central London and to minus 30 m in the estuary in response to a much-lowered sea level in the North Sea. Shallow trough-like valleys were eroded in the London Clay which later, as sea level rose, were filled with silts, clays, sands, gravels and brickearth 6–18 m thick in Westminster to a level up to 10 m above present sea level. Still later the Thames cut a channel in the gravelly deposits which was itself in turn later filled with alluvium. The floodplain alluvium varies in width but generally narrows upstream from the estuary. It was sufficiently narrow at the sites of London Bridge and Westminster Bridge, to be bridged in Roman times. In the latter case the crossing was facilitated by the existence of the Isle of Thorney a small circum-alluviated knoll of Flood Plain terrace gravels which became the site of the Palace of Westminster. The Flood Plain gravels contain much water and tunnels in the Underground have to be continuously pumped; between West Kensington and Temple stations, 6800 m^3 of water are extracted daily. Isolated gravel filled fissures in the London Clay below the Flood Plain gravels to depths of 23 m have been encountered in foundation works at Battersea and elsewhere, and these may be of a periglacial origin.

The construction of river embankments with deep foundations and building on the flood plains has not only prevented flooding but has completely transformed the natural scene. The prevention of the lateral spread of floodwater serves to raise the level of tide and flood peaks and so make necessary further raising of embankment levels. The weight of buildings on the flood plain and the abstraction of groundwater from below has resulted in consolidation of the ground and lowering of the surface level.

14·2 Physiographic Features of Inner London.

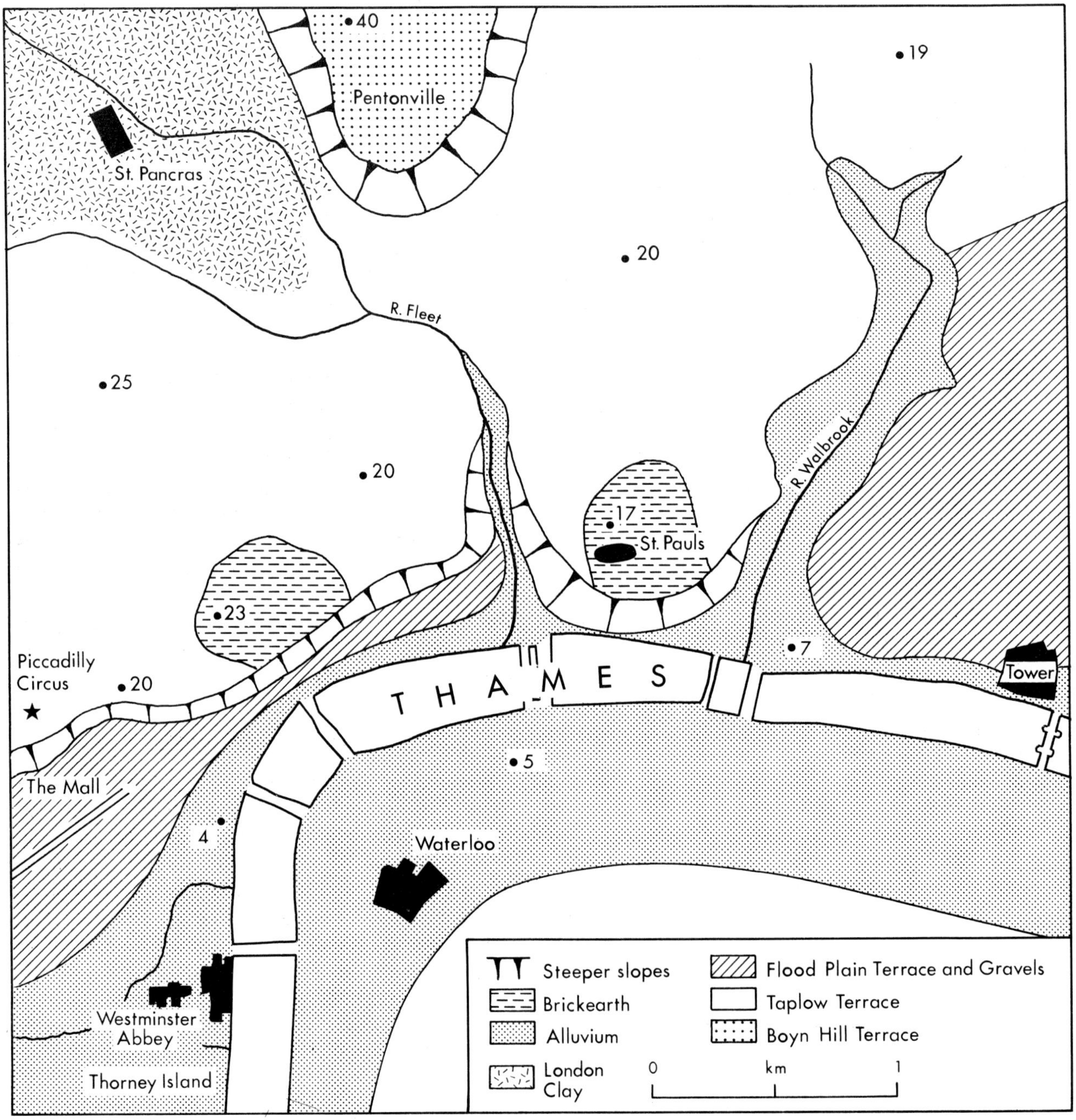

The Thames Terraces through London

Between Southwark and Blackfriars Bridges the Thames pushes against the north side of its valley floor. It has eliminated the Flood Plain terraces and directly undercuts a steep bluff, the flat top of which, some 15 m above the river, formed the site of the Roman city of Londinium. The site crowned by St.

Paul's Cathedral, is a fragment of the Taplow terrace of the Thames, separated from a much more extensive spread of the same terrace throughout the West End, Hyde Park and Kensington by the valley of the Fleet river at Ludgate Circus. The Strand runs along the front edge of the terrace and Trafalgar Square is cut back into the bluff between the Flood Plain and Taplow terraces. Those familiar with the gradients of streets in the West End will appreciate that there is an Upper and a Lower Taplow terrace but the distinction is not always easy to see because of the extent of building. North-eastwards the Taplow terrace underlies Hoxton, Shoreditch and much of Hackney, whilst Whitechapel, Stepney and Tower Hamlets are on the Flood Plain terrace. Upstream broad spreads of the Taplow terrace form the physical foundation of Hounslow, Heathrow Airport and Slough in the core of the great southward loop of the Thames. East of the Lee the same terrace is well preserved through Leyton, Wanstead Flats, Becontree Heath and South Ockendon. But south of the Thames the Taplow terrace is only preserved in scattered fragments, principally in the southwest at Putney and East Sheen.

Whilst extensive spreads of the Flood Plain and Taplow terrace gravels remain relatively undissected and form well-drained flat areas in the heart of London, the higher terraces through London are much more dissected and form flat-topped hills from which it is possible through the bricks and mortar to overlook the sprawl of central London. The Boyn Hill terrace, 30 m above river level, caps Highbury Hill and Hanger Hill north and Clapham Common, Herne Hill, Brockley and Dartford Heath south of the Thames but the most extensive remnants are to be found east of the Lee at Wanstead continuing to Barkingside–Hornchurch, where the terrace gravels rest on glacial drift, and Chadwell. Across the river at Swanscombe a fossil human skull, the oldest human remains in Britain was discovered within Boyn Hill gravels.

The terrace gravels of the Thames may reach a thickness of 10 m or more but are usually less. They comprise, for the most part, pebbles and subangular pieces of flint with many pebbles of quartz and quartzite, the latter derived from glacial gravels. Here and there blocks of Sarsen stone are encountered in the gravel, these were derived from the Reading Beds in the Lower London Tertiaries. The nature and thickness of the gravels testify to river action of high intensity such as is associated with glacial conditions. In places the terraces are covered with brickearth, a mixture of silt and clay up to 6 m thick. Much of it is probably reworked London Clay transported by the Thames and redeposited in relatively still floodwaters but some may have been blown by the wind before deposition. Cappings of brickearth occur on the Taplow terrace in the City and around Covent Garden and Sir Christopher Wren described how it had to be removed in excavating the foundations for St. Pauls. Similar spreads in south-west Middlesex and in the Lee Valley have constituted the pedological base of important market gardening areas.

Whenever holes are dug below the ground surface of the urbanized area of London the rubbish of man-made ground is exposed, not natural earth materials. In the City of Westminster this averages 3·5 m deep. The removal of soil and brickearth prior to building has in many areas counterbalanced this but the precise form and height of the natural land surface is in many areas no longer ascertainable. As its name implies brickearth found a use as a building material and the terrace gravels constitute an important resource for concrete aggregate especially from wet pits west of London where the water table is high and washing of the gravels is relatively easy. In south-west Middlesex in particular the coexistence of extensive spreads of terrace flat lands, gravel and brickearth has given rise to severe land-use competition.

Earlier Valleys of the Thames

The first unequivocable geological evidence of a river Thames is to be found in small remnants of what are undoubtedly its highest terrace gravels, traceable along the southern flank of the Chiltern Hills between the Goring Gap and Bishops Stortford. This Westland Green phase of the Thames falls in height from 146 m above Henley to 104 m in Hertfordshire, where it passes under glacial drift. The Vale of St.

Albans, a 5 km broad linear depression at the margin of the Tertiary rocks parallels this early north-easterly flowing Thames and in all probability represents the first identifiable valley of the Thames. When ice invaded the Thames Valley the Thames was diverted southwards into a second, broad, linear depression through Finchley, between the high ground of Mill Hill and Hampstead Heath. A further incursion of the ice from the north-east pushed the Thames southwards yet again into its present and third valley through London. The two abandoned valleys are prominent features in the relief of north London. Their floors are choked with glacial till and outwash gravels and it is evident from the distribution of the drift that ice tongues extended as far as Bricket Wood and Aldenham in the Vale of St. Albans and Church End Finchley where a mass of boulder clay resting on the floor of the depression and pointing down the Brent Valley is probably the much eroded remains of a terminal moraine. The sub-drift floors of the two abandoned Thames valleys are about 60 m above sea level and the Colne and the Brent are the descendants of the glacial meltwater rivers which drained from the ice tongues. The outwash gravels along the Colne, in the Vale of St. Albans have been a valuable source of concrete aggregate since World War II. As the ice advanced up the valleys it dammed the Thames and created a pro-glacial lake and it was overflow from this lake which probably initiated the breaches which led to the creation of the lower Lee, the Brent and the Colne and the double diversion of the Thames. A smaller linear depression at Borehamwood south of St. Albans may represent a course of the Thames intermediary in age between that of the first and second valleys.

West of the Colne between the Chiltern back slope and Slough and at a higher level than the Flood Plain, Taplow, Boyn Hill and Black Park terrace spreads, which belong to the third Thames valley through London, are three or more terraces, the Winter Hill, Harefield and High Gravel terrain which appear to belong to the second valley through Finchley, from which they are now separated by the Colne and Brent Valleys. Together they constitute the very distinctive if subdued staircase of the Beaconsfield gravel plateau, part of the Chiltern Hundreds.

The north-east of the London region is formed by the south-western fringe of the East Anglia boulder clay plateau—a thick series of glacial deposits drained to the Lee by the Rib, Ash and Stort. Along the latter, upstream of Harlow, run rail and motorway routes linking London with Cambridge via the Cam Valley.

Hill – top Gravels

The highest hills in and around London are all capped with variable thicknesses of gravel deposits. Hampstead Heath, Highgate Hill, Mill Hill, Totteridge, High Barnet, Shenley, in a line north from central London; Oxhey, Bushey Heath, Elstree and Arkley overlooking the Vale of St. Albans; the Epping Forest ridge east of the Lee, Ongar, Brentwood, Billericay and the Laindon Hills in Essex; are all remnants of a plateau surface sloping north and east across the London Basin at a height of approximately 120 m dating from a time the proto-Thames was flowing north-eastwards along the line of the Vale of St. Albans. Across this surface flowed south bank tributaries of the Thames, the ancestors of the Mole and Medway. Included in these hill-top gravels in north London are fragments of chert which could only have come from the Lower Greensand rocks of the Weald. Nothing of this plateau remains south of the Thames, where the highest hills form the Crystal Palace ridge and Shooters Hill.

During the last 2 000 000 years the Thames and its tributaries, under the influence of an episodically falling sea level and periods of arctic climatic conditions involving on occasions incursions of ice, have cut down from a height of about 120 m to their present levels so creating the hill slopes and valleys on which London is built. The superficial deposits which characterize each stage in land form development from the highest, the Pebble Gravel, to the lowest terrace gravel have a tendency to move under gravity down valley and hill slopes. This was particularly so during cold wet glacial episodes. As a consequence most slopes in the London area are draped by a sheet of solifluction material, called head, about a metre thick comprising a trail of intermixed sand, gravel and clay derived from the hill top deposits and the underlying clays which in slope-foot situations and in smaller valleys has accumulated to greater depths. It is this together with made ground which forms the present material of garden soils.

Landform Regions

The combined influence of rock character, and erosion and depositional processes acting through time has produced in the London area a number of distinctive types of physical terrain (Fig. 14·3). They fall into four main categories, two highland and two lowland in character. The lowlands comprise the valley lands of the Thames, its tributaries and former courses together with the clay plains of the London Clay outcrop. The hill lands comprise a great variety of dissected plateau and upland areas together with the bounding scarplands of the Chilterns and North Downs. Altogether there are some nineteen recognizable geomorphological regions over and into

14·3 Landform Regions of Greater London.

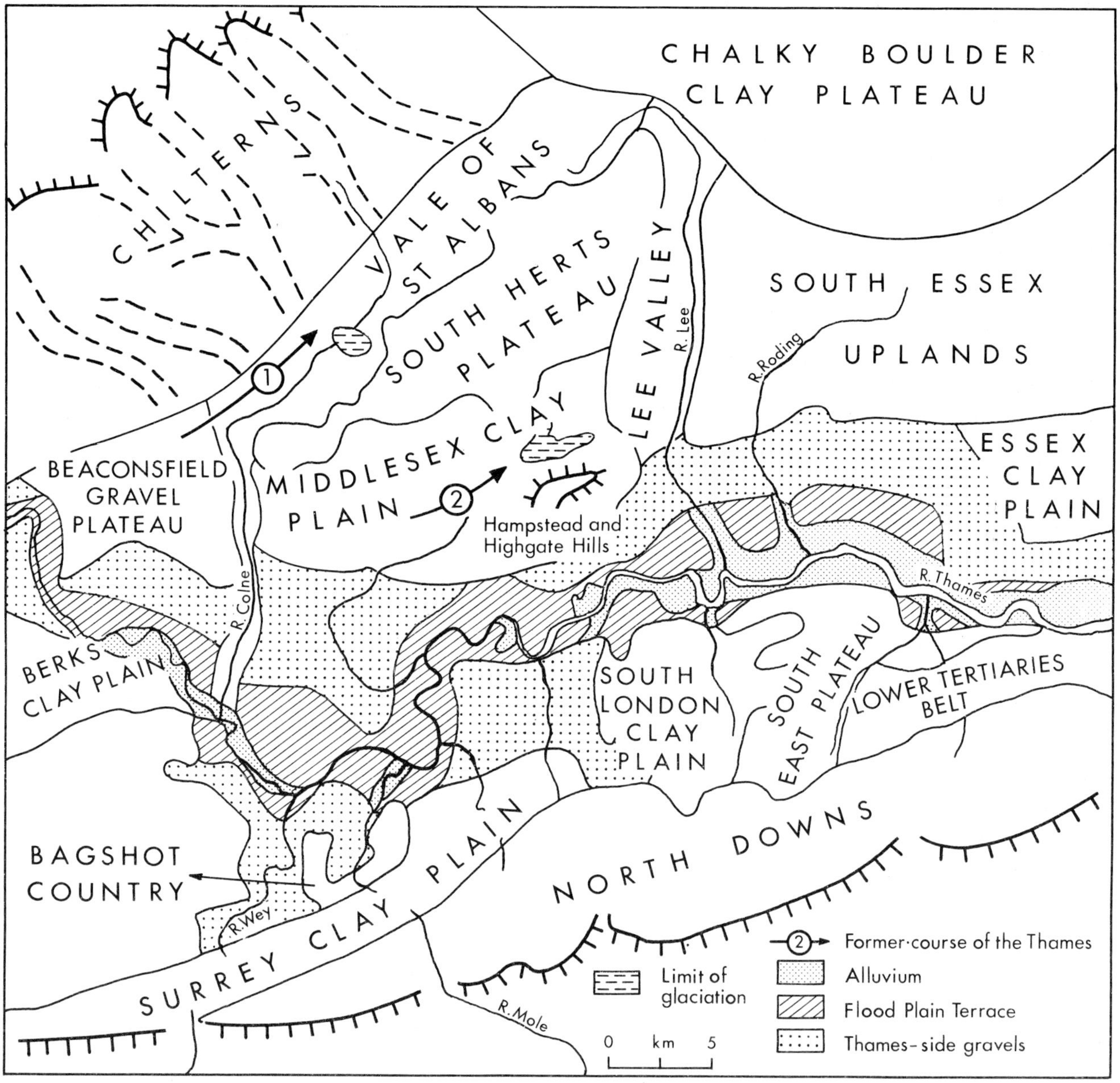

which the urban mesh of London extends.

At the core of the city is the floor of the Thames Valley comprising its alluvial Flood Plain and the associated low gravel Flood Plain terraces. Similar valley floors characterize its main tributaries but that of the Lee is most extensive and merits recognition as a separate region. The broad spreads of the higher terraces of the Thames through London, especially the Taplow terrace, form the characteristic Thamesside gravel tracts. They are particularly prominent north of the river. The abandoned courses of the Thames along the line of the Vale of St. Albans and through the Finchley depression constitute the remaining valley lands. There are five clay plains, which in detail are featureless, gently undulating regions but in places are studded with conspicuous residual hills such as Harrow Hill in Middlesex and the Norwood hills in south London. The clay plains in Middlesex, south London and Essex were areas of great suburban expansion during the interwar years.

The most prominent of the hill lands within the built up area of London are the north London heights of Hampstead and Highgate and their continuation north of the Finchley depression in the flat topped hills of the south Hertfordshire plateau extending north to the Vale of St. Albans. This high ground which rims the Thames Valley to the north continues westwards through Bushey Heath to Harefield and thence across the Colne Valley, westwards into the staircase of higher terraces of the Thames in the Beaconsfield gravel plateau. East of the Lee the South Essex uplands extend eastwards from the Epping ridge to Brentwood giving way northwards to the boulder clay plateau of east Hertfordshire and Essex. The two plateau areas south of the Thames—the Bagshot Country in the south west and that around Chiselhurst and Bromley—owe their distinctive characters to the underlying outcrops of sandy Bagshot Beds and pebbly Blackheath Beds respectively. Their surface characteristics contrast markedly with those of the adjacent clay plains.

The Chilterns and North Downs are Chalk upland plateaux in a state of youthful dissection, trenched by sub-parallel valleys most of which are dry. The interfluves are mantled with a variety of clays, silts, sands and gravels of diverse origins and the valleys are floored with gravels and solifluction deposits such that the Chalk bedrock is rarely to be seen exposed except on the steepest valley sides and on the bounding escarpments, the crests of which reach 240–50 m above sea level. The outcrops of the Lower London Tertiary rocks north of the North Downs form distinctive belts of subdued relief and relatively good and easily worked soils between the outcrops of the Chalk and London Clay.

Conclusion

The physical site of London lacks spectacular features such as the crag and tail of Edinburgh's Castle rock and Royal Mile, Bristol's Avon Gorge and Durdam Downs, New York's Manhattan Island and Palisades and the drowned valley of Sydney's harbour with its intricate alternation of bay and headland. But like most of the world's large cities London's growth and development has, in part at least, been in response to the subdued relief of its site which has not made that growth unduly difficult in terms of the character of its slopes, bedrock and surface drainage. Favourable elements in its situation have allowed relative ease of communication by water and land. Its nucleus was located near the tidal limit of the Thames where the alluvium of the flood plain narrowed and low gravel terraces on either side facilitated bridging. A steep bluff capped by a higher gravel terrace and undercut by the river provided the site of the core of what became the commercial city. Both it and the Royal City of Westminster on the lower gravel terrace upstream and linked to the City by the Strand along the top of the bluff, were able to extend northwards over the level well-drained surface of the Taplow terrace. Farther afield small villages grew up, invariably located on slightly higher ground within the sea of the London Clay outcrop, where permeable caps of sand and gravel provided at one and the same time well-drained soils and foundations and a source of water from springs and shallow wells in the capping. In the nineteenth and twentieth centuries these dry point villages have become the administrative and shopping centres of the suburban boroughs as the tide of bricks, slate, tile, concrete and tarmacadam flowed over the terraces and the clay plains of north and south London. The valleys of tributaries of the Thames served as avenues for London's expansion up valleys such as the Lee and Wandle and lines of communication by road, rail and canal with the rest of England frequently, but not inevitably, made use of valley routes provided by the Thames and its tributaries through and beyond the bounding Chalk uplands. The seemingly unchanging land has made its not unsubstantial contribution to changing London.

Further Reading

British Regional Geology, *London and the Thames Valley* (HMSO, London, 1960)

Davies, G. M., *Geology of London and South-East England* (Murby, London, 1939)

Sparks, B. W. and West, R. G., *The Ice Age in Britain* (Methuen, London, 1972)

Woodward, H. B., *The Geology of the London District* (London, 1922)

Wooldridge, S. W. and Hutchings, G. E., *London's Countryside* (Methuen, London, 1957)

Wooldridge, S. W. and Linton, D. L., *Structure, Surface and Drainage in South-East England* (George Philip, London, 1955)

Index